pg 51

*"It's So Good,
Don't Even Try It Once"*

David E. Smith, M.D.

is Medical Director of the Haight-Ashbury Free Medical Clinic, Assistant Clinical Professor Toxicology in the Department of Pharmacology at the San Francisco Medical Center, and a consultant to the San Francisco Veterans Administration Hospital. He is the editor of the *Journal of Psychedelic Drugs* and author and editor of many books and articles, among them the highly acclaimed *The New Social Drug: Cultural, Medical, and Legal Perspectives on Marijuana* (Prentice-Hall, 1970).

George R. Gay, M.D.

is Chief of the Heroin Section and Director of the Drug Detoxification, Rehabilitation, and Aftercare Project of the Haight-Ashbury Free Medical Clinic. He is also Senior Physician at the San Francisco Veterans Administration Hospital and Lecturer in Toxicology in the Department of Pharmacology at the University of California Medical Center in San Francisco.

"It's So Good, Don't Even Try It Once"

HEROIN IN PERSPECTIVE

Edited by
DAVID E. SMITH, M.D.
and
GEORGE R. GAY, M.D.

A SPECTRUM BOOK

PRENTICE-HALL, INC., ENGLEWOOD CLIFFS, NEW JERSEY

Library of Congress Cataloging in Publication Data

SMITH, DAVID ELVIN
  "It's so good, don't even try it once."

  Includes bibliographical references.
  1. Heroin—Addresses, essays, lectures.   2. Drug
abuse—United States—Addresses, essays, lectures.
I. Gay, George R., joint author.   II. Title.
III. Title: Heroin in perspective.
HV5822.H4S64   362.2′93′0973   72–3966
ISBN 0–13–506592–5
ISBN 0–13–506584–4 (pbk.)

"Taking Care of Business: The Heroin User's Life on the Street" by Edward Prebel and John J. Casey, Jr., originally appeared in *The International Journal of the Addictions* 4, no. 1 (March 1969): 1–24, and is reprinted by permission of the authors and Marcel Dekker, Inc.

"Treatment Techniques for Narcotic Withdrawal" by Donald Wesson, M.D., and David E. Smith, M.D., and "The Journey Beyond Trips" by Allan Y. Cohen, Ph.D., both originally appeared in the *Journal of Psychedelic Drugs* and are reprinted by permission of the authors and the *Journal of Psychedelic Drugs*.

10 9 8 7 6 5 4 3 2 1

Prentice-Hall International, Inc. (*London*)
Prentice-Hall of Australia, Pty. Ltd. (*Sydney*)
Prentice-Hall of Canada, Ltd. (*Toronto*)
Prentice-Hall of India Private Limited (*New Delhi*)
Prentice-Hall of Japan, Inc. (*Tokyo*)

"It's So Good, Don't Even Try It Once"

These are the words of Emmanuel, a young middle-class addict. They catch some of the essential ambiguity in the young heroin user's position. He has gone beyond the counterculture, or around it, to arrive at what seems like simple self-destruction. But is that how he sees it? And is heroin really a universal evil that we can all feel safe in condemning, or could it be that our social-political system is the true culprit? What is heroin, what does it do to you, how "good" is it and where (if anywhere) is the new drug scene leading us? These are some of the questions that will be dealt with by the contributors to this book.

Acknowledgments

The editors wish to thank Ron Wilton, coproducer of the film *Darkness, Darkness,* Haight-Ashbury Films, 701 Irving St., San Francisco, California, for his assistance in the preparation of this volume.

Contents

"It's So Good,
Don't Even Try It Once"

Introduction

David E. Smith, M.D., and George R. Gay, M.D.

In June of 1971 President Nixon declared a "national emergency" and stated that "America's Public Enemy Number 1 is drug abuse." A short time later he asked Congress to create a Special Action Office of Drug Abuse Prevention, to coordinate the activities of the nine federal agencies then fruitlessly trying to control drugs. Named director of this new agency was Dr. Jerome Jaffe, Chief of the Drug Abuse Program for the Illinois Department of Public Health and an advocate of the "multi-modality" approach to rehabilitating drug users. Dr. Jaffe was to develop an overall federal strategy for drug abuse programs and coordinate detoxification, rehabilitation, drug education, and job retraining programs in the military forces. His budget for 1971 was $371 million, $216 million of which was already available.

Creation of this new agency represented a dramatic reorientation in the administration's approach to drug abuse, for during his first two years in office Nixon declared only unrelenting *judicial* war on drugs. "law and order" were emphasized (somehow this term was equated with "justice" in Attorney General Mitchell's mind) and drug abuse continued to be thought of as primarily a legal matter. This attitude led to the passage of stiff new drug-control legislation (beefed up by the Bureau of Narcotics and Dangerous Drugs in the Justice Department), and tightened the U.S. borders against the inflow of drugs. In addition, Nixon publicly dispatched emissaries abroad to persuade other countries, particularly producers of marijuana and opium, to tighten their control over the manufacture and exportation of drugs. Such measures received a great deal of political support from "Middle America," but predictably did little to stem the flow of drugs into urban ghettos and middle-class suburbs. In fact, the only real effects seemed to be a rise in the cost of narcotics in the illegal marketplace and a shift toward more expensive drugs with higher abuse potential.

In 1969, for example, the now infamous "Operation Intercept" caused marijuana to become scarce and thus, possibly more than any other single official action, served as a "trigger mechanism" for the use of harder drugs throughout the country as drug users turned to whatever was available in the marketplace. A significant shift to heroin by drug-experimenting, alienated youth was noted in San Francisco; a shift to "speed" was noted in Seattle; a marked increase in heavy barbiturate usage occurred in Eugene, Oregon; and so on throughout the country.

What has produced such an apparently dramatic change in the government's attitude toward drug-dependent individuals in the United States? Certainly not the plight of thousands of black, brown and yellow American addicts now increasingly crowding the inner-city slums—ghettos that for decades have sought escape from intolerable conditions through heroin. Why this sudden effort on the part of our chief executive to initiate an intensive and apparently humane rehabilitative program? Why this new concern for the plight of the downtrodden and forgotten people who are measuring out their lives in morphine drops? [1]

In truth, these longstanding psychosocial and very personal inequities —the real guts of the heroin problem in the United States—have received little attention in the administration's priority of reorientation and investment. The real explanation for this change in policy lies in the abrupt appearance of the returning Vietnam veteran who is addicted to heroin. We have become aware, almost overnight, not only that heroin (along with many other drugs) is in Vietnam and in other foreign theaters with our Armed Forces, but also that heroin addiction has invaded white middle-class America. We are appalled to read that heroin is easier to buy than liquor in Vietnam, that from 26,000 to 60,000 American GI's in Vietnam are using hard drugs (mainly heroin) at this writing, with an unknown number addicted. And, though an accurate head count of addicts in this country is almost impossible, estimates range up to 500,000 (the figure quoted by Senator Vance Hartke on March 2, 1971). Hartke states that nearly 20 percent of these "new" addicts are teenagers and that heroin has become the major killer of young people between 18 and 35, outpacing deaths from accidents, suicide, or cancer in most major cities. He further points out that addicts in America annually steal $2.5 billion of goods and that they commit 55 percent of crime in the cities.

1. Burroughs, *Junkie* (New York: Ace Books, 1953).

It has become obvious, then, that the heroin epidemic in Vietnam is the real reason for Nixon's apparent turnabout in attitude and policy. Our involvement in Southeast Asia, while achieving no meaningful military objectives and severely compromising the purpose and moral fiber of our nation, has now produced thousands of new heroin addicts for the United States to absorb and certainly demands the highest attention of our government. It must be realized, however, that heroin addiction in America will not end with the war in Vietnam and that a shift in approach to drug abuse is needed not just for the returning veteran addicts but also for the hundreds of thousands of stateside addicts and the even larger number of abusers of nonnarcotic drugs.

After Nixon's dramatic announcement in June 1971, Dr. Bertram Brown, Director of the National Institute of Mental Health, stated that "ultimately our success in efforts to control drug abuse in the United States will rest with knowledge we do not now possess." Such a realization is crucial, for many social planners, government leaders, and American citizens view the drug abuse problem as a simplistic, linear, cause-and-effect relationship. The bitter fact is that heroin dependence and other drug abuse patterns are merely the symptoms of a complex medical, psychological, and social disease whose causes are interwoven with the very fabric of American society. We can cure America's heroin epidemic only by understanding the full dimensions of the problem and developing effective, consistent means of treatment that are based not on preconceptions but on "what works."

Toward that end, this book will examine heroin addiction in America from many perspectives. Heroin addiction seems a far cry from the psychedelic joy that at one time dominated the Haight-Ashbury district, described in the late sixties as the hippie capital of the world, where our work began. We at the Haight-Ashbury Free Clinic, along with the contributing authors of this publication, have watched with frustration as heroin has helped to destroy this and other counterculture communities. We feel it is crucial that all, especially those involved in the counterculture, understand the many dimensions of heroin dependence.

A great deal of existing literature analyzes the chemical, pharmacological, psychological, and social variables of heroin use. Among the studies already available, the classic work is *The Road to H: Narcotics, Delinquency, and Social Policy,* by Isidore Chein and associates, which presents a comprehensive body of research conducted between 1949 and 1962 in the New York area.[2] Unfortunately, most of Chein's recommendations were ignored by government social plan-

2. Isidore Chein et al., *The Road to H: Narcotics, Delinquency, and Social Policy* (New York: Basic Books Inc., 1964).

ners until the recent revelation of the magnitude of addiction in Southeast Asia. The editors of this volume are concerned that, when America finally extracts itself from military involvement in Southeast Asia, we will once again lapse into the "law and order" approach to addiction that has been pursued so relentlessly and so unsuccessfully for years. As Chein stated in 1964:

> We think it is time to call a policy of forcing the addict from degrada- tion to degradation, all in the name of concern for his welfare, just what it is—vicious, sanctimonious, and hypocritical. Every addict is entitled to assessment as an individual and to be offered the best available treat- ment in the light of his condition, his situation, and his needs. No legis- lator, no judge, no district attorney, no director of a narcotics bureau, no police inspector and no narcotics official is qualified to make such an assessment.[3]

In a later publication Chein stated:

> Few of the gatekeepers are willing to listen to people like me. I have been stressing for years now that the crux of the issue is not abstinence, it is what happens to this person. If the person is better off with the drug than without it, insofar as it is humanly possible to do something for him, then he ought to have the drug. If we do not like it, we should find better ways of helping him. The consideration is not does he stay off the drugs, but what is wrong with him. When I see somebody in misery, I respond to his misery, not to the fact that he has to take drugs in order to cope with his misery. It is the man who needs help and not the narcotic.[4]

Our intent is not to duplicate Chein and associates' excellent ma- terial, but rather to contribute contemporary perspectives on the rap- idly changing problem of heroin addiction in America. It is our fervent hope that this book will help keep the fires of enlightenment burning, now that our country is in the midst of a serious heroin epidemic.

SOCIAL POLICY PERSPECTIVES

Nowhere is the pure law-enforcement approach to "victimless crimes" more rigorously practiced than in the case of heroin addiction in Amer- ica. We watched the personal, social, and psychological turmoil in the United States during the sixties create drug problems of unprecedented magnitude, which have culminated in the current heroin epidemic. At

3. Ibid., pp. 379–80.
4. I. Chein, "Psychological, Social and Epidemiological Factors in Drug Addic- tion," in *Rehabilitating the Narcotic Addict*. (Washington, D.C.: Vocational Re- habilitation Administration, HEW, 1966), p. 69.

the beginning of this decade we witnessed the launching of the "big government drug crackdown" in an attempt to control international narcotics traffic. Efforts at drug control were intensified. For example, customs agents made 3,000 seizures involving 37,000 pounds of "illicit drugs" in the third quarter of 1970, more than doubling the amount confiscated in the same period a year earlier. Nonetheless, *heroin has never been more available* in the United States than it is now. One reason is that 94 percent of 1970's haul was marijuana and hashish— drugs that are peripheral to our country's hard-core narcotics problem. Although several thousand pounds of heroin are smuggled into this country each year, customs agents reported only 9.5 pounds of heroin confiscated during the third quarter of 1970. The clampdown on heroin seemed only to *increase the price,* thereby *increasing the criminal activity* that the addict had to engage in to support his habit. This "law and order" approach, although widely heralded at its inception, became a major disappointment even in the eyes of such conservative publications as *U. S. News and World Report,* whose December 7, 1970 article on "Booming Traffic in Drugs" described our latest law enforcement efforts as "a failure." As Spinoza so accurately observed, "He who attempts to determine all by law foments rather than lessens crime."

About four-fifths of the world supply of opium, which serves as a base for heroin, used to be grown in Turkey. It was then smuggled to France, where it was synthesized to heroin. Through a complicated, organized criminal effort it was smuggled into the United States. This source of heroin has recently been greatly augmented by the increasing supply from Southeast Asia.

> According to the United Nations Commission on Drugs and Narcotics, since at least 1966, 80 percent of the world's 12,000 tons of illicit opium has come from Southeast Asia. Eighty-three percent of the world's illegal supply originated in the Fertile Triangle of Northwestern Burma, Northern Thailand, and Laos—the area where opium is controlled by the U.S.-supplied troops of Laos and Nationalist China.[5]

Turkey has recently agreed to provide stricter enforcement of laws controlling opium growing and traffic, but efforts to obtain the same cooperation from Southeast Asian countries have been ineffective. One major reason is that many officials in the South Vietnamese government benefit from the financial rewards of narcotics traffic. It is ironic that at the same time we are attempting to control international narcotics traffic, we are covertly encouraging and sometimes offering open help to the opium traders, hence bolstering the economies of Southeast

5. Frank Browning and Banning Garrett, *Ramparts* (May 1971), p. 38.

Asian countries that the administration feels might otherwise fall
under Communist domination. This ambivalent attitude seems to be
the "Catch-22" of control measures for Southeast Asian opium traffic,
making all attempts self-defeating.

The logical answer would be to reduce the stateside consumer
demand for chemical escape, for "death without permanence, life
without pain." [6]

PSYCHOLOGICAL PERSPECTIVES

For a variety of psychological and pharmacological reasons, heroin
appears to be a drug whose time has come. Many young people with
wide drug experience express the feeling that "junk is as far out as
you can go." [7] A great deal has been written about the psychosocial
variables that serve as the basis for the traditional heroin scene in
America.

There is considerable debate now whether Chein and associates'
traditional heroin user (whose background was economic poverty,
ghetto psychology, and a disrupted family) is substantially different
from the new middle-class junkie. Chein's original personality breakdown defined almost 40 percent of his heroin addict population as
either being overtly schizophrenic or having a borderline schizophrenic
process. Some programs, like the Haight-Ashbury Free Clinic, which
deal with middle-class heroin addicts, are finding approximately the
same percentage of overt and borderline schizophrenics. Both heroin
addict populations appear to have similar pathological family backgrounds and to suffer from a serious lack of self-esteem. Although a
great deal more research is needed in this area, it appears that the
ghetto junkie may be psychologically closer to the middle-class junkie
than we first imagined. Only through in-depth psychological studies
of young heroin users can we understand how and why the current
drug education and prevention programs have failed. Much of traditional drug education seems to have been discredited by excessive
use of "scare tactics" that present distorted and often blatantly dishonest information about drugs (especially marijuana). The "step-
pingstone" theory—that marijuana use leads to heroin addiction—
has been so thoroughly ingrained by misleading films and lectures
that it may take us decades to outgrow it.

Such techniques create credibility gaps whose adverse long-term

6. D. E. Smith and J. Luce, *Love Needs Care* (Boston: Little, Brown & Co., 1971).
7. Patient at Haight-Ashbury Free Clinic. The reader is referred to the glossary
at the end of this volume for explanation of drug terms and other slang expressions
used by members of the drug culture.

effects may be devastating for the adolescent drug experimenter. We must bear in mind that such a young person is a perfect set-up because of two factors: (1) universal drug availability, and (2) intense peer-group pressure. In adolescent turmoil a young person may cultivate a heroin habit for social or psychological reasons, only to discover later that he has developed a true physical addiction. At this stage he may feel his situation is so hopeless that there is "no hope but dope."

SOCIAL AND ECONOMIC PERSPECTIVES

There may be heroin addicts in Vietnam, but they don't become junkies until they reenter the United States. The reason, of course, is that heroin of at least 90 percent purity is readily available in Vietnam for $2 to $3 an ounce. An addict can thus maintain his habit for a few dollars a day, without having to steal to do so. Heroin is used socially; it is smoked, sniffed, or injected in group settings. Many dealers in the United States, however, cut their heroin to a potency of 2–10 percent, depending on their location. In an area with very strict law enforcement, heroin prices may be so high that the addict must steal, engage in prostitution, deal in narcotics, or participate in a wide variety of other illegal activities to support a $50- to $100-a-day habit.

RADICAL AND RACIAL PERSPECTIVES

Chein and associates found that a number of unfavorable feelings toward police, law enforcement, and the Establishment in general were common to the heroin subculture and delinquent youth. It was widely held, for example, that the police were open to bribes, that they practiced open racial discrimination, and that they favored their friends and picked on the youth.

In the eight years since publication of *The Road to H*, these negative attitudes have grown into the full-blown "conspiracy theory" that now permeates the thinking of certain racial and ethnic minorities. Many of these groups feel that both heroin and methadone are the tools for an Establishment conspiracy to prevent violence in the ghetto and to control counterrevolutionary activity among alienated white youth. Also, many ghetto dwellers feel that turning to drugs is basically an adaptive mechanism to deal with the horrors of life and the lack of opportunities in the urban ghetto. Heroin addiction, they say, is a social disease caused by the same individuals who created the ghetto conditions. Political activism is seen by some as an alternative response to ghetto alienation. Thus many black militant groups, in an attempt to foster revolutionary fervor, try to persuade ghetto dwellers not to use heroin.

Cy Carter, Mendocino Family Graduate and now Director of the Northeast Mental Health Center Minority Retraining Program in San Francisco, had a history of eleven years of heroin dependence. At the National Heroin Symposium in San Francisco in June 1971 he was asked why he had used heroin. His response was, "Why not?" Cy elaborated that in the ghetto the individual with the most status is the heroin dealer, the pimp, the hustler. With no other meaningful status hierarchy, the ghetto dweller rarely finds any successful alternative to a heroin life style.

One major reason why America has been unable to come to grips with its heroin problem and make its treatment facilities more effective is that most of its programs spring from the experience of Establishment social planners. Statistics seem to be the major language of these planners, but nothing could appear more conspiratorial to the addict or make him feel more manipulated. He senses the loss of his identity; he feels, like the convict, that his name and personality have been replaced by a number—or worse, a punched-out IBM card.

Within the last few years, however, there has been more involvement of the population at risk, including the use of ex-addicts and minority groups to establish their own treatment facilities. These innovative and often unique modalities of therapy have added a new dimension to drug abuse treatment.

TREATMENT AND PREVENTION

Health Education

Many health educators who talk about the importance of "prevention" or an "overall drug abuse control plan" seem to think of health education as the only component of a preventive plan. Health education is indeed important, but we feel it is only *one* component of a *broad social plan* for preventing drug abuse. The ghetto drug user does not use heroin because he lacks the facts about the drug. He has been raised around the heroin life style. He uses heroin because it seems to him to be the best thing to do at the time. Thus we put our emphasis on a "social alternatives model," rather than a "health education model" which in most areas is simply a factual presentation of the dangers of drugs—heroin being the prototype of the most dangerous drug. The alternative model philosophy is eloquently described in Dr. Allen Cohen's article, "The Journey beyond Trips: Alternatives to Drugs" (reprinted as chapter 16 of this volume).

Methods of Treatment

Of course, prevention is only part of an overall program to reduce consumer demand for heroin. We must also treat the large number of people already afflicted with the psychosocial disease of heroin addiction.

Since traditional treatment approaches have met with such a low cure rate (2–5 percent), the general philosophy that has developed is "once a junkie, always a junkie" or "heroin addiction is incurable." However, Charles Winick has demonstrated that large numbers of addicts "mature out" of heroin.[8] Only recently has it even been considered that perhaps treatment modalities as a whole should be re-evaluated. Failure to evaluate traditional treatment programs, of course, emanates from the fact that they were controlled not by medical specialists, but by rigid law enforcement officials. Dr. Jerome Jaffee has emphasized that because there are so many complex routes to heroin dependence, many different types of treatment modalities would be necessary in finding a successful overall program. Very simply, this "multiple modality treatment approach" could be described as "different strokes for different folks." Only in the context of a *broad* multimodality treatment strategy, drawing on all types of programs, can we begin to analyze the methodology and effectiveness of each specific treatment technique.

In 1970, 1,046 people died of heroin overdose in New York City alone. Heroin has become the leading cause of death among New York City residents between the ages of 18 and 35. The physiology of sudden death from heroin is not clear. In the great majority of cases, no true pharmacological overdose can be demonstrated. In fact, it appears in certain situations that an allergic reaction may be to blame. The relative infrequency of death from heroin (about one death per thousand injections) has made it difficult to investigate the pathogenesis of these deaths. Many of those who die are not naive young heroin experimenters, but long-term addicts who are quite experienced with heroin. The need to learn how to treat acute heroin reaction has become more important as heroin use in Vietnam has increased. In 1971 a GI in Vietnam had a better chance of becoming a heroin addict or of dying from heroin overdose than he did of becoming a combat casualty. Many communities that until now had been unaffected by the heroin epidemic now suddenly find themselves involved.

A wide variety of long-term treatment methods have been advocated, ranging from individual or group psychotherapy through the religious

8. Charles Winick, "Maturing out of Narcotic Addiction," *Bulletin on Narcotics,* vol. XIV, no. 1 (January–March 1962), 1–7.

strategies of the "Jesus freaks" to the so-called British system. None of these approaches have met with widespread acceptance, but some social planners are advocating British-style legalized heroin clinics. One modality that has been successful is the "therapeutic community" or "third community." The first such program was Synanon, which was launched in Santa Monica, California, about twelve years ago. Its founder, Chuck Dederich, an ex-alcoholic, advanced the theory that the addict can change his deviant behavior patterns only by voluntarily joining a strongly disciplined but loving pseudofamily and reexperiencing the process of growing up. This is accomplished through a self-help regime, including physical labor to maintain the program, and the familiar techniques of group encounter and confrontation.[9] The first offshoot of Synanon was Daytop, developed on New York City's Staten Island under the direction of David Deitch, a talented Synanon graduate. Other offshoots include the New York City-sponsored Phoenix complex, Gateway House in Chicago, and the Family Awareness House complex in California and Arizona.

We call this the "third community" approach for the following reasons: the "first community" is the straight world, from which the addict feels both different and alienated; the "second community" is that of hip drug users, whose value system appeals to him but who advocate the use of psychoactive drugs as a means of problem-solving and escape; the "third community" is, in effect, that of the hip non-drug users. As originally proposed, Chuck Dederich felt that Synanon would be effective for only one out of every ten addicts and that Synanon members would never be able to return to the straight world or the hip world without going back to drugs.

As determined by Jaffe in Illinois, however, one of the biggest problems of this treatment modality is that it is applicable only to the few who will accept it. Out of every hundred who seek help in a "third community" program, more than 90 are rejected at the door or leave the program after only a few weeks. Of those who remain, 80–90 percent remain heroin-free and crime-free for at least one year. But this is only 8 or 9 percent of the total number needing help.

Methadone Maintenance

According to Chein and associates:

> In extreme cases it may be that the best that can be offered an addict is to help him stay chronically narcotized. If so, such a case is entitled

9. The history and function of Synanon is accurately described in Dr. Lewis Yablonsky's excellent book *Synanon: The Tunnel Back* (New York: Penguin Books, 1970).

to treatment as is a terminal cancer patient or a diabetic patient. If the best that our society has to offer is narcosis, what moral right do we have to withhold it from them? Dare we in our ignorance take the position that it is proper to keep these people from finding relief merely because we find their method of finding relief offensive to us? [10]

10. Chein, *The Road to H,* pp. 380–81.

When Chein and associates wrote their book, the technique of methadone maintenance that has now evolved as the most successful of the current treatment modalities had not been developed. The originators of this technique, Vincent Dole and Marie Nyswander, were not even mentioned by Chein, which shows how rapidly both social problems and approaches to solving them change in our society. The advantages of methadone over heroin are that methadone is long-acting and can be administered orally. An individual can escape both the life of the criminal and the destructive needle.

Methadone maintenance has many critics at both ends of the political spectrum. Conservatives claim that methadone is just another addictive drug, while radicals insist that methadone is just another form of white Establishment drug control proffered without any concomitant attempt to cure the underlying causes of the disease.

Treatment in Perspective

No treatment approach has yet eradicated a social disease like heroin dependence, so we must explore new means of preventing drug abuse. Rather than declaring the drug abuse problem to be "Public Enemy Number 1," we must realize that the true enemy is ourselves— witness our immoral and unjust involvement in Southeast Asia, our racist attitudes and inability to deal with problems of minority ghettos, and our ineffectiveness in developing alternative living arrangements to compensate for the decline of the monogamous nuclear family. Our country must undergo an immediate and dramatic reorientation of national priorities and we must look for contemporary solutions to contemporary problems.

Time is running out, however. In fact, it may already be too late. Titus Livy described a parallel situation when he spoke of the decline of Rome: "We reached those last days when we could endure neither our vices nor their remedies."

THE BACKGROUND

1

Evolution of a Drug Culture
in a Decade of Mendacity[1]

Anne C. Gay, M.A., and George R. Gay, M.D.

It is no longer buried in Black and Puerto Rican ghettoes, no longer confined to the "ignorant" poor. Heroin is in the suburbs, and white parents are beginning to know the impotent rage of fear and despair that black parents have lived with for decades: the call from school, from the police, from a hospital somewhere. The call that rips you from complacency and tells you the cold, neon, streetcorner truth: your kid has been arrested; your kid is a junkie.

Your daughter—the lovely, clear-eyed child who was going to marry a nice, attractive, sensible, hard-working young man, who was going to give you grandchildren and comfort in your old age—well . . . she ran off with a greasy slob on a motorcycle. When he got tired of fucking her, he split, so now she is turning tricks on the street, hustling for enough bread to cop a balloon.

Or maybe your son, who was decorated in Vietnam, has come home from the war acting "strange," and you find the rig in his drawer one day, contrasting sickeningly with the model cars and airplanes still on his shelves, the plaid bedspread he picked out when he was ten, and the smiling graduation picture on his wall.

Maybe they're your kids we have here at the Haight-Ashbury Medical Clinic's Heroin Detox Unit. We don't know all their real names; a lot of them sign in as "Jane Doe" or "John Smith," and they show up at our door, sometimes up to 500 of them a week, O.D.'d, or comatose, or catatonic, or just plain sick. You won't see their names in the

1. "Mendacity [lying] is a system that we live in. *Liquor is one way out an' death's the other. . . .*" Brick to Big Daddy. (Tennessee Williams, *Cat on A Hot Tin Roof*, 1955.)

newspaper, either, unless you're a parent of one of the 1,046 kids who died of heroin overdose in New York last year. (76 died in San Francisco last year.) Or maybe a friend of yours is one of the 60,000 GIs snorting, shooting, smoking junk in Vietnam—is it really 2.5 percent? Or 4 percent? Or 16 percent? No one really seems to know.

Some of the GI junkies die nice, peaceful deaths because they are so high up there on smack that they never knew what hit them. ("I saw one guy so high that he took fifteen bullets before he went down. I figured if smack could do that for *him*, then maybe I could take one bullet and still live.") Maybe they are the lucky ones. The ones who are still alive, back here in the States, have to spend every waking hour in the hustle for more junk. Malnutrition, venereal disease, and hepatitis are quite familiar to them. Their eyes no longer mirror the hopes of Mom and Dad. Instead they reflect the cynicism and the ravages of a life style never imagined by you, their parents, who thought you had given them everything.

You can retreat into a scotch and soda, you can retreat into the psychiatrist's office, or you can retreat into despair . . . but the problem still remains. You can blame the pushers, you can blame the police, you can blame the war, the schools, the government, or you can even blame yourself . . . but the problem, although it may never become this personal to you, still remains. We are in the midst of a heroin epidemic the likes of which the credit-card comfort of the white middle class has never known.

In the history of the recorded epidemiology of drug use, there has never been a concentrated pattern of multiple drug abuse like that seen and documented in the Haight-Ashbury section of San Francisco from 1967 to the present.

Three years ago, a year after the "Summer of Love" had made San Francisco's Haight-Ashbury a household word, we were seeing about four patients a week with the symptoms of heroin intoxication. The kids were into LSD and speed then. In the last two and one-half years, however, we have seen and treated over 2000 heroin addicts at our clinic alone. Some of them are old-style, hard-core junkies, but most of them are kids—kids in their early and middle twenties—you've heard of Janis Joplin, James Taylor, and Jimi Hendrix; Joan Baez • and David Harris; Bob Dylan and the Beatles; Bernardine Dohrn and William Calley; Stokeley and Huey; David and Julie; Tricia and Ed; Luci Baines and Lynda Byrd; Angela Davis; Muhammed Ali. That is the generation we are talking about: the war babies, the Sputnik kids, the Drug Generation. They come from all over the country—from San Francisco, Los Angeles, Twin Forks, Indianapolis, Sioux City—you name it, they're here, and the long road they took from the suburbs of America to a heroin clinic in San Francisco had its origins in the subtle interactions of our history and our people.

THE PAST IS PROLOGUE

The Drug Generation first drew breath in a heady and arrogant time in our nation's history. There was no drug scene in those years because it was difficult to smuggle with a world war going on. San Francisco was in the news in those days for playing midwife to the birth of the United Nations. The United States was riding high. *We* had won the war! *We* were Colossus—bestriding the world in triumph. The self-acknowledged preserve of DEMOCRACY, we felt only too committed to re-creating the war-ravaged world in our own image. Somehow we believed in our own propaganda: in the words of Colonel Purdy, "We'll democratize these people if we have to kill every last one of them to do it!!" MacArthur warned of Armageddon, but nobody much seemed to notice any inconsistency in welcoming World Law in June and blasting Hiroshima to bits in August. When Ho Chi Minh, an obscure little man from an obscure little country called Vietnam, asked for U.S. support in his country's bid for independence, nobody bothered to answer his appeals.

In our postwar elation, we declared that we'd "never be caught unprepared again." That meant we had to be prepared to smell smoke before the match was lit. We changed the name of our Department of War to the Department of Defense, pulled in our talons, sat on our atomic bomb, and looked around for new threats to our primacy on which to unleash all our unspent patriotism. But Hitler was dead (*really?*), and so was Mussolini, and we had crushed Japan. Russia, however, was being skittish about currency in Berlin, so we spread our wings and joined the heroic airlift. If we were not for God, for Harry, and for England, at least we could prove we were for God and for Harry—against the specter of International Communism. Our president, our Commander-in-Chief, embodied this vestigial pioneer spirit: "Give 'em hell, Harry!"

We were ripe for paranoia, and it appeared: McCarthyism, the Hollywood Loyalty Hearings. ("Chiang Kai-shek can't be a despot, dear. He's anti-Communist!") When the French asked our support in Vietnam, MacArthur said, "If there is anything that makes my blood boil, it is to see our Allies in Indochina and Java deploying Japanese troops to conquer the little people we promised to liberate. It is the most ignoble kind of betrayal." We didn't say anything then, either.

Then there was Korea. "Patriotic consensus" was still with us in

1950, when we plunged into the first of our most recent series of un-declared wars. The United Nations offered its blessing, however in-effectual, and we saw our first "peacetime" conscription begin. Those who were drafted were, of course, too young to vote. The Silent Gener-ation, still mesmerized by the vision of U.S. omnipotence, went in to fight our first one-to-one battle with the new enemy and, like the British in our own Revolution, came up against an adversary who would not play fair. Brainwashing! Heretofore war had been waged against bodies, not against minds—or so we had thought. We saw an appalling number of your young men (our junkies' older brothers?) collapse under this new pressure. ("Who do those dirty Commies think they are, anyway? They ought to play by *our* rules!")

"Gooks" were not only cheats, but they were ungrateful as well—hadn't we saved them from the dirty Japs? But somehow, now, the "dirty Japs" were our friends, and the Chinese had become evil. So the Korean war ("police action," "conflict"—whatever) was fought—and talked—and talked—and finally settled. We now had divided Ber-lin *and* divided Korea to watch over. ("Syngman Rhee can't be a Communist, dear, he's an anti-Communist!")

We, the white, middle-class people of America—still worshipping our Panglossian priests, Norman Vincent Peale and Norman Rockwell, and with our newly proliferating TV sets urging us to be "happy" with the deluge of new wonder drugs developed during World War II —were again "right" in our course to save the world. We were not aware, however, that heroin was becoming a real problem in the slums. As a matter of fact, we were not aware of the slums. Anyway, heroin was cheap then, only a couple of bucks—and everyone knew you couldn't expect much from the "colored." If they got to be a nuisance, they could be put in jail—it was for their own good.

As we strolled into the fifties we were tired. Maintaining self-right-eousness is hard work. We had come out of a depression, fought two wars, kept the Commies at bay, and made ourselves the technological giant of the world. We put on Eisenhower like a comfortable old shoe. A father figure, he would take care of us; a war hero, he would take care of the Communists; a personification of all that was good, decent, and American, he could do no wrong. We could go to sleep. Howdy-Doody would take care of our kids and we had discovered tranquilizers. This was the best of all possible worlds.

True, there were a few cranks writing books like *The Hidden Per-suaders* and there was always somebody worrying about the H-bomb. Someone named Martin Luther King was causing trouble in the South ("Probably a Communist"), but we could turn on "Gunsmoke" and be soothed by illusions of a more bearable America.

True, there were a few embarrassing incidents, like the U-2 spy plane. "Why in the hell didn't we get in there and rescue the poor guy?" ("Take a Librium.") And there was John Foster Dulles with his "Cold War" and his "Brinkmanship." ("Take an Excedrin.") But essentially we managed to skirt further confrontation on an international level. Indeed, we remained virtuously aloof over the Suez Canal and we clucked our tongues sadly over poor Hungary. But we proved that our intellectual powers were still functioning by discussing them both over cocktails. Good old Ike would muddle through.

In October, 1957, the Russians orbited Sputnik I.

In August, 1960, in Cuernavaca, a man named Timothy Leary ate his first mushroom.

1960–1970: DECADE OF MENDACITY

If an increasing pattern of dissatisfaction and outright alienation from the "Establishment" or from society in general has been noted in the past decade; if a selfless dedication to the high-level decisions of our elected government officials (particularly in regard to the war in Vietnam) has been gradually replaced in our young people with feelings of disillusionment, impotence, and rage, it was surely not apparent as we entered the sixties.

Born into unparalleled prosperity, the Drug Generation spent their childhood in a land where the "good guys" were still US and the "bad guys" THEM. Reared on TV, Wonder bread, and vitamin pills, when they arrived at school, they were hit by the post-Sputnik anxiety of a generation of parents who were discovering that "Johnny can't read." Glutted with science and "scientific" learning, they all dutifully learned their chemistry lessons. They learned how bombs work, but the moon holds no poetry for them. They know about the "Six Day War," but Dachau is ancient history—Hitler might just as well have been Tamburlaine. They were still on their pottie chairs when Stalin died. For them, Jews were part of the Establishment. "Black Rage" had not broken through. Entering the fifties as war babies, they emerged from that decade as the Sputnik Generation. It was a time of hope. Penicillin and the New Math solved all problems. Cresting the sixties on a wave of social optimism, they were not yet ready to believe that Daddy could bullshit them.

With the election of John Kennedy, white America saw an economy on the rise, plentiful jobs, and steady progress being promised and achieved in racial desegregation. Most of our Sputnik kids, then approaching their teens, felt a great affinity for the handsome young president and his elegant first lady. Camelot was upon us. The Golden Age was at hand: "Let the word go forth from this time and place, to friend and foe alike, that the torch has been passed to a new generation of Americans—born in this century, tempered by war, disciplined by a hard and bitter peace, proud of our ancient heritage. . . ."

As we stood over our kitchen sinks that morning, some long dormant creative spirit moved inside us: our lives suddenly swelled with purpose and courage. Scores of kids, ministers, and housewives joined ranks with Martin Luther King as the civil rights marches began to be taken seriously by the white intelligentsia. We saw George Wallace stand at the door of the University of Alabama; we saw Robert Kennedy back him down. (Who were the "good guys" now? Hadn't Wallace fought for America in World War II?)

John Kennedy focused the idealism of youth on becoming involved: "Ask not what your country can do for you . . ." (Nobody had ever said *that* to them before!) They were to be part of the tremendous upsurge of personally rewarding political experience. The Peace Corps was created for them. But as the Sputnik kids approached puberty, cracks were appearing in the New Frontier. Underneath the inspired rhetoric, we were discovering that things wouldn't move just because a Kennedy told them to. Desegregation was slow and frustrating; many of our idealistic young were being brutalized in the South.

Kennedy had also failed to heed Eisenhower's last warning: beware the military-industrial complex. The awesome bureaucracies of the government, the Pentagon, big business, and the CIA went seemingly unchecked. We were all too busy being inspired to notice; we were all too busy being busy. Again we looked for a scapegoat and, sure enough, the Commies were still there—they were behind all those civil rights marches ("If only there weren't any Communists, we'd have peace." "Take a Bufferin. Buy a Bond.") In close succession then came the Cuban Missile Crisis, the Bay of Pigs fiasco, and the assassination of John Kennedy. When we looked around for a Communist conspiracy, what did we find? Lee Harvey Oswald, a frightened, sociopathic kid. A misfit product of our own megasociety . . . and Excedrin wouldn't make any of it go away.

LBJ: LESS BULLSHIT, JESUS!

In the trauma of readjustment, we were faced with Lyndon Johnson, a political monolith incapable of communicating with our newly vocal, radical young. Something had happened to the kids after Michael Schwerner et al. got bulldozed into the red Southern mud. They had all gone south in quest of the Holy Grail. When they came back they were changed forever: idealism had hardened into cynicism. They had been lured into involvement and had been blasted with reality. The credibility gap was born.

Another election, and Lyndon Johnson flapped back into the White House on the great gray wings of the dove. He would not abuse the Tonkin Resolution. He wanted the Asians to fight their own wars. But Ho Chi Minh was predicting that the American people could not last in his country for the ten years the struggle would take.

APRIL FOOL! On April 1, 1965, President Johnson decided to use American ground troops for offensive action in South Vietnam. In June, Chet Huntley remarked on a five-minute radio news analysis that whatever we wanted to call it, what was going on over there in Indochina was *war*. Our involvement in a country that few of us could find on a map had somehow expanded while we had been laughing at *I Love Lucy* and lapping up the fatherly concern of Daddy Cartwright. Behind the scenes, our young men began going off to war in large numbers. It was so easy. Our continuing fear of Communism had led us to the maintenance of the draft system. A limitless supply of young men—the oldest of the baby boom Sputnik kids—was at the disposal of our president, and without the hassle of congressional approval or the "nicety" of a declaration of war. As a growing stream of American resources, materials, and lives were channeled into a struggle that nobody wanted, but that nobody seemed to be able to avoid, most of us retreated into philosophical arguments about the Tonkin Resolution—over cocktails—or buried ourselves in jobs and homes, desperately trying to make them mean something apart from the world out there that was full of Commies and gooks and situations we couldn't seem to handle.

MacArthur had warned us about a land war in Asia, but swept up in the defense of our illusions, we barged in, destroying Hue "in order to save it." The ivory towers of intellectualism, our universities, began to be caught up against their will in the practicalities of war as draft boards began demanding a B average in exchange for a young man's life. The march on the Pentagon by a group of our more outspoken intellectuals and students marked the first major "white-versus-white" middle-class confrontation, while Johnson's own Polonius, General Westmoreland, even when skewered behind the cloak of his own military curtain, kept promising "a light [Napalm, perhaps?] at the end of the tunnel." Somebody, somewhere, was lying.

With the assassination of Malcolm X, whose integrity and ever-expanding mind had promised a bridge to racial adjustment, disillusionment erupted into open violence in Watts in the summer of '65, the first of the "long hot summers." Over a bottle of beer, Middle

America wondered "why?" The Free Speech Movement in Berkeley, the first confrontation of the new radical student leaders with the educational establishment, had dug its heels in and wouldn't go away. Grabbing for the bottle of Maalox, Middle-America wondered "why?" Cesar Chavez led Mexican farmworkers out on strike—Middle America could no longer hear. Experiencing culture shock for the first time, they were beginning to be afraid of their own kids.

The Sputnik kids, the TV Generation, reared in an era of instant worldwide communication, with its increasing focus on sociopolitical problems at home and abroad, were well aware by now that all was not well with our society. Somehow Dick and Jane and Puff and Spot had not prepared them for a real world where Bull Connor's fire hoses vied for newspaper space with the Jack Armstrong smiles of a new batch of astronauts, a TV world of tastelessly nonchalant juxtapositions: bloody corpses displayed in living color interrupted by the nubile and idiotic faces who complained, "Do you use Dial? Don't you wish everybody did?"

The war babies heard their parents complain, but remain unwilling to give up the American Dream for the American Reality: Communism has to be bad for us to be good; therefore, anything that is bad is Communist. Many of the kids were only too glad to confirm their parents' fears. Maoists, Leninists, Marxists, and Trotskyites seeped from every campus. They saw their own ponderous government grow more and more self-defensive, more removed, more unwilling to look at what they saw from their perspective. Mom and Dad kept pontificating: "When you get to be our age you'll wish. . . ." The Peace Corps was not what it had seemed. The draft hung over their heads like the sword of Damocles. Their comrades from the civil rights marches were beginning to say, "Black is beautiful. We don't need you, honky." Mom and Dad nagged about getting into college—the baby boom had produced intense competition for grades. Something had to give.

They had several alternatives, the Sputnik kids, as they approached their college years: they could do like Mom and Dad said, work like hell, get all A's and end up in a gray flannel suit, sipping martinis in the evening. But to get there, it was becoming increasingly obvious, you had to go by way of Vietnam. Another alternative was to let your hair grow, scream "motherfucker" at the registrar, and throw bombs at Bank of America buildings. Or third, and sometimes this seemed the only way out of the intolerable pressures caused by the opposition of the other two, was to say "fuck it" and drop out.

Born into optimism, educated in panic, the baby boom Sputnik kids, well versed in chemistry, brainwashed by TV into believing in the magic of pills, had metamorphosed in the sixties into the Drug Generation.

THE THIRD ALTERNATIVE

San Francisco has traditionally been a haven for the adventuresome, the disillusioned, the disenfranchised, the psychopathic, the runaway, and for any other stray soul who felt psychologically out of joint with society . . . whatever his reasons. In the days of the gold rush, it was the "Barbary Coast." In the days of the "Beats," it was North Beach. But when Tim Leary, Ken Kesey, and Augustus Owsley Stanley III discovered LSD, it was the Haight-Ashbury, and they invited everybody to come along on their trip: "Turn on, tune in, drop out. Expand your mind; turn on those billions of unused neurons like light-bulbs! We are composed of organic chemical compounds; therefore, we should be free to take into our bodies any of these substances we wish!" And as Tim, the Super Libra, became more evangelical, he cried, "You can be anything you want to be . . . this time!" Were we truly out of Scorpio? Was the Age of Aquarius to be? Or was it just another medicine show, a Pied Piper, a music man with a new snake oil for the seventies? To many it was a promise of hope, a way of circumventing intolerable realities, of avoiding the fact that "Yes, Virginia, Daddy *can* bullshit you."

The new hip community in the Haight was made up of a new breed of cat who was either stoned out of his mind or on the path to a *new society of man* . . . nobody could quite figure out which. After the three-day "Trips Festival" at Longshoreman's Hall in January 1966, thousands came out to see for themselves, and as they came, they brought with them a voracious press that was only too delighted to turn from the depressing facts of Vietnam to the San Francisco sound and the psychedelic scene. The press called them hippies, but they didn't really call themselves anything except pet names like "Teddybear" and "White Rabbit" and "Chocolate George."

The press heralded the onslaught of the "Summer of Love." The Haight, according to *Time* magazine that spring, was the "vibrant epicenter of America's hippie movement." Kids with flowers in their hair poured in; on any given day you might find (literally) as many as 25,000 kids, all from different drug backgrounds and all stuffed into six blocks of Haight Street. Empty kids from all over, anxious to be filled. God knows what made them come—like lemmings. It was the new Fort Lauderdale, and they surged around the street sign that said "Haight" and "Ashbury"; they overflowed into the Panhandle; they overran Golden Gate Park.

Some of them were intensely sincere. Still searching for the Holy Grail, they arrived in the Haight hoping to find it in the psychedelic experience of LSD . . . and out of this, they developed the ethic of the "dropped out." ("If you take LSD in the right circumstances, everything's cool.") They believed, with a religious fervor they believed, in expanding their consciousness and awareness through the use of chemicals. ("Better living through chemistry.") Lysergic acid diethylamide (LSD-25) and its cousins, mescaline, DMT, STP, MDA, and psilocybin provided a magic world of "mind expansion" which was unrelated to and, better yet, very much opposed to the ordered existence of the world their parents wanted them to believe in. If acid was the religious drug of this growing counterculture, then marijuana was its "social drug," used in group situations like Mom and Dad used booze. The very illegality of pot became the symbol of opposition to the "straight" world of war, academic achievement, and "bullshit."

Pitying the "uptight" Establishment, all the hippies, would-be hippies, borderline schizos, "walking crazies," and misplaced teeny-boppers grooved along in the counterculture, soaking up good vibes and righteous Owsley acid. Barefoot, they wandered through garbage, broken glass, and dog droppings, high on their magic pills. ("They all moved in here because they believed it was like the newspapers said.") Great God Acid would take care of them; it never occurred to them that they could ever get sick.

But it turned out *not* "to be like the newspapers said." To have a good trip on acid, it has to be peaceful and calm and uncrowded, and it's nice to have someone who's been there before—a guide or a guru —someone you can trust. With too many seekers and not enough guides, the Haight became like an overcrowded cage full of rats. They choked Golden Gate Park, all hopelessly looking for some secluded corner to trip out in. Soon there were no corners left and the righteous scene began to be a bummer.

The Diggers had predicted a lot of people, but the San Francisco Public Health Service had chosen to ignore the predictions, feeling apparently, that if they ignored the scene, the scene would just die or go away. But it didn't, and the only medical facility available to the tens of thousands of kids who were beginning to seek help was the Haight-Ashbury Free Medical Clinic, a band of dedicated innocents, led by Dr. David Smith, who had opened up shop in an old house on Clayton Street in the Haight that June.

"GIVE ME LIBRIUM, OR GIVE ME METH!"

As the summer wore on, Smith and his overworked volunteers perfected techniques for treating bad trips—they had "calm rooms" and "talk downs," and were able to send many of the confused trippers back out with a minimum of bad effects. But there were just too many people. The scene on the street was rapidly changing, and back to the street was where, after treatment, they all went. The big carnival had attracted the bikers, the bully-boys, Hell's Angels and Gypsy Jokers, who adopted the fashions of the hippie, but never his philosophy of love. They came for one thing—to exploit the scene—and the idealistic acid-heads had to be raped or ripped off a few times before they realized the speed scene was beginning to take over.

Eventually the disastrous "Summer of Love" ended, spewing literally thousands upon thousands of pill-poppers back to their home towns or colleges—to Des Moines, to Kansas City, to Great Falls, Montana— carrying visions and bizarre drug experiences back with them as the ripple effect of overt drug use crested back into Middle America. At the same time, the country plunged into an election year.

NEW HOPE WITH "CLEAN GENE"

The Drug Generation had a short resurgence of hope in 1968. If our political structure still had viability for our young, it seemed to be with "Clean Gene" McCarthy. First in New Hampshire, and then gathering spontaneous momentum across the country, youngsters were willing to shave and to trade their beads for narrow ties and neatly pressed suits; here was a chance to fight and win on the enemy's own battle-field, a last flash of the Sputnik challenge. The Establishment was faltering. Bobby Kennedy entered the fight and LBJ fled in disarray to the Pedernales. Then came the brief, exhilarating final moments of Robert Kennedy. The signs of an aggressive young fighter who had begun to glimpse the real needs of his country ended in a moment of tenuous triumph, then despair in the confusion of a Los Angeles hotel kitchen.

They had touched and felt victory. Now they held only a confused, sick, and bitter young Arab nationalist who, for whatever internal dissatisfactions, had attacked and murdered the emerging champion of the young.

The death of Robert Kennedy only seemed to complete the stroke that had cut down Martin Luther King scarcely two months before. King, peaceful but passionate, had joined Medgar Evers, Malcolm X, and a host of others among the martyrs of the civil rights movement. Black Americans were left with appeasing Uncle Toms pitched against an emerging nucleus of bitter, cynical young radical leaders. Polarization continued: there were major confrontations at San Francisco

State and Columbia University between the old, inflexible, established authority and the new, but as yet unorganized, student leaders. Demonstrations continued at the Oakland Induction Center.

Now Gene McCarthy, the poet-philosopher, not the in-fighter that Kennedy had been, abruptly quit the fight. If Norman Mailer loved him, the kids who had fought for him from New Hampshire to California felt deserted and betrayed. With the Democratic Convention in Chicago came worldwide TV coverage of a major riot: Richard Daley, the archetypal old political boss, sparred with the bratty antics of Jerry Rubin and overwhelmed with muscle the idealistic, but by now confused and disillusioned group of young political activists who had hoped for political change through the existing system.

1968: GRAY FLANNEL AND FLANNEL MOUTH

In the election of '68, we were suddenly faced with two candidates who fell far short of the personal charisma we had begun to expect from our political candidates: *Richard Nixon or HHH?* Tweedle-Dum or Tweedle-Dee? In either case, instant turn-off.

Having been packaged and sold like a can of Right Guard, Richard Milhous Nixon arrived, promising an "honorable end" to the war in Vietnam. With him came John Mitchell, the humorless Alfred Hitchcock of the law and order regime. Desegregation slowed down to appease the "Southern strategy"; Black radical leaders were jailed; and the Chicago Seven went through the tragicomic paces of trial before Judge Julius Hoffman, a senescent septuagenarian whose dusty Victorian sense of law was as currently relevant as asafetida was to acid.

Spiro T. Agnew was unleashed and we laughed, but the virulence of his polemics continued the polarization of elements within the country. The Cambodian invasion proved that our Congress and our State Department were helpless in the face of a president's midnight decisions.

Paternalism was on the land: Nixon experienced untold ecstasies with his television and his telephone as the first astronaut strolled on the moon. Martha Mitchell, like a latter-day Marie Antoinette in a cheap waxworks rendition of French history, was giving us the uncomfortable feeling that this crew of irritatingly ordinary people was being carried away on the wings of its own publicity. Martha might just as well have burbled, "Let them eat cake," as she peevishly stamped her feet, requesting a "compound" for government families . . . to be protected, no doubt, from the "liberal Communists" then swarming the streets of Washington in search of peace. The rest of us let down our fear of Communism as we began to feel terror of the Black

Panthers, the Yippies, the Weathermen. Guilt? Truly, our society appeared to have declared war on its children.

Nixon himself, pondering the generation gap, betook his presence to the throngs of demonstrators camped across from the White House, confident that a little chat about their hometown football teams and California surfing would help him "relate." To the young pacifists, the ghost of Hamlet's father would have felt more sincerity from Rosencrantz and Guildenstern. These were kids who had bummed across the country and partaken fully in the psychic rewards of chemistry; kids who had been hosed and beaten in Alabama; kids who had been clubbed and gassed and shot at by the pigs in Berkeley and Oakland; kids who had been, some of them, to Vietnam; kids who walked in the shadow of Napalm and the bomb—No, Richard, they did not come to discuss football.

THE AGE OF AQUARIUS AND THE END
OF INNOCENCE

If Woodstock was a fading glimpse of an idyllic Aquarian Age, the concert at Altamont proved to be a nightmare of violence and the inability of the young to cooperate, to do their own thing, or to love one another on a large-scale basis. They were, after all, not saints and genuises, just kids. Our kids, and they'd been on page one for a long time.

In the Haight-Ashbury, the halcyon days of early hippiedom, full of happy, smiling youngsters, were long past. The colorful shops that had been filled with psychedelic knickknacks, the flower children who had strolled Haight Street and tossed frisbees in Golden Gate Park, the tourists in their Grayline buses, gawking at the freaks—only to find themselves staring into hippie-held mirrors—were long gone. By 1968 a general boredom and discouragement had set in. People were wondering what had happened to the beautiful thing that had been the press-agent's Haight. Born out of optimism, good vibes, warm hearts, and acid, whatever the hope had been, it had not been sustained for lack of those manual and commercial skills so vital to the building and maintaining of a community.

Things were going downhill: buildings and people were deteriorating. Imbued with television's pharmacological overkill ("A Pill for Every Ill"), the street people were turning to their own pharmacopoeia of medications to alleviate all their psychedelic bad trips. They turned to speed to overcome the tension and anxiety produced by bummers. Speed did that; but it did a great deal more. Shooting speed produces a different personality from that of the peaceful acid-head. You get tense, jumpy—you can't stop talking; and if you take enough, you get paranoid and the probability of violence greatly increases.

On the street there was increasing malnutrition from the appetite suppression and sleeplessness of amphetamine abuse. Everybody was more and more susceptible to the diseases of bad hygiene. The street got dirtier, stores were boarded up, and more and more police were on patrol. Bizarre and lurid headlines screamed: "Superspade is Dead!" and another righteous dealer was murdered and dismembered. Other murders followed. The Haight had become a rip-off scene.

CHANGING DRUG PATTERNS IN THE HAIGHT

The speed scene lasted until October of 1969, but thankfully, the amphetamines were largely self-limiting; the very intensity of the speed trip eventually wears you out (and you stop taking it entirely), or it drives you to the use of a downer (primarily, at that time, barbiturates—'barbs'). As discouragement, disillusionment, and fear took over, the population of the Haight, still using their own pharmacopoeia, sought a social anaesthetic. Downers or dopers became prevalent and the Haight entered the upper-downer sequence.

The upper-downer (speed-barb) sequence was actually a reflection of the elements of drug abuse that were hawked daily on television in Madison Avenue's most persuasive terms. It was a macrocosm of the drugs found in any home medicine cabinet, wherein are contained legitimately prescribed amphetamines for weight control, pep pills for getting to work when you are suffering from "headache, neuritis, or neuralgia," sleeping pills, tranquilizers, and a plethora of other related medications that were all too easy to come by, by a visit either to the local doc (and a "script" doc was *always* available to prescribe by phone) or to the local pharmacist.

When the speed freak turned to barbs, there was another abrupt change in personality. No longer perpetually on the run, now he was "on the nod"—not the serene cool of an acid trip—he was sloppy, he talked at $33\frac{1}{3}$ rpm, he didn't comb his hair, sometimes he drooled or burned holes in his clothes with his cigarette. He may have found relief from his anxiety and from the intense depression which often follows an extended speed run, but he had become the biggest slob around. (In the hierarchy of drug users, the doper is only one step up from the glue-sniffer—one pattern that the drug abusing population of the Haight has been too sophisticated for.)

The personality of the Haight never became one of pure barbs because the continuing presence of speed masked the passive, dull scene of the barbiturates. In retrospect, however, the Haight-Ashbury neighborhood proved to be a selective end product in itself for prevailing drug abuse patterns. As one drug arrived on the scene and became more prevalent (or dominant), it pushed the previous one into the background.

SUCH STUFF AS DREAMS ARE MADE ON

The kids who had turned to the self-administered psychopharmacology of speed and barbs were, by the summer of 1969, using other depressants: alcohol, tranquilizers, PCP, other sedative-hypnotics, and opiates. It was perhaps no coincidence a few months later that, as "Operation Intercept" was being carried out on the Mexican border, drug patterns all over the country underwent a change. In the Haight, the kids turned to heroin. By November, the Haight Clinic was seeing up to sixty patients a day with symptoms of heroin intoxication.

To the almost totally alienated population in the Haight, the early thrill of subterfuge, the paraphernalia involved, and the routine one had to go through to acquire the drug—its very illegality—tempted them to follow what seemed to be a natural pattern of evolution to this perfect drug of social escape.

But beyond the initial thrills, heroin, unlike acid or speed, produces a true physical dependence. Although withdrawal from heroin won't kill you (and does not produce the convulsions and occasional deaths seen with barbiturate, alcohol, and tranquilizer withdrawals), the process of withdrawal can be discomforting in the extreme. One addict described it as "super flu."

As physical tolerance develops, the limiting factor in heroin use or abuse is economic: it costs too much to go over a $200-a-day habit because you have to deal or steal $400 (or more) worth of goods to get that. There is also the tremendous physical and psychological drain on anyone attempting to acquire the daily money for this habit. Brought up in comfort, many of the new "middle-class" junkies just can't hack it—the hassle gets to be too much.

The pharmacologic effect of heroin, given in controlled (sterile, or at least clean) situations, is not in itself harmful. (Indeed, the medical profession and its legitimate patients have been the ultimate losers in the illegalization of heroin, because its pain-relieving and euphoriant properties are not available to such people as terminal cancer victims.) The way you die from heroin is from overdose—you stop breathing— or from a secondary infection that is either masked by the pain-killing properties of the drug and thus not treated or related to the unsterile conditions surrounding the fix.

The greatest chance of overdose and death with heroin occurs in the nontolerant individual and in the person who combines it with other potent respiratory depressant drugs (such as alcohol or barbiturates). Janis Joplin and Jimi Hendrix were victims of such multiple drug abuse.

As might be predicted, the atmosphere of the Haight is now the dead cool of the smack-head, who is introverted and selfish to a remarkable degree. In belonging to an illegitimatized population, he lives in the shadows of success-oriented America. He accepts deception and dishonesty as part of his daily life; to survive he becomes a master manipulator and a rip-off artist, but he avoids violence and headlines or confrontation at all times.

Maybe it was all a press-agent's dream; maybe the "New Community" of love and hope had never really existed; maybe we had been misled by the columnists who wrote that the Haight was so beautiful— so bent on an ecstatic and fulfilling future—bent on an alternative to the materialism, nationalism, deception, and alienation of our time. It is a sad paradox: the flower child, so intent on personal freedom, has come full circle to the drug of complete personal slavery—the ultimate pharmacological cop-out—heroin. The ragged remnants of the baby boom, the shards of a million chemistry experiments (on themselves), the nation's new "niggers"—our own kids—are no longer dreaming of becoming astronauts. Promised a vicarious trip to the moon (LSD is faster) or a very real trip to Vietnam, they are now scheming how to get their next fix; they lives are pinned on the point of a dirty needle.

In considering the overall patterns of drug abuse in the Haight-Ashbury and elsewhere, these factors stand out:

1. There is a historically unparalleled availability of (and familiarity with) an almost endless range of drugs—often of undetermined nature or strength.

2. Parallel to this is a powerful peer-group pressure. We can expect youngsters from any family and any walk of life to have a surprisingly complete knowledge of, and wide range of experience with, all the common street drugs—and they inevitably "turn on" their friends.

3. The only consistent factor noted in drug abuse in the Haight-Ashbury has been change itself—with a predictability seen only in retrospect. We have seen the psychedelics crest and give way to amphetamines, the use of which, in turn, led to barbiturates—and now heroin. Invariably, one drug is taken to make you feel good because the last one you took got too heavy.

4. Drug patterns in the Haight have been seen, in the years be-

tween 1965 and the present, to spread throughout the rest of the country in a ripple effect as those who heard the call in the early sixties gave up on the Haight and went back home, back to school, or to a thousand different scenes, taking the Haight's acquired drug patterns with them.

AND WHAT ROUGH BEAST, ITS HOUR COME ROUND AT LAST . . .

Heroin is only about seventy years old. At the turn of the century, the only addicts in this country were a few Chinese opium smokers and many unsuspecting housewives who sipped patent medicines that contained opiates for their attacks of the "vapors." But in 1906 the Pure Food and Drug Act made all that illegal and by 1910 doctors also discovered that heroin, which had been developed in Germany in 1898, and was at first thought by some to be a cure for morphine addiction, was itself addictive. Since that time we have become progressively sillier in our legislation concerning narcotic drugs. Our moralistic tendencies continue to lead us to produce monsters in order for us to appear virtuous to ourselves. We have spent the last sixty-five years developing a highly complicated, but also highly profitable "illegal" schematic: two groups of fat cats sit in the middle, feeding on each other and draining dry those above and below them. These are (1) the Federal Bureau of Narcotics and the CIA, and (2) the Man, organized crime, who imports diacetylmorphine from Marseilles, Lisbon, and Tunis. This source is being bypassed more and more, however; as our involvement in Southeast Asia has increased since World War II, the supply of heroin from Indochina has increased and now it is estimated that 80 percent of the world's 1200 tons of illicit opium comes through the hands of the small countries in the fertile triangle that we are "liberating" in the cause of "democracy."

Below the fat cats are the junkies—bloodsucked dry by the frenzied hustle to procure heroin by dealing, stealing, or turning tricks until they reach the economic ceiling (about $200 a day). Above are the rest of us—good Puritan-bred Americans, the great, silent, bewildered majority whose automobiles (the symbol of our potency), electronic gadgets (the symbol of our prosperity), and TV sets (the means by which we keep ourselves "informed") are the objects of the junkie rip-off. They steal from us to go for broke with the guys in the middle —to pay for a habit that we have made both illegal and possible by idiotic legislation. We have created this cute little game of cops-and-robbers for the men in the middle to play, while the junkie below shakes for a fix and we above shake in fear of being robbed.

There is one solution, of course, and that is to remove heroin from the streets. Until recently, the application of the law of supply and demand worked quite well in England, where a junkie could go for a legal and medically regulated fix. (Now, however, in a misguided attempt to legislate morality, the English have substituted methadone for heroin and have, in effect, created an illicit market on the street where none existed before.)

Another effective, if hard-nosed, approach has worked in parts of Harlem and Oakland where the "pusher man" has simply been "offed" —a local problem handled by local community action; no intervention by civil or government conscience money, just a break in the chain that eliminates one of the major determinants in the spread of the addiction and abuse process—availability.

However, what past administrations have done and what Nixon is continuing to do is to pass more and more punitive legislation that gluts our jails with smack-heads, but does nothing to get at the root of the problem. One junkie said, "with all the new arrests here in San Francisco, it's really hard to get junk. Today it took me *three* hours!" Nixon's administration has inherited mendacity and seems to be perpetuating it. The president is still promising that we will "leave Vietnam with honor" (and 60,000 junkies); he promises us $155 million for addict rehabilitation, but he apparently does not see the tons of raw opium being processed and fed yearly into the United States as a direct result of our presence in Southeast Asia. He dons his television "look of concern" and states bluntly that we must cut off foreign aid to countries that produce opium. ("What? And turn Laos over to the Commies?") Nixon, reacting to overwhelming pressure from all sides, has now declared drug abuse "America's new Public Enemy Number 1." In creating a Special Action Office of Drug Abuse Prevention to develop overall strategy, he has in some respects reversed John Mitchell's Napoleonic approach (arrest an individual *before* he has committed a crime) and has offered clemency to veterans who admit they are addicts.

Either this is a direct sham or else the Penatgon generals have missed Nixon's cue, for they claim that the military shares no responsibility for drug addiction and that GI benefits must be denied for this "non-service-related" disability. Attempts to clean up GI's for thirty days before releasing them to points of debarcation (like San Francisco) seem to be an attempt by the Armed Services to evade the issue and wash their hands of the whole affair. Enforced detoxification does not work; certainly not unless prolonged supportive aftercare goes along with it. And the slap-dash, get-em-moving approach demonstrated by the Army recently in Vietnam leaves much to be desired.

It is time to stop lying, both to ourselves and to each other. We are dealing with a medical and psychosocial problem that, although it appears staggering simply because of our abhorrence of what the "junkie" represents, *can* be reversed. The small, short-term smack habit (and the preponderant availability in Vietnam is just a little over two years old) *is* reversible . . . but not by arresting and harassing individuals, some of whom are already at the breaking point. We must stop creating hysterical legislation. Addiction must be faced by the AMA and Public Health Services at local, state, and national levels. Careful funding of well-conceived programs must be facilitated with money perhaps freed from such items as SSTs, guns, tanks, moon walks —and Agnew's rhino-watching. Innovative techniques should be explored (such as the self-sufficient commune to remove young people from the dope-saturated inner-city-sanctums), and we must explore and expand old and proven modalities of treatment (such as methadone maintenance *with aftercare* and ambulatory methadone withdrawal).

VIETNAM, LOVE IT OR LEAVE IT!

Now split the decade like a stack of smudged and greasy Tarot cards. October 16, 1965. At the Berkeley campus at the Vietnam Day Rally. Up turns Kesey, painted like the Fool in Merry Prankster Day-Glo.

> There's only one thing to do . . . there's only one thing's gonna do any good at all . . . and that's everybody just look at it, look at the war, and turn your backs and say . . . Fuck it! . . . Just look at it and turn away and say Fuck it! . . . *Fuck it!*

There is *no way* to leave Vietnam "with honor." With that country Democracy-, Dope-, and Napalm-ravaged, and millions dead, translate "honor" into "horror" . . . or into silent rage.

Faced with a problem of such magnitude and immediacy, we can no longer wish it away or lie it out of existence. If our "honor" is lost, perhaps we can at least salvage our youth.

Mendacity . . . no more!

2

A Brief History of Heroin Addiction in America

John C. Kramer, M.D.

When people get together to talk about heroin dependence, the discussion quite properly centers around the question of how to solve the problem. But there is another question that bears discussion: How did we get to where we are?

Archaeologic studies suggest that opium was used at least as early as 4000 B.C. in Sumeria and about 3500 B.C. in Egypt. There is evidence that it was used in ancient Assyria, Babylonia, Persia, and Greece. Egyptian papyri of 1550 B.C. list opium as one of 7000 remedies, and Assyrian medical tablets of the seventh century B.C. also mention it. Pliny the Elder, during the first century A.D., was aware of some of the risks of the drug and described opium poisoning.

Albert Fields and Peter Tararin have summarized some of this early history.[1] They describe how the opium trade and addiction were spread throughout the Arab empire after the seventh century. Opium's dissemination in the Near East may have been enhanced by the prohibition of alcohol in the Koran. During the last 2000 years opium use has spread widely throughout Europe, Asia, and North Africa both as a remedy for a variety of symptoms and, in many places, as a pleasure-giving drug. Nonetheless, there was no noticeable concern over addiction until well into the nineteenth century. This is not to say that the effects of withdrawal of the drug after prolonged use were never seen. In fact, the Portuguese physician Acosta wrote in 1655 of the difficulty some patients experienced in giving up the drug.[2]

1. Albert Fields and Peter A. Tararin, "Opium in China," *British Journal of Addiction* 64 (1970): 371–382.
2. As quoted in M. Goldsmith, *The Trail of Opium: The Eleventh Plague* (London: Robert Hale, Ltd., 1939), pp. 000.

Rather it appeared to be an accidental and occasional phenomenon. The Emperor Yung Ching of China forbade the domestic sale of smoking opium in 1729. However, since a previous Chinese emperor had forbidden the use of tobacco, the significance of Yung Ching's prohibition is uncertain.

In 1701 the English physician John Jones noted that some people used opium regularly.[3] He described the symptoms of withdrawal "after long and lavish use thereof," as well as the relief provided by resuming the use of the drug. Despite this, he argued for moderation in the use of opium, not for abstinence. About fifty years later another physician, George Young of Edinburgh, wrote a treatise on opium's indications and contraindications.[4] He described an addicted patient whose friends had suggested that she lay aside opium before it became a habit and went on to say that his patient would rather lay aside her friends. Clearly, even in the eighteenth century it was common knowledge that opium could be addictive and that the habit was cause for concern. Young also describes habituation, physical dependence, tolerance, and euphoria (he does not, of course, use this vocabulary), yet he did not view the phenomenon that was later to be called addiction as a serious problem. Thomas DeQuincy, the English opium eater, wrote of a book by an apothecary named Awsiter, whose essay on the effects of opium had been published in 1763.[5] Awsiter feared that widespread habituation would occur if the properties of the drug became universally known, and he thought such a situation would be a general misfortune.

During the eighteenth century, then, the phenomenon of dependence on opium was recognized, heavy and extensive use in the Orient was described, and it was known that some people in Western nations took the drug regularly but without ill effects so long as they did not discontinue its use. In the early nineteenth century the autobiographical reminiscences of Thomas DeQuincy and descriptions of Samuel Taylor Coleridge's use of opium in vast quantities brought to light the possibility of heavy use among non-Asiatics, but even these revelations did not inspire wide concern.

The *American Journal of Medical Sciences* for 1832 discussed a British civil suit concerning an addicted nobleman who had taken an insurance policy on his life. Upon his demise the insurance company

3. As quoted in G. Sonnedecker, "Emergence and Concept of the Addiction Problem," in *Narcotic Drug Addiction Problems,* ed. R. B. Livingston (Washington: U.S. Public Health Service, 1963).

4. George Young, *A Treatise on Opium* (London: A. Millar, 1753).

5. Anonymous: Review of "Apologia; or Confessions of an English Opium Eater: Being an Extract from the Life of a Scholar, *"Medico-Chirurgical Review* 2 (1822): 881–901.

refused to pay because they claimed that his addiction had compromised his health. Expert evidence presented during the hearing cast doubt on the part that addiction played in his death. The American physician who commented on this case described several of his own addicted patients and speculated on the medical aspects of opium addiction in general. The doctor's speculations are of less importance than is the revelation that the habitual use of opium was frequent enough in the United States for a single physician to have noted several cases in his own practice. In 1856 George B. Wood described "enormous abuse" of opium and suggested that apothecaries were more aware of its true extent in the United States than physicians.[6] Dr. Wood indicated that only through the occasional observation of withdrawal symptoms did physicians become aware of the presence of an opium habit. Horace Day described his successful effort to withdraw from fifteen years of addiction.[7] When he wrote in 1868, he had been abstinent for about ten years. At that time he estimated that opium eaters in the United States numbered between 80,000 and 100,000, which would be about one addict for every 350 people. Though the recent Civil War had added to these numbers, Day implied that many had become habituated before that conflict. In his view, businessmen and laborers seldom became addicted, but professional and literary men, people with protracted nervous disorders, hard-working women, prostitutes, and the injured from the Civil War were particularly susceptible. The observation that addicts generally did not reveal their addiction by their appearance or by any defect in their morals was notable. Nevertheless, the regular use of opium was occasionally referred to as a vice and DeQuincy either chose to call his autobiographical sketch "confessions" or allowed someone else to do so. It was clear even at the beginning of the nineteenth century that whatever pleasures opium provoked and however easily its pains could be held at bay, dependence on it sooner or later was felt to be a bondage, tolerable only because life without the drug was more intolerable.

It appears, then, that through the middle of the nineteenth century a recognition was gradually growing that the regular use of opium could lead to habituation. Travelers to the East told of the habit being both widespread and heavy in various areas, but few suggested that it was detrimental to life and health in very many cases. Concern about the abuse of alcohol sprang up earlier than serious concern about the opium habit. Many advocates of temperance proposed not merely that drunkenness was bad, but that any imbibing at all inevitably led

6. George B. Wood, *A Treatise on Therapeutics and Pharmacology or Materia Medica*, 2 vols. (Philadelphia: J. B. Lippincott and Co., 1856).

7. Anonymous (attributed to Horace Day), *The Opium Habit, with Suggestions as to the Remedy* (New York: Harper & Bros., 1868).

to destruction. The temperance movement flourished steadily and reached its crescendo in 1920 with the onset of prohibition. The same year, in effect, marked the onset of prohibitions against medical management of addicts.

Several events of the mid-nineteenth century altered the picture of dependence on opiates. Among them were the Civil War; the introduction of opium smoking; the temperance movement, which brought about local prohibition in some areas; the introduction of the hypodermic needle; and the advertising of opium-bearing patent medicines. C. E. Terry and N. Pellens, the most prominent compilers of data on opium dependence, have, like most of the subsequent reviewers of this history, given the Civil War a foremost place in creating the problem.[8] However, this event may have been a less significant influence than is generally believed. Throughout the latter half of the nineteenth century substantially more women than men were addicted, which is the reverse of the situation we would expect if Civil War veterans made up a predominant proportion of the addicts. Civil War veterans did add to the numbers of the addicted, but there appear to have been a substantial number of American addicts before the war and only a portion of the addiction afterward could be attributed to the war.

After the middle of the nineteenth century we thus see a changing picture. First, the rate of dependence was rising, though perhaps not as fast as is sometimes suggested; second, awareness of the dependence-producing qualities of opium drugs was increasing; and third, opium and morphine addiction were beginning to be identified with criminals. Nevertheless, it would be erroneous to assume that the era was marked by a clamor for immediate action. From 1884 to 1893 the *Journal of the American Medical Association* published only about twenty items relating to opiate dependence. The mood was neither one of total apathy nor one of pressing concern. The addiction rate was high, but addicts were generally unobtrusive because opiates were readily and cheaply available. Though action was taken against opium smoking, other forms of the drug were not only available but advertised.

By the beginning of the twentieth century physicians and pharmacists had become aware that any continued use of opiates carried a risk of addiction and they exercised more care in dispensing than had their predecessors. Importation of opium from 1900 to 1909 shows a per capita decrease over the previous decade.

Ironically, it was a Southeast Asian war that planted the first seeds of both the later international negotiations on narcotics control and the American control laws. The Spanish American War had given the

8. C. E. Terry and M. Pellens, *The Opium Problem* (New York: Bureau of Social Hygiene, Inc., 1928).

United States dominion over the Philippine Islands. Subsequently several commissions were assigned to investigate various questions of the health and welfare of the Islands, including the use of opium in the Philippines and throughout the Far East. In 1903 the American Pharmaceutical Association had reported an alarming increase in opium use by American troops stationed in the Philippines and concern over these findings may have influenced undertaking the investigation. The commission found that opium smoking was less extensive in the Philippines than elsewhere in the Orient and that it was primarily a practice of the Chinese, not the Filipinos. Nevertheless, the commission anticipated the worst and assumed that the practice would grow if not strongly checked. One of the members of that commission, Episcopal Bishop Charles Brent, several years later wrote to President Theodore Roosevelt about the immoral opium trade in the Far East. Activist as he was, Roosevelt proposed an international conference to discuss the problem. The meeting convened in Shanghai in 1909 and, under pressure from the American delegation, struck out in favor of strong international drug control, specifically, "in favor of immediate opium prohibition as the goal everywhere." A group of resolutions were adopted, which were to be followed by a treaty. To that end a conference was convened at the Hague, where a multilateral treaty was proposed that required unanimous approval to become effective. Though the requirement for unanimity was later abrogated, the vote to abrogate was less than unanimous and therefore of doubtful authority. Strictly speaking, the treaty was not in effect until after World War I, when ratification of the Treaty of Versailles and the other treaties of peace included ratification of the Hague Convention of 1912. However, the United States had ratified the treaty on December 10, 1913, and immediately claimed it to be in force. One reason why this was so vital was that the constitutionality of the proposed Harrison Narcotics Act had been challenged on the basis that its presentation as a revenue measure was a subterfuge to allow federal control in an area reserved to the states by the Constitution. Presenting the act as a fulfillment of a treaty obligation would help to quiet such opposition. Thus, though it is usually stated that the Harrison Act was passed to fulfill our international obligations under the Hague Convention, it might be more accurate to state that the Hague Convention was organized so that the Harrison Act could be passed. Despite hesitancy about this or that provision and despite the enforced delay in final ratification due to the more immediate business of World War I, none of the nations really questioned the assumption that control of international and internal commerce in opium, opiates, and cocaine was necessary. However, having had centuries of experience with opiate dependence, most nations realized that it was impossible to abruptly deny addicts the use of opiates without creating immense turmoil and perhaps dooming the efforts.

It was largely American willfulness that initiated and propelled the international control of narcotics. The nineteenth century was an era of reform movements. Since man was learning to shape and control his environment through the application of scientific discoveries, it must have seemed appropriate to control and shape his own behavior as well. Antislavery, antiliquor, antiprostitution, and antidrug movements all sought to better mankind through legislation. The United States was characterized by a directness and an impatience both in its international negotiations and at home. Internationally, its will was tempered by other nations; at home it was not and the U.S. approached the problem of addiction with surgical simplicity.

The Harrison Narcotics Act was by no means the first federal law regulating opiates. In 1842 a tariff had been applied to imported opium. The rate varied over the years and at times the tax profoundly affected the quantity of opium legally imported. As early as 1888 consideration was given to the possibility of prohibiting the importation of smoking opium. By 1909 many states and localities had banned opium smoking and federal statute had forbidden it in the Philippines. Meanwhile the product was still imported quite legally, with the tariff collected for revenue. In February 1909 Congress finally acted to prohibit its importation as of April 1909, and declared that after April 1913 all smoking opium discovered would be presumed to have been smuggled. Prohibiting the importation of smoking opium did not prevent the diversion of medicinal opium for conversion to smoking opium within the United States, so in January 1914 the manufacture of smoking opium was effectively prohibited by a federal law that set a licensing fee of $100,000 for the manufacture and a tax of $100 per pound on the product.

Since we are now talking about the turn of the century, it is appropriate to discuss the introduction of heroin (diacetylmorphine). The substance was first synthesized in the 1870s, but was evidently left unstudied until about 1890, when some of its effects were examined in dogs. In 1898 the Bayer Chemical Company of Germany placed heroin on the market for general medical use. Though the story has often been told, and has even been dignified by appearing in print, I have found no evidence for the contention that heroin was introduced as a cure for the morphine habit. The journals of the day describe it as merely a cough suppressant when taken orally in doses of 3 to 5 milligrams. Some early reports indicated that heroin did not appear to be addictive, while still other reports suggested that it did not have analgesic effects. In the doses prescribed, neither of these two eventualities were likely. A report appeared in 1900 and another in

1901 stating that in a few individual cases heroin had been found to alleviate symptoms of morphine withdrawal. Dr. Maurice B. Ahlborn in the *Medical Summary* of Philadelphia, February, 1901, reported having been able to relieve the withdrawal symptoms from morphine dependence in three cases by using relatively small quantities of heroin. Several nonprescription patent remedies for the cure of the morphine habit contained heroin, but a much larger number of home remedies for the treatment of the morphine habit contained morphine itself. By 1903 there was no longer a question that heroin had a substantial capacity to induce dependence. In short, there appears to be no foundation for the notion that heroin was introduced as a morphine cure, nor does its possible use in alleviating withdrawal symptoms appear to have been given any more than transitory consideration.

Let us return to the question of federal narcotics laws. Despite the real intent of Congress to control rather than to tax and despite the uncertain status of the 1912 treaty when the Harrison Narcotics Act was passed, it was ultimately declared constitutional. Without a doubt, effective control over the distribution of opiates and cocaine was necessary. Aside from its questionable constitutionality, the Harrison Narcotics Act was a reasonable piece of legislation. With that tool in hand, it seemed merely a matter of time before the addiction problem would be solved.

But even before the passage of the act, there was one overriding question, which remains to this day the source of debate: should people who are already addicted, who have developed a compulsive need for opiates, continue to receive their drug, under careful supervision? It had been common practice for physicians to continue prescribing opiates for patients who were unable, or unwilling, to live without them. Most addicts had maintained their habits with regular doses purchased quite legally from pharmacists. As far as can be determined now, in retrospect, they continued to function fairly well. The passage of the Harrison Act caused considerable concern among physicians about what limitations the law might place on their privilege to prescribe as they saw fit within the bounds of accepted medical practice. The part of the act that helped allay their fears stated: *Harrison Act*

> Nothing contained in this section [prohibiting distribution of opium, opiates, and cocaine] shall apply:
> a) to the dispensing or distribution of any of the aforesaid drugs to a patient by a physician, dentist, or veterinary surgeon registered under this act during the course of his professional practice.

Shortly before the act became law, Dr. Charles E. Terry, who had worked with addicts for several years, wrote in the *American Journal of Public Health* of the need for more information on the problem of addiction and the need to provide a supply of drugs for certain users. Shortly after the law became effective, an editorial in the *Journal of the American Medical Association* stressed the importance of preventing illicit traffic without interfering with the legitimate use of these drugs by physicians. Many articles, comments, and notes followed in the journal informing physicians of their obligations to register and of the requirements for prescription-writing and dispensing of opiates and cocaine. One editorial is of particular interest. First it describes some of the international negotiations that had preceded the Harrison Act, then goes on to discuss some practical matters:

> But what about old habitués, persons suffering from painful and incurable diseases, and others to whom opium in some form is absolutely necessary? Every physician knows of such cases. For them the physician so long as he complies with the law of his own state can prescribe whatever he sees fit. But it must be done openly and without attempt at evasion and the physician must be ready and able at any time to justify his acts. The whole purpose of the law is to restrict use of opium and cocaine to legitimate channels.[9]

The journal's repeated reaffirmation of the physician's privilege to prescribe narcotics for his addicted patients ceased abruptly after the journal noted Treasury Decision 2200. Announced May 11, 1915. The decision stated that physicians' prescriptions for narcotics for addicts must show decreasing doses over time; were this not the case, the physician would be presumed to be violating the law. The abruptness with which this order appeared and its contradiction to the editorial opinions that had been expressed in the journal right up to the date of the order suggested that it was a Treasury Department decision, which was made unencumbered by medical opinion. Treasury Department officials had made a decision as to what was proper medical practice and then proceeded to enforce this decision through their police power. This order, issued a few weeks after the Harrison Act took effect, authorized what was later to be called the "ambulatory reductive" treatment. In this, the doctor could prescribe narcotics to an addict so long as the dose prescribed was gradually diminished. Over the next few years Treasury Department orders became more and more restrictive until ultimately it became a prosecutable offense to prescribe or provide any narcotics whatever to an unhospitalized addict. The concept that "control"equalled prohibition had also been promulgated by the United States government in international conferences, but few other nations had found this interpretation reasonable or acceptable, not because it was undesirable, but because it was impractical.

9. Editorial, *Journal of the American Medical Association* 64 (1915): 834–835.

For several years the constitutionality of the Harrison Narcotics Act remained in question, finally reaching a test in the United States Supreme Court in the case of the United States *vs.* Doremus in the spring of 1919. The Court decided, five to four, that "the act may not be declared unconstitutional because its effect may be to accomplish another purpose as well as the raising of revenue." The majority of the court refused to recognize that raising revenue was in no way the objective of the act. On the same day the Doremus decision was announced, the Supreme Court disclosed its views in the case of Webb and Goldbaum *vs.* the United States. Going beyond the case at hand, the United States Attorney had asked this question of the court:

> If a practicing and registered physician issued an order for morphine to an habitual user thereof, the order not being issued by him in the course of professional treatment in the attempted cure of the habit, but being issued for the purpose of providing the user with morphine sufficient to keep him comfortable by maintaining his customary use, is such order a physician's prescription under [the meaning of the law]?

Although a majority of the Court ruled that such a prescription was not in the course of professional practice, four of the nine justices once again dissented. It is possible that the Court failed to note the curious phrasing of the question, which assumed that in all cases "treatment" was identical with "attempted cure." The attorney who asked the question and the five justices who ruled against it failed to recognize that where a physician cannot cure, it is equally "professional practice" to sustain a patient and retard his deterioration. It was widely known that most opiate addicts continued to function adequately while receiving their drugs, but, if denied legitimate supplies, would turn to illicit sources of drugs and ultimately, to the detriment of themselves and society, to illicit enterprises. Even if scientific evidence could have been presented to show that maintaining addicts on drugs was unwise in the long run, the Court's declaration that it was a "perversion of the meaning" of medical practice was a gross and grievous error. It had, in fact, been acceptable medical practice for ages, continued to be so until the moment of the decision, remained acceptable medical practice in most civilized nations, and under certain limitations has again become acceptable medical practice in the United States. The Treasury Department continued to assume the role of physician and to restrict doctors' prerogatives to prescribe. In the summer of 1919 the Treasury Department declared that "mere addiction alone is not recognized as an incurable disease," a simplistic statement that abjectly disregarded the known chronicity and relative intractability of dependence on opiates.

Though the first narcotic maintenance clinic was opened in Jacksonville, Florida, in 1912 and performed quite well, the real era of the narcotic clinics spanned a relatively short period during 1919 and 1920. The clinic in New York City was poorly run, and unfortunately it has been presented as exemplifying all the narcotic clinics. It was opened as an emergency measure on April 10, 1919, less than two days after the arrest of six physicians and four pharmacists for prescribing and dispensing drugs to addicts. There were probably more physicians and pharmacists engaged in this practice, but the arrests undoubtedly caused the others to cease. Over the next nine months nearly 7500 addicts used the New York Clinic. Records were poorly kept and lines of waiting addicts stretched down the street. After having received their morphine, addicts could return to the end of the line and many did. Police agents could enter the line and receive morphine and they too did.

The clinics cannot be said to have failed, because, with one or two exceptions, they were not open long enough for reliable evaluation. The only criticism that can be substantiated is that some clinics were poorly run, a condition that would have been more likely remedied by keeping them open and improving their management than by shutting them down and thereby depriving both the nation and the addicts of one possible option in the management of addiction. The clinic in Shreveport, Louisiana remained open for about four years, operated first by the state of Louisiana and subsequently by the city of Shreveport. Case records were carefully kept, medical and drug histories were recorded, and curability was evaluated. Efforts to reduce and eliminate the habit were made in cases that were deemed curable. Where appropriate, addicts were hospitalized and intercurrent diseases were treated. Terry and Pellens[10] document enthusiastic support for the clinic among local physicians and community authorities. On the other hand, arguments presented many years later by opponents of the clinics take the form of such vague generalities as "Several prostitutes attended the clinic" or "The addicts said they would take less drugs if the costs were higher" or of such anonymous quotations as "One citizen of Shreveport stated, 'the clinic is outrageous.' "

It has also been stated that local officials decided on their own to close the clinics. Though this may be true of some instances, the position of the Treasury Department was at that time so firm and their influence so great that it does not seem unfair to say that Treasury itself was responsible for closing the clinics. The *Illinois State Medical Journal* for September 1920 made the terse announcement that the Federal Prohibition Commissioner, John F. Kramer (no relation to the author) had ordered all the clinics closed. Another erroneous view

10. Terry and Pellens, *The Opium Problem.*

that has been stated frequently is that the weight of medical opinion of the day was opposed to the maintenance approach. A reading of the contemporary journals suggests, quite to the contrary, that the preponderance of physicians, especially of those concerned with addiction problems, argued for the need for narcotic maintenance of many addicts.

Many physicians were concerned that if the wrong people were appointed to the new drug committee of the American Medical Association, the position of American medicine might be misrepresented.[11] Precisely this event occurred. One member of the four-man committee was Thomas S. Blair, who mocked the concern of physicians for the suffering of their addict patients and advocated abrupt withdrawal of narcotics.[12] It was also his view that imprisoning addicts accomplished the best results. He urged physicians to accept police policy with "sweet reason" and stated that the narcotic laws could help the doctor by relieving him of the burden of caring for addicts.[13] Another member of this committee was Dr. Alfred P. Prentice, who wrote of "sinister propaganda" to create popular sentiment against the Harrison Act and of a widespread conspiracy to defeat the purpose of the law.[14] In condemning any opinions that the Harrison Act was unconstitutional as sinister or as a conspiracy, Prentice lost sight of the fact that four of nine Supreme Court justices had voted that way in the Doremus case. As promulgators of "fallacies" he cited such professional journals as *American Medicine,* the *Illinois Medical Journal,* the *American Journal of Clinical Medicine,* the *Medical Record,* and the *American Journal of Public Health,* as well as such lay publications as the Washington *Post,* the New York *Tribune,* the *New York Times,* the New York *World,* the Chicago *Tribune,* the New York *American,* and *New Republic.* In essence, he damned to hell every physician who disagreed with him and concluded pompously and with the finality of a judge rendering a death sentence: "and may God have mercy on their souls." These two unreasonable men made up half the American Medical Association's committee to judge the new restrictions on physicians' prerogatives to prescribe opiates. In 1921 this committee presented to the House of Delegates of the American Medical Association a resolution that stated that the American Medical Association should condemn any "ambulatory methods of treatment." The House of Delegates

11. D. Brown, "Letter to editor," *American Medicine* 27 (1921): 264–265.

12. T. S. Blair, "Narcotic Drug Addiction as Regulated by a State Department of Health, *Journal of the American Medical Association* 72 (1919): 1441–1445.

13. T. S. Blair, "Making the Narcotic Laws Help the Doctor and Not Hinder Him in His Work," *American Medicine* 26 (1920) 373–380; and "The Doctor, the Law and the Drug Addict," *American Medicine* 27 (1921): 581–588.

14. A. C. Prentice, "The Problem of the Narcotic Drug Addict," *Journal of the American Medical Association* 76 (1921): 1551–1554.

rejected this proposal in its 1921 meeting; it rejected it in its 1922 meeting; in 1923 the House of Delegates again rejected the proposal and officially protested the prohibition commissioner's ill-advised interference with the practice of medicine. However, in 1924, the House of Delegates finally accepted the proposal. In retrospect, that acceptance looks meaningless, since by then American physicians had already been prohibited, to all intents and purposes, from prescribing opiates to addicts for four years.

Over the years the notion has been falsely promulgated that ambulatory treatment of narcotics addicts was rejected by American physicians. Closer inspection of the record shows that, in fact, the decision was forced upon them. Whether or not it should have been judged constitutional, the Harrison Act itself was not a bad law. It offered an excellent opportunity to control indiscriminate over-the-counter sales and to control the indiscriminately prescribing physician. Had American physicians been more determined to resist unfair and politically inspired interpretations of the act, it seems likely that a reasonable approach could have been found to supply the intractably addicted without serious abuses of the system. When doctors lost their privilege to prescribe for addicts, they also lost the opportunity to treat addicts, whether with drugs or without. Although hospital treatment was permitted, there were virtually no hospital facilities. A breach was made between the addict and the physician that has only recently been narrowed.

Through the middle and late nineteenth century most American addicts were initiated in their habit through medical treatment, whether self-medication or a physician's prescription. By the latter third of the nineteenth century opium smoking and subsequently other means of ingestion were used by members of the demimonde. Addicts who used intramuscular or subcutaneous injections often suffered from multiple abcesses, but those who used the drug orally, though firmly addicted, tended to function fairly well. In going from early 1915, when opiates were available over the counter, to 1920, when it became illegal even for a physician to prescribe opiates to addicts, we turned a large number of our citizens into criminals and opened the door to a very profitable illicit market. Data has been presented that suggest a sharp and steady drop in the addiction rate between 1920 and 1945, but the validity of this information has been questioned. The prevalence of addiction probably did decline during this era, but the drop was not so sharp as has sometimes been depicted.

The intravenous use of heroin that is today's usual pattern seems to have started in the United States about 1925, but was not widespread prior to 1930. This pattern spread very rapidly between 1930 and 1940, which according to John O'Donnell and Judith Jones suggests that a drug subculture had been formed that facilitated the spread of drug use techniques.[15]

Our ancestors, in their naïveté, failed to recognize opium's considerable potential for producing dependence. Ultimately, addicts have recognized that the tragedy of addiction to opiates lies in the bondage to the drug. The addict contracts a mortgage, with payments due regularly. When the problem was finally recognized, the United States led the world in establishing necessary controls. Unfortunately, in an excess of zeal, we demanded absolute abstinence from all American addicts. Physicians were, in effect, prohibited from treating addicts.

Looking back, we can see that a series of small things—several letters by an Episcopal bishop to the president of the United States, several five-to-four votes in the United States Supreme Court that went the wrong way, an unfortunate choice of two of the four members of an American Medical Association committee—may have influenced the course of history. We can only hope that the examination of past error will guide us to future wisdom.

15. J. A. O'Donnell and Judith P. Jones, "Diffusion of the Intravenous Technique among Narcotic Addicts," *Journal of Health and Social Behavior* 9 (1968): 120–130.

3

Pharmacology of the Opiate Narcotics

George R. Gay, M.D., and E. Leong Way, Ph.D.

Heroin (from the German *heroisch,* meaning "large" or "powerful") is currently a word with high emotional content. The mention of heroin brings visions of the most blatant social and moral degradation. One envisions William Burroughs' *Junkie:*

> Doolie, sick, was an unnerving sight. The envelope of personality was gone, dissolved by his junk-hungry cells. Viscera and cells, galvanized into a loathsome insect-like activity, seemed on the point of breaking through the surface. His face was blurred, unrecognizable.[1] *

Structurally, heroin is *diacetylmorphine hydrochloride.* It is manufactured by the diacetylation of morphine, that is, by the action of acetic anhydride or acetylchloride on morphine. It is a white, odorless, crystalline powder that dissolves readily in water (Mexican heroin is brown). Pharmacologically, heroin is a highly effective *narcotic analgesic.* Developed by the Bayer Company in Germany in 1898, it was thought at first to be nonaddicting and actually to be a cure for morphine addiction. Not until 1910 were the addictive properties of heroin noted.

NARCOTIC ANALGESIC: CONFUSION OF TERMS

Pharmacologists prefer to categorize drugs in terms of their chemical structure, their effects on cellular biochemistry or physiological systems, and their effects on behavior.[2] Unfortunately, however, society itself chooses to classify drugs according to the prevailing attitudes of the dominant cultural group or of a more vocal minority. These views

---

* References for this chapter will be found on pp. 57–58.

are reflected by the lawmakers who impose legal sanctions on drug sellers and users.

Because of this confusion between pharmacological and legal terminology, there is considerable misformation regarding the pharmacology of various abused drug groups. Until very recently the legal definition of *narcotics* (from the Greek *narkōtikos,* meaning "benumbing, deadening" included not only opium and its surrogates, but also marijuana and cocaine, whose effects are wholly unrelated to morphine. Indeed, cocaine causes reactions that are quite the opposite.[3] Although recent legislation attempts to be more precise in categorizing narcotics, the lay press and law enforcement officials insist on perpetuating earlier errors.

Pharmacologically, a *narcotic analgesic* is a substance that combines the actions of an analgesic (it relieves pain), a hypnotic (it produces sleep), and a euphoriant (it causes a feeling of well-being or a loss of care). The classic narcotic analgesic is morphine, which is the main alkaloid present in opium. It exerts a two-fold analgesic action on the central nervous system: the pain threshold is elevated and the psychological response to pain is altered. Pain may still be present, but the individual is now indifferent to it.[4] To the junkie, the classic effects of narcotics have other meanings: analgesia can result in one's walking around with undetected abscessed teeth; changes in mood or drowsiness are known as "nodding out"; respiratory depression as a result of an overdose can be fatal. In those who are feeling fatigue, worry, tension, or anxiety, the euphoriant effects afford considerable relief and may allow the individual to feel "larger than life." Although opium and the morphine alkaloids are not generally used therapeutically for mood alteration, because of their physical dependence liability, they are highly effective tranquilizers. Anxiety disappears, as do feelings of inferiority. Since the user no longer cares about life's problems in general, everything looks rosy, until the pleasurable drug effects wear off, at which time he needs a pharmacologic restoration of this euphoria with another dose.

The euphoriant and anxiety-relieving properties of the narcotic analgesics principally account for their dependence liability. Further, this type of drug produces *tolerance* and *physical dependence;* frequently repeated administration results in a diminished response and bodily processes become modified so that continued administration is required to prevent uncomfortable withdrawal symptoms. The term "addiction" was once associated only with drugs that produce physical dependence. It is now recognized that physical dependence is not the primary motivation for drug-seeking behavior, although it may be a strong reinforcing factor. For this reason it would be better to drop the term "addiction" and substitute "narcotic dependence." The undue emphasis given to physical dependence is now readily acknowledged. Curing physical dependence is a relatively simple medical procedure. However, a far greater problem occurs *after* detoxification, when the psychological or emotional dependence on the drug results in relapse or recidivism. The personality of the user and environmental factors become extremely important at this crucial stage.

A SHORT HISTORY OF OPIUM [5,6,8]

The euphoriant effects of the opium poppy are implied in Sumarian records of 4000 B.C. Greek and Roman records are replete with historical references.

> Now Helen, the daughter of Zeus, turned her thoughts elsewhere. Straightway she cast into the wine of which they drunk, a drug which quenches pain and strife and brings forgetfulness of every ill.
> —Homer, *The Odyssey*

Aesculapius, the Greek god of medicine, was supposed to have used a potion called "nepenthe" (probably containing opium) to produce insensitivity to pain. Theophrastus referred to the pharmacology of opium in the third century B.C.

In the sixteenth century, Paracelcus compounded an alcoholic tincture of opium called "laudanum." In 1680 Thomas Sydenham wrote:

> Among the remedies which it has pleased almighty God to give to man to relieve his sufferings, none is so universal and so efficacious as opium.

References to the narcotic and analgesic effects of opium are sprinkled liberally throughout the works of Shakespeare:

> Look where he comes! Not poppy, nor mandragora,
> Nor all the drowsy syrups of the world,
> Shall ever medicine thee to that sweet sleep
> Which thou owdst yesterday.
> —*Othello*, III. iii. 330–333

Opium (from the Greek *opion,* meaning "poppy juice") comes from the milky exudate of the incised, unripe seed pods (which later become a sticky brown resin or gum) of the poppy *Papaver somniferum,* which grows best in moist climates at elevations above 2000 feet. The major areas of its growth are the Middle East (Turkey, Lebanon, Yugoslavia, and Iran), the "fertile triangle" of Southeast Asia (northwestern Burma and northern Thailand and Laos), Communist China, and scattered hilly areas of Central and South America. Opium was probably first cultivated in Asia Minor and was used medicinally in

Egypt and later in Greece as a cough suppressant, a sedative, a suppressant of dysentery, and for relief of pain and anxiety.

Arab traders then introduced the drug to India and China and, indeed, opium eating has been known in Asia for many centuries. Opium smoking appeared only after American tobacco was introduced to the Orient. (Opium and heroin smoking are peculiarly prevalent modes of drug use among U.S. troops in Vietnam at this time.)

Smoking is a common mode of administration of heroin by addicts in the Far East. Two inhalation techniques are used. A relatively mild form of dependence may be produced by smoking nearly pure heroin mixed with tobacco in a cigarette. The high temperature of the burning cigarette, however, destroys about 80 percent of the heroin. A more pronounced dependence is obtained with a second inhalation procedure, wherein heroin is volatilized after mixing with a suitable vehicle, such as barbital. This serves to effect sublimation of heroin at a much lower temperature and prevent its decomposition.[7] Fortunately, the milder cigarette procedure is more popular among U.S. soldiers.

Composition of Opium

Over twenty-five alkaloids are contained in opium, but only morphine, codeine, and papaverine have wide clinical use. Opium also contains organic acids, resins, gums, oils, sugars, and proteinlike bodies that comprise about 75 percent of its weight, but do not contribute significantly to the pharmacodynamic properties of the drug. Table 3.1 shows the approximate percentage of natural alkaloids present in opium.

TABLE 3.1. THE NATURALLY OCCURRING ALKALOIDS OF OPIUM

Class	Natural Alkaloid	Percentage in Opium
1. Phenanthrene	Morphine	10.0
	Codeine	0.5
	Thebaine	0.2
2. Benzylisoquinoline	Papaverine	1.0
	Narcotine	6.0
	Narceine	0.3

The Discovery of Morphine

In 1806, Friedrich Wilhelm Serturner, a pharmacist in Westphalia, poured liquid ammonia over opium and obtained a white powder.

He found this substance to be basic (alkaloid) and to be the cause of the soporific properties of opium. He named the drug "morphium" (after the Greek god of dreams, Morphius). The name was later modified to "morphine."

The British East India Company's expanding opium empire (based on importation of opium to China) fought and easily won the so-called Opium War of 1839–1842, which led to the legalization of opium in China. The opium-smoking Chinese were later to introduce the habit to the West Coast of the United States. Patent nostrums containing opium extracts, like "Dover's Powder" and "Dr. Barton's Brown Mixture," flourished in the nineteenth century. By 1900 it was estimated that one in 400 Americans (including many housewives and individuals with such chronic painful diseases as gout or arthritis) were addicted.

The naturally occurring narcotic analgesics are morphine and codeine. In addition, many synthesized and semisynthetic surrogates possess pharmacologic properties similar to those of the naturally occurring drugs (see Table 3.2). Table 3.3 shows a relative value scale of dosages of opium, its alkaloids, and certain synthetic narcotic analgesics. The dosages given are those that would be administered to an individual who weighed seventy kilograms (about 155 pounds) to achieve relief of surgical pain.

HEROIN

Morphine is acetylated to heroin by a simple chemical process and reaches the United States through France, Mexico, Italy, Canada, the Far East, and other divergent illicit routes.

A kilogram of 80 percent pure heroin may be bought by an importer for about $5000–$7000.[10] The white powder is then easily concealed, and a careful smuggler usually has little difficulty in eluding detection. Once in the United States, the heroin may pass through as many as seven different "cuts," or "dealer dilutions," yielding an eventual net profit of $250,000 or more. The heroin may be diluted with milk sugar, quinine, cornstarch, or almost any white powdery substance (even cleansing powder, arsenic, or strychnine, if the user is labelled for a "hot shot," or fatal dose). The junk that eventually results may contain as little as 1–3 percent pure heroin. This material is sold in glassine packets, "bags," or rubber "balloons" in quantities of about 350 to 400 milligrams. Each bag or balloon may cost as much as $25 (or more).[11]

The user then "cooks up" his adulterated heroin in a spoon (it takes four bags to make a spoon) or bottle cap held with wire or tweezers. Tap water is used as the diluent. A "fit" or "outfit" is then used to draw

TABLE 3.2. NATURALLY OCCURRING AND SOME SEMISYNTHETIC OPIATES

Opiate	R_1	R_2	Double Bond between C_7 and C_8	R_3	R_4
Morphine	—OH	—OH	present	—H	—H
Codeine (Methylmorphine)	—O—CH₃	—OH	present	—H	—H
Thebaine	—O—CH₃	—O—CH₃	double bonds between C_6 and C_7 and between C_8 and C_{14}	—H	—H
Heroin (Diacetylmorphine)	—O—C(=O)—CH₃	—O—C(=O)—CH₃	present	—H	—H
Oxymorphone (Dihydrohydroxy-morphinone—"Numorphan")	—OH	=O	absent	—OH	—H
Hydromorphone (Dihydro-morphinone—"Dilaudid")	—OH	=O	absent	—H	—H
Methyldihydromorphinone ("Metopon")	—OH	=O	absent	—H	—CH₃
Dihydrocodeine ("Paracodin")	—O—CH₃	—OH	absent	—H	—H
Hydrocodone (Dihydro-codeinone, in "Hycodan")	—CH₃	=O	absent	—H	—H
Oxycodone (Dihydrohydroxy-codeinone, in "Percodan")	—CH₃	=O	absent	—OH	—H

TABLE 3.3. DOSAGES: A RELATIVE VALUE SCALE

Drug	Dosage	Route
1. Raw opium	0.3–0.6 gm	oral
2. Morphine	8–16 mg	intramuscular or subcutaneous injection
3. Codeine	15–60 mg	oral or intramuscular injection
4. Heroin (diacetylmorphine)	2–5 mg	intramuscular injection
5. Dilaudid (dihydromorphinone)	1–4 mg	intramuscular injection
6. Demerol (meperidine)	50–150 mg	intramuscular injection
7. Dolophine (methadone)	15–75 mg	oral or subcutaneous injection

up the solution. This unsterile instrument consists of a 22- to 25-gauge needle fitted onto an eyedropper (the rubber eyedropper top is preferred to a conventional syringe because it is more easily manipulated for self-injection and because the backflow of blood can easily be seen as the needle enters a vein). The solution is drawn up through a "cotton" to filter out the more gross impurities. The very nature of the drug creates this haphazard attitude about sterility; even if a new, surgically sterile outfit were available, it would likely be disregarded, as the ceremony of needle sharing contributes to the overall effect (at least early in the experimental junkie experience). Used "cottons" are saved for a rainy day.

This frighteningly unsterile game certainly contributes to both primary and secondary infections (abscesses, transmission of hepatitis, septicemia, endocarditis, etc.), as well as to the overall unsavory reputation of the junkie. If the same heroin injections were given in sterile and controlled situations, this individual and social hazard would be greatly lessened and the injection of heroin would cause little more concern than that of morphine administered by the crisply starched nurses on hospital wards. Indeed, medical use of heroin is still legal in Great Britain and has been widely used by many physicians without serious consequences.

Pharmacology of Heroin[5,8,9]

The addictive potential of heroin is greater than that of *any other* drug, due to its marked euphoriant properties and rapid onset of action. Heroin's properties are very similar to those of morphine and, in fact, much of its effect is due to conversion to morphine in the body. A junkie however, can differentiate heroin from morphine given intravenously; the pleasurable, whole-body, warm, orgasmic rush comes on more rapidly and is more intense after a heroin injection. After subcutaneous or intramuscular injection ("skin-popping"), however, he cannot distinguish between the two substances. Like morphine, heroin constricts the pupils. Heroin depresses respiration by its depressant action on the central nervous system, and respiratory failure and death may result from medullary paralysis. Both rate and depth of respiration are affected, and hypoxia and hypercapnea occur. Cyanosis is noted, and the "O.D.'d" junkie may turn as blue as his jeans. (And he may suffer cardiac arrest secondary to hypoxia!)

Although alveolar carbon dioxide tension is increased, the response of the respiratory center to carbon dioxide stimulation is greatly reduced. Not uncommonly, respiratory rate is depressed to three or four breaths per minute. The greatest chance of accidental overdose and death occurs in the heroin-susceptible or nontolerant individual (such as a beginner or someone who has been off the drug for a while) or in the individual who concurrently injects or ingests a combination of respiratory depressant drugs (such as opiates and/or alcohol and barbiturates). Narcotic antagonists like nalorphine, levallorphan, or naloxone will dramatically reverse the respiratory depression resulting from overdose of heroin or other narcotic substances.

Heroin depresses the respiratory center and the cough reflex more effectively than morphine and is two to five times more efficient as an analgesic. Although heroin is an excellent rapid-acting reliever of postoperative pain, its medical use has been denied in the United States since it was illegalized in 1956.

An interesting physiological phenomenon is the depression of libido in the heroin user.

> Junk short-circuits sex. The drive to nonsexual sociability (as well) comes from the same place sex comes from, so when I have an H or M shooting habit, I am non-sociable,

says William Burroughs in *Junkie*.[12] Sexual relationships dissolve into nonsexual "partnerships" dedicated to the daily acquisition of heroin.[13] Histamine release may be seen following heroin injection, as may anaphylactic shock, collapse, and death. The "itching nose" that is commonly seen is probably due to histamine release. "Cotton fever," marked by general shakes and collapse following injection of heroin, may be due either to an allergic phenomenon or to a septicemia secondary to an infected outfit or needle. Constipation occurs after heroin use due to decreased propulsive activity throughout the gastrointestinal tract. Nausea and vomiting are not uncommon and are more likely to occur if the user is up and moving around. Nausea and vomiting are probably related to vestibular movements and may be counteracted by various antiemetic drugs (such as diphenhydramine or thorazine). Tolerance to these effects appears rapidly and, once the habit is firmly established in the addict, nausea and vomiting are rarely seen. With a gross overdose of heroin a general cardiovascular collapse may occur. Otherwise, in the tolerant individual there may be only a slight drop in blood pressure following injection. Postural hypotension is commonly seen and collapse (or "fainting") may occur if the individual suddenly sits up or moves about. Vasodilatation of the skin occurs and sweating may be stimulated.

Heroin is rapidly hydrolyzed by the liver and other body organs and tissues and is largely excreted in the urine as morphine and its glucuronide conjugate. (This is the basis of the classic urine test.) Heroin also appears as morphine in breast milk, in the sweat, and in saliva. It also readily crosses the placental barrier and may produce a narcotized and addicted fetus.] The pregnant junkie mother who delivers must be treated for her withdrawal (or maintained on narcotics) while in the hospital, and her baby must be carefully withdrawn from its own unintentional habit during the first week of its life.] Small amounts of paregoric—a camphorated tincture of opium—may be utilized in the baby's formula on a reducing dosage scale. Likewise, alcoholic tincture of opium or small amounts of methadone in decreasing dosage may be used. Within a week to ten days the infant will then effectively "kick" its habit.

HEROIN VERSUS OTHER FORMS OF DRUG DEPENDENCE

The pervading Puritan ethic of our American culture, which insists upon placing moral value judgment on drugs, has caused the illegalization of heroin and the criminalization of those who would use it. In truth a drug is merely a chemical compound, which has no inherent moral connotation. A drug remains completely innocuous until ingested or injected.

From a pharmacologic viewpoint, the seriousness of a drug problem may be assessed by (1) the immediate psychic and physical effects of the drug on the individual and (2) the social consequences of continued abuse.[14] In other words, we must consider whether a particular drug has effects on the brain that tend to promote compulsive self-administration and whether this behavior may be hazardous to the individual and to society. Based on these considerations, alcohol (our legal social drug) is far more hazardous than all other drugs combined. There may be as many as twelve million alcoholics in the United States, but even the most pessimistic estimates of the number of heroin addicts do not rise above 500,000 and most estimates are well below that figure. (Recent surveys indicate that we may have an additional 25,000–60,000 heroin users in, or recently returned from, Vietnam.)[15] In terms of incidence of use, complications from acute overdose, long-term effects on the physical and mental state of an individual, and ultimate consequences for society, there is no close second to alcohol. Our ambivalent attitude toward drugs has long been apparent. While waiting with anticipation for our own cocktail hour each evening, we may read an article in the *Journal of the American Medical Association* decrying the adverse effects of marijuana and "unwind" while watching a TV news analysis of the growing drug problem among the military.

Heroin, if stripped of its emotional overcoat, has proven pharmacologic and medicinal benefits. It is an excellent suppressant of diarrhea and cough. It is a highly effective, short-acting pain reliever and a tranquilizer of enormous effectiveness. The established clinical usefulness of heroin in the operating room and in the treatment of cancer patients has been denied for nearly two decades by our own hysterical fear of the junkie, promoted to a large extent by certain overzealous law enforcement officials.

Heroin's chief drawbacks are the ease with which psychic and physical dependence are produced and the concurrent strong drive that is developed to obtain the drug by illegal means. Antisocial behavior, however, abates immediately when the drug is made available. It should be pointed out that good health and productive work are not necessarily incompatible with dependence on narcotics. Even when the addict is "on the nod" he can be aroused and can perform with little loss in motor coordination. During a research study in Hong Kong, one of us (ELW) met several addicts who were able to function adequately while on high doses of heroin. These included tailors performing fine needlework, construction workers on high-rise apartments, coolie laborers, and barbers. (It is well recognized today that addicts on high daily oral doses of methadone can also carry on their daily tasks and hold responsible positions.) The main point is that the ill health, social irresponsibility, and criminal activity that often accompany heroin dependence result not from the pharmacologic effects of the drug, but from the addict's need to satisfy his compulsion by means of a superimposed illegal life style when those effects are wearing off.

Dependence on alcohol or other general depressants, such as barbiturates and meprobamate, is much more difficult to produce than heroin addiction. Once established, however, these dependencies become far more hazardous to the individual. During severe withdrawal from such depressants, grand mal seizures and severe psychosis may occur. Even among patients under intensive care, there is a relatively high incidence of mortality. Heroin abstinence, on the other hand, although extremely uncomfortable, rarely results in death.

Severe heroin abstinence symptoms can be made endurable by administration of low doses of methadone. Ten to twenty milligrams administered subcutaneously at six- to eight-hour intervals will prevent most withdrawal signs and symptoms. Discontinuing the methadone after several days results in a relatively mild withdrawal. This use of methadone for detoxification purposes has been a widely accepted medical practice for many years and should not be confused with the use of high oral doses of methadone for maintenance.

The rationale for methadone maintenance is based on established pharmacologic principles. As pointed out earlier, individuals who are tolerant to narcotics can still function after high doses. Narcotic analgesic drugs exhibit cross dependence and cross tolerance, which means that any narcotic will allay or prevent heroin abstinence and that an individual who is tolerant to heroin is also tolerant to other narcotics. For practical purposes then, any narcotic that is orally effective and that has a relatively long duration of action can be used in a maintenance program, especially if tolerance is developed to a degree that the euphoric responses to heroin injection become blocked. Theoretically, even heroin itself could be used, but its poor oral efficacy and the short duration of its effect make it highly impractical. At the present time, the drug that most nearly fills the requisites for a maintenance program is methadone. However, it *would* be desirable to have a much longer-acting substitute. It should also be emphasized that when methadone is mainlined it produces an excellent "high" and, hence strict precautions must be made to prevent the diversion of methadone for such purposes.

Blockade of heroin effects can also be achieved by the use of narcotic antagonists. The best-known antagonist is nalorphine (Nalline), but its low oral efficacy, short duration of action, and disturbing side effects preclude its use. Two other narcotic antagonists are being studied at present—naloxone[16] and cyclazocine[17,18]—but both appear to have shortcomings. Naloxone has low oral efficacy and is too short-acting; cyclazocine, although orally effective and reasonably long-acting, produces undesirable psychotomimetic side effects. Studies are in progress to overcome these deficiencies. Unlike methadone, an antagonist can be administered to an addict *only* after he has been detoxified. Giving an antagonist to a heroin-dependent person would precipitate a severe abstinence syndrome (instant "cold turkey"). Preliminary studies suggest that the strongly motivated are most likely to remain in antagonist maintenance programs, but an extensive evaluation of antagonist program must still be made.

CONCLUSION— *my own*

It is high time that we quit passing laws to make criminals out of persons who possess and use drugs. The core of the problem is people, not drugs. Outlawing any drug is no solution. For every drug banned, there have always been and will continue to be hundreds of others available to the compulsive drug-seeker. At this time in our history, the major "scare" drug is heroin; and its users, both the classic and the "new" junkie,[11,19,20] are the cause of sudden national concern. This is the right response for the wrong reasons (fear of property loss by junkie "rip-offs," a Communist conspiracy to enslave our youth, and the like). We must replace emotion and hysteria with some modicum of logic and common sense. We must explore the multimodality techniques of rehabilitation for the recidivists—uncontrolled free clinics, halfway

TABLE 3.4. PERTINENT DRUG ABUSE LEGISLATION

1906	*Pure Food and Drug Act:* Removed patent medicines containing opiates from the market.
1912	*Hague Conference:* Agreement that production and trade of opiates and opium be limited to amounts necessary for medical and scientific use.
1914	*Harrison Narcotics Act:* Basically a tax act (or law); persons authorized to handle or manufacture drugs are required to register, pay a fee, and keep records of all narcotics in their possession.
1920	*Volstead Act ("Prohibition"):* Nonmedical usage of alcoholic beverages prohibited.
1919–1924	*Public Outpatient Narcotic Clinics:* Opened in hopes of rehabilitating the addict and preventing his involvement with criminal drug distributors. In general badly managed, all clinics were forced to close by 1924 by public pressure brought about by a moralizing and crusading press and the Federal Bureau of Narcotics.
1922	*Behrman Case:* Prevented MDs from legally supplying drugs to addicts for self-administration. Implied that addicts must be isolated and hospitalized. Illegal narcotics then became the addict's only source of supply. Led eventually to the Public Health Service Hospitals in Lexington, Kentucky (1935), and Fort Worth, Texas (1938).
1922	*The Jones-Miller Act (Narcotics Drug Import and Export Act):* Established firm penalties for violation of the Harrison Act.
1924	Prohibition of manufacture of heroin in the United States.
1925	Supreme Court ruled that a physician may administer narcotics to allay withdrawal symptoms, if done "in good faith." The Federal Bureau of Narcotics has ignored this, and continued to punish physicians who give narcotics to addicts.
1933	*Repeal of Prohibition:* Illicit drug traffic turns from alcohol to heroin.
1937	*The Marijuana Tax Act:* Marijuana brought under stern control similar to that of the opiates.
1951	*Boggs Act:* Graduated sentences with mandatory minimum sentences applicable to *all* narcotic drug offences. Subsequent to the Boggs Act, many state legislatures enacted "little Boggs Acts."
1956	*Narcotic Drug Control Act:* Even more punitive than the Boggs Act, it did, however, differentiate between drug *possession*, drug *sale*, and drug *sale to minors. Medical use of heroin prohibited.*
1956	All existing heroin supplies in the United States ordered surrendered to the government.
1963	*Supreme Court (Robinson v. California):* Declared that addiction is a *disease,* not a *crime.* Legally then, an addict cannot be arrested for being "high" (internal possession), but he *can* be arrested for the external possession and/or sale of drugs.
1966	*Narcotic Addict Rehabilitation Act:* Views narcotic addiction as being symptomatic of a treatable disease and not of a criminal condition.
1966	*Drug Abuse Control Amendments:* Law became effective whereby sedatives, stimulants, and tranquilizers came under tighter controls. Hallucinogens were specifically added to the law in 1966. Enforcement of this law became the responsibility of the Bureau of Drug Abuse Control in the Food and Drug Administration.

TABLE 3.4. (Continued)

1968	*The Bureau of Narcotics and Dangerous Drugs (Department of Justice)*: Was given responsibility on a federal level for the entire drug problem. The Bureau of Narcotics was removed from the Department of the Treasury and the Bureau of Drug Abuse Control from the Food and Drug Administration.
1969	*Operation Intercept:* An attempt to block import of marijuana at the Mexican border. It effectively increased use of "harder drugs" throughout the country.
1970	*Comprehensive Drug Abuse Prevention and Control Act of 1970:* Replaces previous acts for control of narcotics, marijuana, sedatives, and stimulants under the Department of Justice. Drugs are classified into five schedules according to their potential for abuse and therapeutic usefulness. First time illegitimate possession of any drug in the five schedules is considered to be a misdemeanor and penalties are reduced. Provisions are made for rehabilitation, education and research. House search legalized ("no-knock" law).
1969–1971	Tightening of controls at a federal level and urging of foreign governments to apply firmer restrictions in regard to manufacture and exportation of drugs.
1971	An apparent turnabout in "law-and-order" approach brought about by public fear of increasing drug use among U.S. troops in Vietnam and general drug use in United States. Creation of Special Action Office of Drug Abuse Prevention (an attempt to coordinate the nine federal agencies already active in trying to control drugs) to develop overall federal strategies for drug programs in general, and specifically for those within the military. Direct responsibilities stated to be major federal drug abuse prevention, education, treatment, rehabilitation, training and research; total budget $371,000,000, of which $155,000,000 earmarked for "rehabilitation."

houses, group and individual therapy, pharmacologic blockade, and narcotic maintenance when all else fails.

Only concerted and prolonged efforts at rehabilitation and after-care and the exploration of innovative techniques in these areas can reverse the social stigma of addiction and return the addict to a level of social existence that is tolerable both to himself and to his community.

REFERENCES

1. William Burroughs, *Junkie* (New York: Ace Books, 1953), p. 62.
2. S. Einstein, *The Use and Misuse of Drugs* (Belmont, Cal.: Wadsworth, 1970).
3. E. L. Way, "Contemporary Classification, Pharmacology, and Abuse Potential of Psychotropic Substances," in J. R. Wittenborn, ed., *Drugs and Youth* (Springfield, Ill.: Charles C. Thomas, 1969).

4. J. Adriani, *The Chemistry and Physics of Anesthesia,* 2nd ed. (Springfield, Ill.: Charles C. Thomas, 1962).

5. F. H. Meyers, E. Jawetz, and A. Goldfein, *Review of Medical Pharmacology* (Los Altos, Cal.: Lange Medical Publications, 1968), p. 270.

6. T. E. Keys, *The History of Surgical Anesthesia* (New York: Dover, 1963).

7. B. P. Mo and E. L. Way, "An Assessment of Inhalation as a Mode of Administration of Heroin by Addicts," *Journal of Pharmacology and Experimental Therapeutics* 154, no. 1 (1966): 142–51.

8. Goodman, L. S., and Gilman, A., *The Pharmacological Basis of Therapeutics,* 2nd ed. (New York: Macmillan, 1960), pp. 216–380.

9. J. A. Lee, and R. S. Atkinson, *A Synopsis of Anaesthesia,* 5th ed. (Baltimore: Williams and Wilkins, 1964), pp. 66–76.

10. E. Preble and J. J. Casey, Jr., "Taking Care of Business," *International Journal of the Addictions* 4, no. 1 (1969): 1–24. Reprinted in this volume, pp. 97–118.

11. G. R. Gay, A. D. Matzger, W. Bathurst, and D. E. Smith, "Short-Term Heroin Detoxification on an Outpatient Basis," *International Journal of the Addictions* 6, no. 2 (1971): 241–64.

12. Burroughs, *Junkie,* p. 16.

13. D. K. Wellisch, G. R. Gay, and R. McEntee, "The Easy Rider Syndrome: A Pattern of Hetero- and Homosexual Relationships in a Heroin Addict Population," *Journal of Family Proceedings,* 9, no. 4 (1970): 425–30.

14. S. Irwin, "Drugs of Abuse: An Introduction to Their Actions and Potential Hazards," *Journal of Psychedelic Drugs,* 3, no. 2 (1971): 5–15.

15. "The New Public Enemy No. 1," *Time,* June 28, 1971, pp. 20–25.

16. M. Fink, A. Zaks, R. Sharoff, A. Moro, A. Bruner, and A. Freedman, "Naloxone in Heroin Dependence," *Clinical and Pharmacological Therapeutics* 9 (1968): 568–77.

17. W. R. Martin, C. W. Gorodetsky, and T. K. McClane, "An Experimental Study in the Treatment of Narcotic Addicts with Cyclazocine," *Clinical and Pharmacological Therapeutics* 7 (1966): 455–65.

18. J. H. Jaffe, "Cyclazocine in the Treatment of Narcotic Addiction," in J. Masserman, ed., *Current Psychiatric Therapies* (New York: Grune & Stratton, 1967), pp. 147–56.

19. C. W. Sheppard, G. R. Gay, and D. E. Smith, "The Changing Patterns of Heroin Addiction in the Haight-Ashbury Subculture," *Journal of Psychedelic Drugs* 3, no. 2 (1971): 22–30.

20. I. Chein et al., *The Road to H: Narcotics, Delinquency, and Social Policy* (New York: Basic Books, 1964).

4

Drug Abuse in Combat:

The Crisis of Drugs and Addiction
among American Troops in Vietnam

David J. Bentel, D. Crim, and David E. Smith, M.D.

> The last few months over there were unbelievable. My first tour
> there in '67, a few of our guys smoked grass, you know. Now the
> guys walk right in the hootch with a jar of heroin or cocain. Al-
> most pure stuff. Getting smack is like getting a bottle of beer.
> Everybody sells it. Half my company is on stuff.
>
> —Returning GI

The recent spread of heroin addiction among the young is frequently
likened to a plague. A Gallup Poll rating shows that since the first
quarter of 1971 drug addiction has risen from seventh to third place
in the public's assessment of the nation's most important problems.[1]
President Nixon recently called drug abuse our Public Enemy Number 1.

Chein and associates, writing almost a decade ago, described addiction as an instrumental device for dealing with human misery.[2] Addiction once was a disease of the lower-class ghetto dweller who dealt with
hopelessness and frustration by shooting dope.

In 1971, however, heroin addiction has suddenly reached epidemic
proportions among the young of the middle and upper classes.[3] The
Deputy Chief New York Medical Examiner reports that overdose by

1. *Newsweek,* 5 July, 1971, p. 28.
2. Isidor Chein et al., *The Road to H: Narcotics, Delinquency, and Social Policy*
(New York: Basic Books, 1964), p. 381.
3. David J. Bentel & David E. Smith, "The Year of the Middle Class Junkie,"
California's Health (Berkeley, Calif.: State Department of Public Health, April 1971),
pp. 1–5.

has become the leading cause of death among teen-agers in New ork City, where over 1,000 persons died from heroin overdose in 1970.[4] Over half of these deaths were among persons twenty-three years old or younger. Heroin dependence is principally an affliction of youth. The average age for discovered addicts has dropped from thirty-five in 1950 to twenty-three today.[5] Youth in various socioeconomic brackets, of different religions and ethnic origins, and in widely differing circumstances have become involved with narcotics and "dangerous drugs" in numbers that have been described as epidemic.

One dramatic dimension of this addiction syndrome has been the sudden increase in the use of illegal drugs by military personnel. Representatives Murphy (D.Ill.) and Steele (R.Conn.) recently reported a "rapid increase in heroin addiction within the United States military forces in South Vietnam, where the best estimates are that as many as 10 to 15 percent of our servicemen are regularly using heroin in one form or another." They also estimated that in some units heroin addiction might be as high as 25 percent.[6] A Special Subcommittee of the Committee on Armed Services concluded that "40 to 50 percent of the men entering military services have at least experimented with drugs, principally marijuana; some 20 percent of our military personnel in Vietnam could be using hard narcotics." [7]

More recently, figures released by the army suggest a much lower rate of addiction—perhaps as little as 2 percent. Blanket figures suggesting either high or low prevalence of addiction among service persons must be examined carefully in context. Even if we assume that no bias was introduced by the attitudes of the researchers, the experimental methodology must still be carefully evaluated. What, for instance, were the ages, ranks, lengths of service, and geographical assignments of the members of the various study samples? What drugs were involved, what was their potency, for what length of time were they used, and how were the validity and reliability of responses determined? We must know the answers to these questions and many others before we can assign anything like scientific credibility to these reports.

Nonetheless, data from many sources generally corroborate the as-

4. Stewart L. Baker, "Drug Abuse in the United States Army," *Bulletin of the New York Academy of Medicine* 47, no. 6 (June 1971): 541.

5. *Newsweek,* 5 July 1971, p. 29.

6. Morgan F. Murphy & Robert H. Steele, "The World Heroin Problem, Report of a Special Study Mission" (Washington, D.C.: Government Printing Office, 27 May 1971), pp. 1, 9.

7. U.S., Congress, Special Subcommittee of the Committee on Armed Services, *Inquiry into Alleged Drug Abuse in the Armed Services,* 91st Cong., 2nd sess., 1971, H.A.S.C. Rept. 92–4, p. 2162.

sumptions that there *is* a major drug abuse problem in military life and that abusable drugs are more readily available than ever before.

PATTERNS OF MILITARY DRUG USE

John Renick and Eric Nelson, two army physicians who have studied the use of drugs in the military, describe abuse patterns as "one-third, one-third, one-third." [8] One-third of combat personnel are "juicers," the heavy "boozing" group that includes older officers and NCOs. The middle group is composed of the younger enlistees, who use both alcohol and marijuana regularly. Both groups suffer high rates of alcoholism and of psychiatric problems related to or exacerbated by alcohol use. The last third is made up of heads and junkies. In this group, regular and compulsive use of hallucinogens, uppers and downers, and opiates is prevalent, and a rising percentage of this group become multiple drug abusers. Members of this group are described in psychiatric language as persons commonly exhibiting "situational maladjustment problems," "immaturity problems," and "more profound and long-standing character and behavior disorders." [9]

The traditional differences between the life styles and values of the boozers and the heads is pronounced in the service. One company officer pointed out the danger in making sweeping generalities about drug use and abuse in the military:

> Its like different ball clubs. One outfit will juice it up the night before patrol and all go out with hangovers. Some will sneak a drink while on the march. Other units stay stoned all the time. The squad leader on down are all heads. Then again, some outfits are real tight. No drugs, or at least nobody is supposed to know if there are. I've even heard of chopper pilots, artillery gunners and tank drivers going out stoned all the time.[10]

Chronic alcoholism still afflicts the upper echelons of the military hierarchy, but the use of alcohol has been institutionalized in military life and alcohol problems are seldom publicized as a chronic military affliction.

If we assume that the "population at risk" includes about two-thirds

8. Personal communication with Dr. John T. Renick, M.D., Coordinator, Drug Treatment Program, Department of Psychiatry, Veterans Administration Hospital, Menlo Park, California; and Dr. Eric Nelson, Department of Psychiatry, Letterman General Hospital, San Francisco, California.

9. George F. Solomon et al., "Three Psychiatric Casualties from Vietnam," *Archives of General Psychiatry*, forthcoming.

10. Personal communication with Dr. Neil R. Scott, M.D., Stanford University School of Medicine, Stanford, California.

of the 255,000 troops in South Vietnam, or roughly 170,000 men,[11] and if we use 10 percent as a convenient, if conservative, compromise estimate of addiction, the number of American servicemen addicted overseas will exceed 17,000 a year beginning July of 1970. Even if all troops are withdrawn from Asia by 1973, at least 50,000 U.S. servicemen will have had some experience with narcotics, whether they are habituated or not.

A study conducted by the army in San Francisco examined the drug habits of army veterans of Vietnam who were returning to be discharged at the Oakland Army Terminal or in the state of Washington. (Only honorable army dischargees of enlisted rank were included in this sample.) In the first quarter of 1971 nearly a quarter of all discharged soliders admitted having used heroin and/or other opiates while in Vietnam. Almost two-thirds of these soldiers had used drugs eleven or more times during their last thirty days in Vietnam. Over a quarter had used heroin, morphine, opium, and other illegal drugs during their tour abroad. Urinalysis revealed traces of narcotics in the systems of some of the admitted "heavy users." [12]

Over 20 percent of the returning veterans in this study had used heroin or opium overseas, but these figures do not suggest how much greater might be the total sample who abuse marijuana, amphetamines, barbiturates, and alcohol during their military service.

It is also misleading to believe that the withdrawal of troops from Vietnam will cause the number of drug abusers to diminish. There is no static number of troops stationed in Vietnam at one time, and thus no static "population risk." Rather, there is a constant turnover and nearly 90-percent replacement each year, since a tour of duty is only one year long. Thus, if nearly a quarter of the troops who remain in Vietnam become involved with narcotics use, over a five-year period rotation could create nearly 375,000 junkies.

Such figures are hypothetical and, when taken out of the context of a complex and changing social environment and without the benefit of careful, long-term study, they lack scientific authority. But they do demonstrate the potential dimensions of the problem that will be encountered. In fact, the Haight-Ashbury Free Medical Clinic in San Francisco and other drug treatment facilities already report a substantial increase in the number of returning GIs seeking help.

Chronic addiction, like the widespread use of mind-altering drugs among combat forces, appears to parallel the current epidemic among young civilians at home. Fatal overdoses are being observed and re-

11. Personal communication with Major Kenneth Eric Nelson, Chief Psychiatric Consultation Service, Letterman General Hospital, San Francisco, California.
12. Personal communication with Dr. Eric Nelson, Letterman General Hospital, San Francisco, California.

corded in military units. Many cases are ambiguous or difficult to determine, however, because the drug-using soldier's shooting partners may make the overdose appear to be either a combat fatality or an accident.[13] In the past years, heroin overdose may thus have been hidden in the almost daily newscast statistics on combat deaths.

Reports from GIs returning to the United States indicate that widespread narcotics usage is a recent phenomenon, that the situation has changed dramatically since the summer of 1970, and that a "J" curve is operating in the increasing supply and demand of illicit drugs.[14] For example, nearly pure heroin is being bought in bulk by soldier-users in Vietnam and is being consumed and resold on post.

WHY HEROIN IN VIETNAM?

If we attempt to find a cause for drug use in Vietnam, we are led ultimately to the despair and boredom of U.S. soldiers stationed there and their lack of a definable mission or objective. In 1968, a detachment of soldiers from Thailand came to South Vietnam to assist American combat forces. They brought with them "Red Rock" heroin, the first large influx of heroin to be introduced directly into American military units.[15] "The impact on American troops—most of them bored, frightened, resentful, ignorant—was immediate. 'I just wanted to get out of Nam and scag took me out for a while, at least' (relates one soldier)." [16]

Using mind-altering drugs in a compulsive and repetitive manner to achieve nearly total anesthesia indicates that drugs are being used as a major problem-solving technique (which is feasible where cheap drugs are as readily available as in Vietnam). Thus apparently a common rationale for using drugs as strong sedatives is to block out the psychic pain of awareness and feelings of personal inadequacy and alienation. For the same reason as in the states, young men have turned to drugs as a means of coping with inadequate selves or an unendurable reality. They find they can instantly alter their mood and their

13. Baker, Drug Abuse in the United States Army," p. 544.
14. Personal interviews with patients in the drug treatment program at the Veterans Administration Hospital in Palo Alto, California, and communication with Dr. James Zarcone, Project Director of the Drug Treatment Program.
15. "Statement by Major Kenneth Eric Nelson, Chief Psychiatric Consultation Service, Letterman General Hospital, San Francisco, California, Department of the Army, before the Special Subcommittee on Alcoholism and Narcotics, Committee on Labor and Public Welfare, United States Senate, Second Session, 91st Congress, "Drug Abuse and Alcoholism in the Armed Services," (reprinted) p. 8.
16. *Newsweek*, 5 July 1971, p. 30.

world by "turning on." [17] Several discharged GIs stated that their heavy indulgence in drugs began at the time they started reading antiwar materials in their barracks in Vietnam. Antiwar slogans and feelings were expressed as part of their explanations of their own drug use. There was frequent mention of the Tet offensive in January of 1968, when they realized, they said, that "we already lost a war we had no business to be in anyway." Increasing drug use and abuse coincides with deterioration of morale and general military discipline. Entire companies, it is reported, are refusing to go into combat and are breaking nearly completely with established military tradition and discipline. [18] General William Westmoreland has said that drugs, race, discipline, and declining public image are major problems of modern military life. He attributes these largely to the "unpopularity of the war in Vietnam" and the major problem of trying to wind down a war while it is still going on. [19]

Returning veterans in recent months report not only problems of drugs and deteriorating morale, but also a pervasive crisis of identity in a complex system that is based on tradition and authority. One GI summarized his recent experience by stating, "I went into the Army as gung-ho as anybody. But right now, morale is terrible, everything is off-limits, and just about everybody is stoned." [20]

The war experience in Vietnam continues to be a source of nearly suicidal despair for many returnees, a high percentage of whom, besides having drug habits, need psychiatric referral. One reported case referral, shocking and probably not typical, but probably not untypical either, describes an 18-year-old marine veteran of Vietnam, transferred from a Veterans Hospital to a nearby naval hospital, who had slashed his wrists and attempted suicide a month before being transferred stateside. He had experienced a severe depressive reaction after six months of duty in Vietnam, and had to be evacuated and discharged early. The patient, interviewed under the influence of amobarbital and methamphetamine, described being brutalized by an alcoholic father at home, enlisting in the Marines to "get the hate out of his system," the pride and satisfaction of "killing gooks," and finally, a traumatic incident where he was ordered by his corporal to shoot a 14-year-old Vietnamese girl after she had refused the corporal's sexual advances. She was shot in the abdomen and killed, then listed in the

17. John Peterson, "Junkie Comes Marching Home," *The National Observer*, June 1971, p. 16; and Donald Kirk, "Morale at Firebase Gladiator," San Francisco *Chronicle*, 30 May 1971, p. 9.

18. Kirk, "Morale at Firebase Gladiator," p. 4.

19. Hugh A. Mulligan, "General Distrustful of Own Guard in New Army," San Francisco *Chronicle*, 23 May 1971, p. 9.

20. Personal interview with patient in the drug treatment program at the Veterans Administration Hospital in Palo Alto, California.

daily body count as another "VC kill." Later the same day, the patient argued with the corporal, drew a bayonet, and stabbed him to death. Shortly thereafter, the patient became acutely disturbed, threatened a number of other Marine personnel, and made suicidal gestures. Eventually he made good his threats and shot himself to death with a .22-caliber rifle.[21]

Whether the availability of self-administered drug therapy may be actually preventing more acute episodes of this type than it is creating should be seriously and carefully researched. To some degree, the drug problem may be therapy in disguise. Nonetheless, for many nonusing officers and NCOs drug use creates a dilemma that allows no honorable compromise. If an officer or NCO countenances drug use by his men, he loses authority or respect or both and his unit will lose efficiency. On the other hand, if he takes a "hard line," policing the compound and disciplining the units involved while trying to single out and punish offenders, he may find himself and his men the victims of "fragging." Most fraggings (throwing of a live grenade into an unpopular officer's or NCO's quarters) occur, say GIs, not because of racial strife or orders to move into combat, but because some "gung-ho" officer is hassling drug users.[22] Officers, on the other hand, report feeling almost helpless to deal with this alarming and unexpected development in previously disciplined military life. One returning officer commented to Dr. Bentel, "To listen to the government talk about controlling drugs over there is just nonsense. Every hootch [barracks] has its own little drug underground. The local mama-sans, the hootch boys, I mean just about everybody from the base commander on down can get you dope inside of five minutes." [23]

WHERE IS THE HEROIN COMING FROM?

Heroin, morphine, and raw opium are cheap and readily available in Vietnam. Crude opium for smoking is even more common than heroin and cheaper. The most frequently asked question is: why has the drug problem suddenly become so acute? There is no single answer. Several changes have occurred concomitantly in both the politics and the drug distribution network of Southeast Asia. In terms of the possible etiology of recent addiction, one returning Army doctor, now at Stanford Medical School, stated that a visible change in military posture and

21. Solomon et al., "Three Psychiatric Casualties from Vietnam," pp. 3–4.

22. Personal interviews with patients in the drug treatment program at the Veterans Administration Hospital in Palo Alto, California.

23. Personal communication with returned medical officers, Letterman General Hospital, San Francisco, California.

troop morale occurred just after the Tet offensive of January 1968. "After that, we weren't at war any more," he said. "We were just marking time." One soldier interviewed by Dr. Bentel stated, "Well, shit, man! Everybody over there knew we had lost the war. It was downhill from then on." [24]

Red Rock heroin was of low grade by more recent standards, only 3–4 percent heroin allegedly laced with strychnine, caffeine, and other bulking agents, which dramatically alter the drug's effect.[25] (No convincing clinical evidence has ever been presented to show that either "street drugs" or heroin from military sources has been regularly adulterated with strychnine, a potent poison.[26]) This variety of heroin, typically smoked by our troops rather than injected, disappeared when the Thai detachment was evacuated.

Sometime in June or July of 1970, large supplies of cheap, high-potency white heroin began entering South Vietnam from processing plants in Laos, Burma, and Thailand. The drugs were allegedly speeded on their way through clandestine channels to American servicemen by high-ranking South Vietnamese military commanders and government officials whose primary motivation was profit. Instead of a political maneuver or a Communist military plot to addict Americans, all indications are that heroin transport to Americans was another form of economic opportunism. Heroin is a high-grade commodity for trade and barter and the profits are enormous.[27]

The "drug of choice" for young Americans in Southeast Asia is the now popular and easily obtainable number 4 white heroin, packed in clear white 100-milligram gelatin capsules. Because of its high purity 95–97 percent) and strength, the user gets a faster, better "kick" and becomes habituated more quickly by simply smoking or sniffing ("horning") the drug.[28] Heroin is processed as either a course, granular white powder with the characteristic bitter taste of quinine or as small purple-red marbles or "soap balls." (One customs agent at Travis Air Force Base in California was fooled for a while into thinking they were ornamental soap balls.)

After only a few experiences with the new heroin, the novice is apt to pick up a "baby habit." This syndrome is in stark contrast to

24. See note 22.

25. "Statement by Major Kenneth Eric Nelson—Drug Abuse and Alcoholism in the Armed Services," p. 8.

26. Personal communications with Dr. David E. Smith, Assistant Clinical Professor of Toxicology, University of California Medical Center, San Francisco, California; and Dr. Frederick H. Meyers, Professor of Pharmacology, University of California Medical Center, San Francisco, California.

27. Frank Browning & Banning Garrett, "The New Opium War," *Ramparts*, May 1971, 32–39.

28. "New Withdrawal Costs," *Time*, 7 June 1971, pp. 9–24.

the long-term ghetto users, whose low-grade habits develop over a period of many years. Crude opium is even more common and cheaper than morphine or heroin. Smoking a marijuana joint dipped in opium has created a new style of drug use, the OJ or "opium joint." The same can be done with heroin. In fact, the new heroin is so powerful that smoking or sniffing (nearly 14 percent of the active agent can be introduced into the user's blood stream by sniffing) rapidly produce physical habituation, along with the withdrawal symptoms that are the result of deprivation. A "spoon" (about a metric ounce) of this heroin can be purchased for a few packs of popular-brand American cigarettes.

SOCIAL USE OF HEROIN IN VIETNAM

Heroin has become a social drug in Vietnam, just as marijuana has become a social drug in the United States. It is so cheap and so easily obtainable that it is a badge of membership in the fraternity of dopers. Dope or scag can be passed around a congenial group in the same way a bottle is shared by buddies. However, the returning veteran finds the heroin scene at home a cynical underworld with more exploitation than brotherhood.

Besides alcohol, marijuana is still the drug most often used by American ground troops. In Vietnam, marijuana is cheap, potent, and readily available, like most other drugs. Vietnamese marijuana is considered by many to be the most potent grown anywhere. In assessing the effects of the drug on troops, therefore, dose and potency become crucial variables. Whereas the weaker, less expendable U.S. marijuana will be consumed only to the point of producing relaxation and some minor time-space distortion, perhaps with feelings of euphoria, the cheap, potent weed of Asia, if taken in large doses, may be acutely hallucinatory, may cause reality distortion or delusions, and may even precipitate a full psychotic episode. Little recent data is available on this aspect of common drug use, but interviews with returning veterans suggest that rather than being used just for escape or to relax, marijuana is taken specifically to facilitate increased sensory awareness. As one young Pfc. explained:

> All our guys used it [marijuana] in my outfit. I was point man for our squad [marched ahead of the squad on patrol to look out for booby traps, mines, and enemy ambush] and I smoked and shot up a little scag [heroin] you know, just to save my own ass! When you get high, in a way it calms you down so that you don't shit your pants. I mean you get so scared out there that you could blow it and get everybody killed. It like makes you more alert and more aware, even more paranoid. When you walk point, man, you get sharp or you get blown away.

> When you are high, you don't miss snake eyes [hidden Vietnamese signs for mined trails] or miss picking up the vibes of the village people who know something is comin' down [an enemy ambush]. You can't do that when you're straight.[29]

Self-titrating the dose of both drugs was important in this example of instrumental usage. When asked by the interviewer if using marijuana and heroin didn't make him drowsy and hung-over, the Pfc. responsed, "No man, you don't get into it that far. Just enough to get up there and alert. Some guys shoot crank for the same reason. But you got to get yourself alert but not really stoned."

OTHER DRUGS OF ABUSE IN VIETNAM

Other commonly abused drugs include scopolamine and atropine, injectables that are contained in CBR (chemical, bacteriological, and radiological) warfare kits to be used as antidotes to nerve gas. Illicit amphetamines and barbiturates are also sold on the Vietnamese black market in large quantities. The most common amphetamines are Maxitone Forte, an ethical (*i.e.,* a legitimate, therapeutic prescription drug) French pharmaceutical sold in two-ounce clear glass ampules containing 100 milligrams of dexedrine tartrate, and Obesitol, another French pharmaceutical product sold as a liquid in six-ounce bottles containing 375 milligrams of phenmetrazine, a central nervous system stimulant. Both are consumed in large quantities by American troops and the indigenous population.[30]

There are four categories of acute conditions created by amphetamine abuse. The worst of these, characterized by auditory and visual hallucinations, is a paranoid delusional system that represents an extreme, if not impossible, problem of therapeutic management. A noteworthy aspect of amphetamine abuse is that it often leads to chronic heroic addiction.[31]

Barbiturates, central nervous system depressants, are also available in Vietnam, are widely abused, and cause the most severe type of physical dependence. Two French ethical drugs, Binoctal and Aminoctal, are both blends of medium- and short-acting sedative hypnotics with doses of 100–125 milligrams. Repeated chronic intoxication with

29. Personal interviews with a patient in the drug treatment unit at the Veterans Administration Hospital in Palo Alto, California.
30. "Statement by Major Kenneth Eric Nelson—Drug Abuse and Alcoholism in the Armed Services," pp. 7–8.
31. David E. Smith, "The Characteristics of Dependence in High-Dose Methamphetamine Abuse," *The International Journal of the Addictions* 4, no. 3 (September 1969): 453–459.

these barbiturates produces acute physical and psychological dependence. Abrupt withdrawal results in a classic withdrawal syndrome, including weakness, anxiety, violent acting out, hallucinations, delirium, and occasionally convulsions and death.[32]

THE RETURNING VIETNAM VETERAN

The second question most frequently asked about the drug problem of military persons abroad is: what happens if they return home undetected and with a desire for drugs? What is the prognosis for rehabilitation or cure? A social habit that might have cost from a few packs of cigarettes a day to $5 or $6 at the most in Asia may be a $100- or $200-a-day habit in this country. (Heroin is only 4–5-percent pure on the East Coast, 2–3-percent pure on the West Coast, and is more costly in the West.) Thus, the mere cost of relieving physical withdrawal discomfort will be almost prohibitive. Some will detoxify, die of overdose, or be hospitalized with needle-induced malaria or hepatitis, but most veteran addicts will return home to become street addicts and hustlers, involving themselves increasingly in a criminal life style and perhaps even going to prison. Addiction is not merely a chemical affinity, but also a life style and a social hierarchy. The addict will often seek out and join a neighborhood "copping community," part of the urban street scene where one can deal in drugs and easily obtain the necessary supply.

Many drug program administrators and coordinators for the Veterans Administration hospitals contend that the GI returning for discharge who is heavily into drugs will not be likely to clean up and seek treatment for at least six months to a year.[33] And many of those will volunteer for detoxification and treatment only in order to temporarily reduce the cost of their habit and their dependence.

The U.S. Army, which can boast the largest addicted population of all the military services, has attempted to introduce detoxification and treatment through their amnesty program. Immunity from prosecution is allegedly provided to soldiers who report their addiction or illicit use and volunteer for treatment. There is to be no criminal or punitive action unless the user is also peddling drugs or is guilty of other crimes. The actual credibility of this provision among troops

32. David E. Smith, "New Developments in Barbiturate Abuse," *Clinical Toxicology* 3, no. 1 (March 1970): 57–65.

33. Remarks made at the National Heroin Symposium, San Francisco, June 20, 1971, by William Dunn, Program Coordinator, and Steve Petty, Program Director, at the Drug Treatment Unit, Veterans Administration Hospital, Palo Alto, California.

is questionable. Some addicts report later suffering the same penalties as if they had been caught. Army treatment centers, including the Veterans Administration hospitals here in the United States, will undoubtedly play a significant role in addict rehabilitation. This paper cannot encompass the great volume of current legislation and policy making that will attempt to deal with the crisis of drug abuse in the military. The difficulties of the returning veteran with a history of drug abuse are compounded by the social and economic conditions he must cope with when he returns. There is high rate of unemployment among veterans and little regard for the servicemen returning from *this* war. Deeply impressed by the hatred, cynicism, and violence of an especially cruel war, many returning GIs seek little more than total anonymity in the colorful, transient, marginal world of the street and ghetto. They relinquish old affiliations and identities, including home and family, and join hippie and radical youth groups, who now comprise almost another army of alien discontents in this nation. Unfortunately, many of these veterans are naive persons, formerly from middle-class homes, who do not possess street hustling skills and thus are additionally disadvantaged.

ADDITIONAL COSTS OF THE VIETNAM WAR

Drug use and drug dependence are only one parameter of the returning Vietnam veteran's much larger problem. Instead of returning home to a proud America to the accompaniment of drums, fluttering flags, and the sound of bugles, many "vets" hide their service identity. "Everybody hates us and the war and acts like we are all My Lai killers," one soldier complained. Most report finding no understanding at home, and no jobs. By recent figures, the unemployment rate for veterans is at least 18 percent. These figures include all ranks of all services, including older, professionally trained personnel who possess highly demanded specialties. The unemployment rate would be much higher for the more typical veteran—a young, unskilled combat veteran, who may be part of a racial minority that is already only marginally employed. Many returning GIs don't even foster hope of finding decent work or a satisfying life. "My brother was over there ahead of me and wrote me from home that the best job you could get was $1.50 an hour at a carwash. I guess I'll live off of food stamps and hustle like all the rest of the hippies," one black veteran lamented.

The drug problem overseas may have helped create a permanent population of estranged, alienated, second-class citizens who will swell the ranks of the unemployed street drifters and add substantially to America's already epidemic drug abuse problem.

Part Two

SOCIAL AND PSYCHOLOGICAL PERSPECTIVES ON HEROIN USE

5

The Haight-Ashbury Free Medical Clinic

George R. Gay, M.D., John A. Newmeyer, Ph.D., and John J. Winkler, B.A.

> Junk is the ideal product . . . the ultimate merchandise. No sales talk is necessary. The client will crawl through the sewer to beg and buy . . . the junk merchant does not sell his product to the consumer, he sells the consumer to his product. He does not improve and simplify his merchandise, he degrades and simplifies his client.
>
> —William Burroughs, *Junkie*

THE HAIGHT-ASHBURY FREE CLINIC

Founded with the avowed ethic that "love needs Care," we have long been identified as a "hippie clinic." [1] Since the opening of our special Heroin Section in November of 1969, we have seen and treated approximately 1600 abusers of heroin; all referrals and "walk-ins" have been accepted. Our workers have included many idealistic unpaid volunteers (who found the junkie "shuck" and "jive" a far cry from the early psychedelic days) and, more recently, "street workers" and ex-addicts. We have always emphasized confidentiality and the "one-to-one" approach and have deemphasized professionalism. We work within the existing California laws, which prohibit dispensing methadone or other narcotic medications for outpatient withdrawal. Most

1. P. Schubart, D. E. Smith, and R. Conrich, "The Concept and Design of a Regionalized Health Facility for the Haight-Ashbury Subculture," *Journal of Psychedelic Drugs* 1, no. 1 (1967): 113–15.

heroin users seem to feel at ease with us; certainly, we see a population that uniformly avoids the more structured and formal medical institutions.

INTAKE METHODOLOGY

Originally our concept of confidentiality precluded lengthy history or intake forms. When we witnessed the changing patterns of drug abuse, however, we began to record not only name, residence, sex, marital status, and the like, but also heavy or habitual use of other drugs (both before and after the commencement of heroin use), the course of heroin use, attempts at withdrawal, and so forth.

In the past several months, moreover, we have begun to use a more sophisticated, "in-depth" psychosocial intake procedure devised by the psychology staff at San Francisco State College. We now explore more deeply the family and educational background of the patient, early childhood deprivation, and experience in the armed forces (especially with regard to all aspects of drug taking).

The data presented in this paper are based upon a review of the medical charts of 1539 patients from our heroin abusing population, who were seen between November 1969 and July 1971.

RESULTS

The Haight Population

Although we are nominally a community clinic, our patient population shows the following residential breakdown: 17 percent of patients report addresses in the Haight-Ashbury; 58.5 percent report addresses in other areas of San Francisco; 23.6 percent report addresses in the surrounding Bay Area; and some patients and their families, about 1 percent, travel hundreds of miles—from such places as Sacramento and Southern California—for our particular care.

Classification of Addicts

In a previous paper,[2] we arbitrarily chose as a baseline of classification the year of first heroin use, because of distinctive temporal socio-

2. C. W. Sheppard, G. R. Gay, and D. E. Smith, "The Changing Patterns of Heroin Addiction in the Haight-Ashbury Subculture," *Journal of Psychedelic Drugs* 3, no. 2 (1971): 22–30.

logical correlates. We subdivided our addict population into the following categories:

1. The "New Junkie" (NJ), who began using heroin after January 1967. He entered the heroin scene during the demise of the hippie movement and at a time of general disillusionment in the counterculture.
2. The "Transition Junkie" (TJ), who began using heroin between January 1964 and January 1967. This individual's initial drug experience paralleled the era of the psychedelics. It is our observation that this was the most socially optimistic period in our drug scene, with the widespread use of "consciousness-expanding" drugs.
3. The "Old Style Junkie" (OSJ), who began using heroin prior to January 1964. He more closely fits the classical definition of a ghetto-bred individual born into conditions of abject human misery.

The "New Junkie" (NJ) now composes by far the largest category studied (see Table 5.1). The NJ has experienced a wide range of drug experimentation prior to heroin usage (see Table 5.2). Nearly fifty-five

TABLE 5.1. CATEGORIES OF ADDICTS

Category	Number	Percent of Total
NJ	882	57.3
TJ	301	19.6
OSJ	356	23.1
Total	1,539	100.0

percent report heavy (daily) prior use of amphetamines (it is of interest to note that all returning Vietnam veterans in this group told of amphetamines being issued by medics to men going out on patrol); 50.1 percent report heavy (two or three or more times per week) use of LSD (and/or other psychedelics); and 37.4 percent report heavy (daily) prior use of barbiturates. A significant jump has been noted in the proportion of NJs reporting heavy (daily) prior use of cocaine: 16.3 percent among those seen since May 1970, as compared to 0.5 percent among those seen before May 1970. Six NJs reported having smoked heroin in Vietnam.[3]

3. G. R. Gay and E. L. Way, "Sane Pharmacological Perspectives of the Opiate Narcotics, with Special Consideration of Heroin," *Journal of Psychedelic Drugs,* 4, no. 1 (1971).

TABLE 5.2. DRUGS USED HEAVILY PRIOR TO HEROIN,
BY ADDICT CATEGORY

	NJ		TJ		OSJ	
Drug	Number	Percent of Category	Number	Percent of Category	Number	Percent of Category
Marijuana	635	72.1	210	69.8	189	53.2
LSD	442	50.1	148	49.3	62	17.4
Amphetamines	481	54.6	168	55.8	107	30.1
Barbiturates	330	37.4	102	33.9	85	23.8
Alcohol	290	32.9	110	36.6	102	28.6
Cocaine	75	8.5[a]	26	8.6	23	6.4
Opium	13	1.5	10	3.3	9	2.1

[a] 0.5 percent from November 1969 to May 1970; 16.3 percent from May 1970 through July 1971.

Among NJs, 91.2 percent have habits of less than $100-a-day (see Table 5.3) and the NJ averages only 1.52 withdrawals prior to his first visit to our clinic (see Table 5.4). Of these withdrawals, 51.7 percent were accomplished "cold turkey," 20.2 percent were self-medicated, and only 10.6 percent were attempted under a physician's supervision.

The "Transition Junkie" (TJ) composes our smallest addict subsegment (see Table 5.1). He has little in common with the "Old Style Junkie" (OSJ), but differences blur between the TJ and the NJ, who both exhibit a significantly greater history of heavy multiple drug use than does the OSJ (see Table 5.2). In particular, the NJ/TJ group has heavily used LSD far more than the OSJ group and has had much more heavy usage of amphetamines. The difference is less marked for marijuana, still less so for barbiturates, and negligible for alcohol.

TABLE 5.3. SIZE OF HABIT, BY ADDICT CATEGORY

	NJ		TJ		OSJ	
Cost per Day	Number	Percent of Category	Number	Percent of Category	Number	Percent of Category
Less than $50	574	66.6	157	53.9	166	47.0
$50–$90	212	24.6	87	29.9	122	34.6
$100–$200	72	8.4	42	14.4	59	16.7
More than $200	4	0.5	5	1.7	6	1.7
Total	862	100.1	291	99.9	353	100.1

TABLE 5.4. WITHDRAWAL FREQUENCY AND METHODS,
BY ADDICT CATEGORY

	NJ		TJ		OSJ	
Number of Withdrawals per Addict	1.52		2.44		3.16	
Method	Number	Percent of Category	Number	Percent of Category	Number	Percent of Category
Cold	685	51.9	345	46.8	599	53.3
Methadone[a]	246	18.3	143	19.4	236	21.0
Self-medicated	272	20.2	180	24.4	174	15.5
MD-treated	143	10.6	69	9.4	114	10.1
Total	1,346	101.0	737	100.0	1,123	99.9

[a] Methadone includes both "street" and physician administered.

By comparison to both the NJ and the OSJ, the TJ reports more self-medicated withdrawals from heroin, and fewer cold withdrawals. This may reflect a greater subcultural sophistication about (or confidence in) drugs extant during the TJ's initiation into drug usage.

Finally, the TJ is less apt to be divorced or separated than the OSJ, but is more apt to be cohabiting or single (see Table 5.5); this may simply be due to the younger age of the average TJ.

TABLE 5.5. MARITAL STATUS, BY ADDICT CATEGORY

Status	NJ		TJ		OSJ	
	Number	Percent of Category	Number	Percent of Category	Number	Percent of Category
Single	454	51.7	159	52.8	117	32.9
Married	220	25.1	68	22.6	111	31.2
Cohabiting	124	14.1	34	11.3	23	6.5
Divorced	36	4.1	26	8.6	62	17.4
Widowed	5	0.6	1	0.3	11	3.1
Separated	39	4.4	13	4.3	32	9.0
Total	878	100.0	301	99.9	356	100.1

The third subsegment to be examined is the "Old Style Junkie" (OSJ), who classically has a long-term, heavy habit and first used heroin prior to January 1964. He is more apt to be divorced or separated, but less likely to have remained single (see Table 5.5). The OSJ has more children to support than do the other two groups (see Table 5.6). Again, this may simply be a result of the older mean age of the OSJ.

TABLE 5.6. NUMBER OF DEPENDENT CHILDREN, BY ADDICT CATEGORY

Number of Children	NJ Number	NJ Percent of Category	TJ Number	TJ Percent of Category	OSJ Number	OSJ Percent of Category
None	620	70.6	211	70.1	196	55.1
One	146	16.6	51	16.9	69	19.4
Two	63	7.2	19	6.3	39	11.0
Three	30	3.4	10	3.3	27	7.6
Four or more	19	2.2	10	3.3	25	7.0
Total	878	100.0	301	99.9	356	100.1

TABLE 5.7. RACE, BY ADDICT CATEGORY

Race	NJ Number	NJ Percent of Category	TJ Number	TJ Percent of Category	OSJ Number	OSJ Percent of Category
White	689	78.5	211	70.1	214	60.1
Black	137	15.6	63	20.9	98	27.5
Mexican-American	42	4.8	21	7.0	39	11.0
Oriental	7	0.8	4	1.3	4	1.1
Indian	2	9.2	0	0.0	0	0.0
Mixed	1	0.1	2	0.7	1	0.3
Total	878	100.0	301	100.0	356	100.0

The higher proportion of nonwhites among the OSJs (see Table 5.7) suggests that this group is largely ghetto-bred. The significantly less frequent involvement of the OSJ in heavy prior use of marijuana, LSD, and amphetamines (see Table 5.2) indicates that this group participated less in the "age of hallucinogens" (1964–1967) and the "age of speed" (1968–1969) than did the TJ and NJ. As with the TJ and NJ groups, however, we are seeing significantly more frequent heavy use of cocaine among the OSJs who have come to us in the past year than among those of the year before.

The OSJ's habit is more likely to be over $100-a-day than the NJ's or the TJ's, and less apt to be less than $50-a-day (see Table 5.3). The realistic habit ceiling appears to be at about $200-a-day, because in none of the three categories were more than 1–2 percent of all habits greater than this amount. In all likelihood, the cause is the difficulty of sustaining a habit of this size through the routine of illicit stealing, dealing, or prostitution.

In regard to therapeutic results, the OSJ has a slightly higher cure rate than the NJ and a lower cure rate than the TJ (see Table 5.8; "cure"

TABLE 5.8. THERAPEUTIC STATUS, BY ADDICT CATEGORY

Status	NJ		TJ		OSJ	
	Number	Percent of Category	Number	Percent of Category	Number	Percent of Category
Clean[a]	47	5.4	24	8.0	24	6.7
Markedly improved[b]	170	19.3	41	13.6	86	24.2
Lost to follow-up	636	72.4	225	74.8	236	66.3
In treatment	26	3.0	11	3.7	10	2.8
Total	879	100.1	301	100.1	356	100.0

[a] "Clean" indicates those patients who have not used for at least one month.

[b] "Markedly improved" indicates using no more than once a week (i.e., use as a tranquilizer for relief of intolerable tension) and with no evidence of abstinence syndrome.

here indicates being totally clean for one month or more) but the OSJ shows a significantly higher rate of marked improvement than does the TJ or the NJ. The OSJ group has a higher percentage of patients with more than ten visits (see Table 5.9) and a significantly

TABLE 5.9. NUMBER OF CLINIC VISITS, BY ADDICT CATEGORY

Number of Visits	NJ		TJ		OSJ	
	Number	Percent of Category	Number	Percent of Category	Number	Percent of Category
One	309	35.2	108	35.9	124	35.0
Two	168	19.1	49	16.3	57	16.1
Three	104	11.8	37	12.3	44	12.4
Four	70	8.0	13	4.3	24	6.8
Five–Ten	154	17.5	64	21.3	59	16.6
Over ten	74	8.4	30	10.0	47	13.2
Total	879	100.0	301	100.1	355	100.1

lower lost to follow-up percentage than do the other two groups (see Table 5.8).

The GI Junkie

Like others, we have seen increasing evidence of heroin abuse occurring in the military. We have consequently expanded our questionnaires to include more specific data concerning military service records. Of the 105 patients seen since January 1971 whose location of addiction is known, twelve were first hooked while in the military (see Table 5.10). Our sample is small and our generalization is therefore

TABLE 5.10. NUMBER OF ADDICTS "HOOKED" IN THE MILITARY SERVICE AND ELSEWHERE, BY ADDICT CATEGORY[a]

	NJ		TJ		OSJ	
Place "Hooked"	Number	Percent of Category	Number	Percent of Category	Number	Percent of Category
Military Service	4	6.6	5	31.2	3	13.1
Elsewhere	62	93.4	11	68.8	20	86.9
Total	66	100.0	16	100.0	23	100.0

[a] Includes only those patients seen from January to July 1971 who have voluntarily reported location of addiction.

guarded, but we detect a definite trend toward increasing addiction in the military. With an increasing military veteran patient population, we anticipate meaningful data that will clarify this disturbing trend more clearly.

DISCUSSION

Since November of 1969 we have noted an unabating increase in patients seeking relief from heroin addiction. In reviewing our data, it becomes readily apparent that the heroin epidemic is of rather recent advent. Figure 5.1, which adds the new data for the period from January 1971 to July 1971, shows clearly the increased proportion of addicts who first used heroin in the last few years, and yet have only recently sought treatment at our facility. We do not feel that the small number of patients who first used heroin in very recent years—1970 and 1971—is an indication of abatement of the heroin epidemic. Rather, the explanation seems to be a decrease in total patient load necessitated by a curtailment of funds in the past year (see Table 5.11) and, more importantly, by a phenomenon we call the "lag phase."

Fig. 5.1 Number of Addicts Who First Used Heroin, Expressed as a Function of the Year

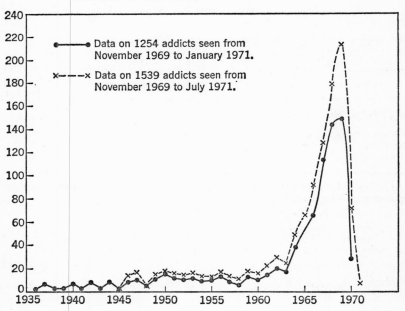

The lag phase is a period, usually one to three years in length, between the first use of heroin and the time when addiction has occurred and conditions that are no longer tolerable finally drive the addict to seek treatment. Because of the lag phase and the unmistakable national evidence of spiraling heroin abuse, it is apparent that we are still seeing only a small segment of the actual heroin abusing population. It should be added that this lag phase also applies to our returning soldiers and that we expect to see in the future a greatly increased percentage of TJs and NJs who were first hooked in the military service (in Vietnam or elsewhere).

TABLE 5.11. NUMBER OF PATIENTS SEEN, BY ADDICT CATEGORY

	NJ		TJ		OSJ	
		Percent of		Percent of		Percent of
Time Period	Num-ber	Total Seen	Num-ber	Total Seen	Num-ber	Total Seen
November 1969–May 1970[a]	433	56.0	149	19.3	191	24.7
May 1970–January 1971[b] (new clients only)	271	56.4	102	21.2	108	22.4
January 1971–July 1971[c] (new clients only)	178	62.5	50	17.5	57	20.0

[a] Total clients seen = 773.
[b] Total clients seen = 481.
[c] Total clients seen = 285.

Figure 5.2 demonstrates a slight upward trend in the age at first use of heroin. The median age is shifting from 18 for the OSJ and TJ to 20 for the NJ. With a multitude of other evidence indicating that drug abuse is spreading to younger and younger age groups, we suggest several explanations for this apparent paradox. First is the lag phase that was mentioned above. There is also an inherent adolescent distrust of all medical facilities and early attempts to withdraw are probably self-treated. Also one may consider our graph to be skewed to the right by a year or two, since underage clients (legal age for treatment at the clinic is 18) may represent themselves as being older.

We must now examine our addict categories (NJ, TJ, and OSJ), which are based on the supposition that homogeneous social environments and Zeitgeists affect each of them. However, it is clearly evident that we at the Haight Clinic are not dealing with a cohesive or stable subculture, so our three stereotypes can only be regarded as rough approximations. Although the proportions of the NJ, TJ, and OSJ divisions have remained rather constant during different time periods (see Table 5.11), their character has changed subtly.

It is most difficult to ascribe stable characteristics to the NJ, for his social and drug patterns are much more variable than those of his older counterparts. He exists in a more frustrating and anomic day-to-day existence. (The hippie movement of his older brother, the TJ, is adulterated if not dead and the war goes on.)

FIG. 5.2 AGE OF FIRST USE OF HEROIN

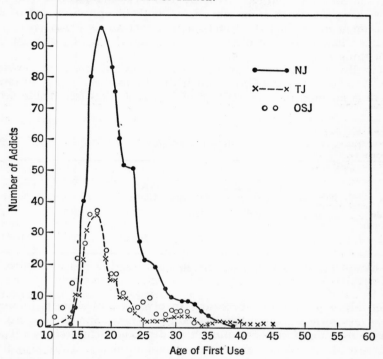

Whereas the TJ generally experienced a more lengthy experimental phase with many drugs prior to heroin (consistent with his immediate subculture's optimistic, mind-expansive attitude), and whereas the TJ repeatedly reports an initial contact with heroin as a downer for an extensive speed run or an LSD bummer, the NJ appears to find his way to heroin more directly—smack now being more available and "acceptable." The NJ, like the TJ, has seen the paranoia and violence of speed and the "freak-out" of indiscriminate LSD use, and so in many cases has found and settled on the euphoria of heroin.

However, NJ/TJ demarcations are blurring in the recent period of increasing multiple drug abuse. Reared in an era of multiple medication, many of our clients are merely shoppers, wandering from one drug treatment facility to the next, their pockets often bulging with collected pills (downers, or those that "give a buzz," are preferred), as they prepare for the next dry spell of heroin or use the medications directly to supplement the very low-potency heroin available on the streets.

Our original OSJ has changed as well. When we first saw him, he was someone who had repeatedly tried to kick, and was trying us as a new thing. As words from our clients, both of optimism and of disillusionment, reached the streets, a new type of OSJ was seen—still trying a new thing, but often with more knowledge of just what this new thing was.

Finally, and perhaps most significantly, several trends are evident that progress from the OSJ through the TJ to the NJ. For instance, there is an increasing percentage of female addicts (see Table 5.12),

TABLE 5.12. SEX, BY ADDICT CATEGORY[a]

Sex	NJ Number	NJ Percent of Category	TJ Number	TJ Percent of Category	OSJ Number	OSJ Percent of Category
Male	587	66.6	234	77.8	305	85.6
Female	295	33.4	67	22.2	51	14.5
Total	882	100.0	301	100.0	356	100.1

[a] Transvestites are listed according to their original sex.

probably reflecting the increasing involvement of women in many aspects of society previously relegated to the male. Similar progressions are seen in the decreasing number of dependent children (see Table 5.6) and the increasing amount of cohabitation (see Table 5.5) from the OSJ to the NJ, which are probably simply a factor of decreasing mean age. Furthermore, the average number of withdrawals increases with habit duration (see Table 5.4).

RIPPLE EFFECT

In the spread of heroin abuse, a "ripple effect" was noticed. The drug pattern of the Haight (and, simultaneously, of New York's East Village) seemed to spread in waves through American society. The movement was generally "outward" from urban, East or West Coast, young, "hip" persons, but with a more complex pattern as far as socioeconomic class and educational level were concerned.[4] The "agent of contagion" might have been Haight emigrés, "summer hippies," itinerant drug merchants, the mass media, or a combination of all of these, but it was clear that those communities with the greatest similarity and the shortest lines of communication to the Haight or the East Village (Berkeley, for example) tended to imitate their drug patterns most closely and with the shortest time lag.

Why, though, should the Haight and the East Village have been the epicenters of these "ripples"? Here we might make another analogy to the physical universe: the situation resembled the cores of dwarf stars, where the extreme pressure of the layers above causes atomic structures to collapse and strange nuclear distortions to occur. In a certain sense, the Haight and the East Village were "ultrahigh-pressure cores": over-populated, ceaselessly seething with life, the focus of a tremendous amount of attention, and (perhaps most important) *the* places for the ambitious chemical-psychic voyager to make his mark. Under these intense conditions, we saw that interpersonal and intrapsychic structures often caved in, and strangely distorted forms made their appearance, providing the perfect crucible for the germination of new patterns of drug abuse. Such conditions were duplicated at the Altamont festival in an even more intense, although temporary, form. The inner core of that crowd was said to approach 20,000 persons per acre in density; Grace Slick, standing stunned at the very center of focus of this human crush, could only observe, "Man—it's *weird* up here!"

DIFFICULTIES

Certainly, we do not reach every addict segment. We are, for example, continually aware of difficulties in reaching much of the black community. (The Haight-Ashbury community is 70 percent black, but only 20 percent of our addict population is black.)

Also, we continue to be limited by the treatment modalities available to us—nonnarcotic drug detoxification and counseling on an outpatient basis—and by the very real scarcity of referral agencies for inpatient care and for intermediate and long-term rehabilitation.

In many ways, our inability to use methadone or other narcotic medications has been a blessing in disguise. We come to know the junkie as a person as the layers of learned manipulative behavior peel

4. G. R. Gay, A. D. Matzger, W. Bathurst, and D. E. Smith, "Short-Term Heroin Detoxification on an Outpatient Basis," *International Journal of the Addictions* 6, no. 2 (1971): 241–64.

from him while he kicks his habit—with the discomfort of withdrawal eased, but not masked, by our relatively mild symptomatic medications. As he reemerges, we can use what we have learned from this observation in referring him to such aftercare as is available to him. His counselors therefore become acutely aware of his underlying problems: environmental, psychological, and physical.

SUMMARY

We feel that our subdivision into New Junkie, Transition Junkie, and Old Style Junkie, although inexact in many ways, has enabled us better to understand the heroin abusers of our population, who may well have common environmental, psychosocial, and personal problems, but who are, of course, individual and unique.

Current trends noted at the Haight Clinic have been:

1. *The GI Junkie:* the returning U.S. serviceman, especially from Vietnam, who reveals a marked increase in contact with and heavy use of heroin and cocaine. An interesting mode of self-administration is the reported smoking of heroin.

2. *An increase of multiple concurrent drug abuse:* especially the use of alcohol, barbiturates, and other downers with heroin.

3. *A lag phase* of from one to three years between initial use of heroin and the time a patient seeks help at our clinic.

4. *The ripple effect:* although we are not yet advanced to the point where we can determine how a pattern of drug use is spread by our transient population or what channels will be selected for its spread, we nonetheless feel that the trends of drug abuse chartered within our patient population will serve a useful predictive purpose as heroin abuse appears elsewhere. This is important for future public mental health policies— for example, in pinpointing where heroin epidemics might be imminent or in rebuilding credibility among marijuana-using youth (credibility that is lost because of useless campaigns against marijuana is often sorely missed when hard drugs subsequently invade the community). Hopefully, our therapeutic experience, as well as our demographic data, will be of help.

Perhaps in the end such arbitrary divisions as those we have chosen will not hold up statistically. If, however, they can now provide a starting point for designing detoxification, rehabilitation, and aftercare programs, they will have served a valid purpose. It has been said that heroin addiction should be approached with a "disillusioned optimism" [5]—the point, of course, being how very much we have yet to learn.

> "We have forty million reasons for failure, but not a single excuse."
>
> —Kipling, *The Lesson*

5. Isidor Chein et al., *The Road to H: Narcotics, Delinquency, and Social Policy* (New York: Basic Books, 1964).

6

The Economics of Heroin Addiction:
A New Interpretation of the Facts

Garrett O'Connor, M.D., Leon Wurmser, M.D.,

Torrey C. Brown, M.D., and Judith Smith, Ph.D.

The illicit narcotics[1] industry is in large part maintained and supported by financial contributions from the general public. A combination of economic and sociopsychological factors, together with misguided legislation, help to maintain an equilibrium that allows for continuing expansion of the industry.

INTRODUCTION

In recent years public concern about law and order has become a preoccupation in the United States. Crime and disorder of all kinds appear to be increasing, and there is evidence of corruption in every stratum of society. The atmosphere is one in which politicians who promise reform are propelled rather than elected into office.

From a historical point of view repressive measures directed against relatively small but highly visible social groups have tended to force such groups to assume increasingly deviant postures vis-à-vis society. In this country, legislation has not only failed to solve the problem of drug abuse, but, on the contrary, has served to force the addicts into a criminally deviant role, which is then rationalized to justify the continuing use of a repressive approach. By the same token, however, addicts and other workers in the narcotics industry may actually be

1. In the context of this paper, the term narcotics refers only to "hard narcotics" such as heroin and morphine.

afforded protection by being compelled to continue operations in the underground realms of society, where their illegal activities are effectively hidden from public scrutiny.

Statistical evidence of a connection between narcotics addiction and crimes against property and person has been parlayed into a massive self-perpetuating stereotypical system which encourages the nonaddicted population to believe that illicit drugs, and especially narcotics, constitute a menace which threatens to undermine the moral fabric of the nation.

Drug addicts are currently the nation's number one choice at the polls of deviance. In selecting a deviant group for special attention and thereby conveniently localizing evil in one place, society can absolve itself from any responsibility for complicity in the matter, and in addition, avoid the recognition of widespread corruption within itself.

Society has declared war on drug addiction. For some reason, however, this war is not realizing its *announced* objectives. The abuse of opiates and other drugs is thought to be more widespread than ever. Indeed, the industry which controls the supply seems to be flourishing. Is it possible that, like another war more familiar to us all, the war against addiction is perpetuated even while it fails because of hidden economic interests which benefit from its continuance?

METHODS

Between December 1969 and August 1970, one of us (LW) administered a crime and drug addiction questionnaire to a group of 115 patients who voluntarily sought treatment at the Johns Hopkins Drug Abuse Center.

Two-thirds of the patients resided in poverty areas of the inner city. Almost half were black. The vast majority were heroin addicts; a few were occasional heroin users. Duration of addiction ranged from six months to thirty-five years.

The questionnaires were completed at the time of intake or shortly after admission to the Center. A professional interviewer or an ex-addict counselor monitored the completion of each form. The replies were unsigned, and confidentiality was assured.

Some measure of validity was obtained in the cases of twenty patients who were subsequently followed in psychotherapy by LW for varying lengths of time. Further validity was derived from reviewing the results of the study with other addicts in treatment who confirmed that the statements made by the experimental group were generally true.

A supplementary series of unstructured interviews was carried out
by GO'C with addicts not included in the experimental group, with
nonaddicted residents of the community in which the center is located, with ex-addict counselors, and with police officers assigned to the
Narcotics Squad of Baltimore City.

RESULTS

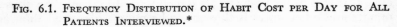

1. *The median cost of heroin to patients in the group was $35
per day.*

   Amounts ranged from $10 twice a week (heroin users) to
$250 a day (dealer's habit). As can be seen from Figure 6.1,

FIG. 6.1. FREQUENCY DISTRIBUTION OF HABIT COST PER DAY FOR ALL
PATIENTS INTERVIEWED.*

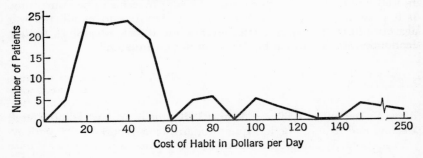

the distribution of estimated habit-costs is skewed positively
(i.e., the bulk of cases fall into the lower part of the range of
scores). Since the mean is more sensitive to extreme scores,
the median is used as an estimate of the central tendency.

2. *Ninety-three percent of the patients supported their drug
habits by illegal activities.*

   The remainder reported habits averaging $10–$15 a day,
which they were able to maintain by income from a combination of legitimate work and family support. Various
types of illegal activities reported are listed in Table 6.1.

* Absolute values for patients reporting a range of habit costs were obtained by
using the lower values reported, i.e. an estimate of $250–$300 is represented in the
distribution as $250.

TABLE 6.1. THE NUMBER OF PATIENTS PARTICIPATING IN ANY ONE ACTIVITY RELATIVE TO THE TOTAL NUMBER OF PATIENTS PARTICIPATING IN ILLEGAL ACTIVITIES.

Means	Number of Patients
Shoplifting	68
Selling (Dealing)	56
Burglary	37
Robbery & Mugging	19
Gambling	16
Flim flam, Conning & Forging Checks	8
Borrowing & Stealing from Family	5
Prostitution	5

3. *Eighty percent of the patients reported that the sale of stolen goods realized profits in the amount of one-third their retail value.*

Vignettes of four cases in the study group convey a general picture of the nature and extent of the illegal activities reported.

Case 24. A 31-year-old heroin addict abandoned his practice of mugging people on a regular schedule of three nights a week with profit of $150 a night, and instead switched to dealing. He obtained 150 bags a day, sold between 100 and 130, and used the rest himself. Most of his $500 daily income was paid to the supplier.

Case 35. On the day preceding the interview, this patient, who reported a habit of $80–100 a day, stole thirty watches, each valued at $9, from a drugstore, and seventy packs of razor blades valued at $2 a pack. He sold the merchandise, which had a store value of $400, for $110. He further estimated that he shoplifted about $150,000 worth of merchandise each year.

Case 39. This patient, aged 22, was addicted to heroin and dilaudid. He paid $65 a day for his drugs. He specialized in stealing tape decks from cars, and estimated that he had removed about 20 of them in a six-month period. In addition, his haul during the same period included forty to fifty leather coats, fifty TV sets, forty radios, one mink stole, and a few hundred dollars from private homes.

Case 46. This man, who spent $70 a day on his habit, limited his activities to department stores. One day's work netted two coats and one suit in the store value of $300.

The results of the "street" interviews and interviews with police and ex-addict counselors are incorporated in the discussion and interpretation of the responses to the questionnaire.

INTERPRETATION OF RESULTS

In common with all attempts to obtain accurate information about the nature and extent of opiate abuse and related activities, the data reported here contain many sources of possible error. A few of these are as follows:

1. The sample of 115 subjects who compose the experimental group for this study may not be representative of the addicted population at large.
2. The actual number of addicts in Baltimore City is unknown. The estimate used as a base for calculation in this paper is in agreement with that of the Baltimore City Police Department and the State Drug Abuse Authority. Even so, it must at best be regarded as approximate.
3. Our speculations as to the total amount of merchandise stolen may be high. It is possible that drug dealing is a more prevalent way of deriving income from depradation of the environment.
4. The average addict is not in street circulation 365 days a year. Episodes of incarceration, periods of reduction in drug use, efforts to kick the habit, etc., may limit his activities.
5. The accuracy of the subjects' personal estimates about the extent of their opiate use must be held in question, especially as these estimates were obtained at a time when it may well have been in the interests of individual patients to exaggerate the severity of their habits in the hope of receiving higher doses of methadone.

Despite these objections, however, the data are nevertheless useful because when they are coupled with conclusions from the supplementary interviews mentioned above, persuasive trends emerge which provide a legitimate basis for speculative interpretation.

Approximately 6000 opiate addicts are known to diverse agencies in the state of Maryland. The vast majority live in Baltimore City. A conservative estimate of the *actual* number of addicts puts the figure in the neighborhood of 12,000.

Discussions with the Baltimore City Police Department indicate that organized fencing operations are virtually nonexistent in the city. Interviews with addicts and residents of poverty areas suggest that members of the nonaddicted population are the major receivers of stolen goods in the city.

Using the data from questionnaire as a base for calculations, we estimate that merchandise with a retail value of between $166,780,000 and $313,560,000 is stolen each year by addicts in Baltimore City. These figures are derived from the following considerations: (a) the total cost of heroin to the addicts, i.e., what they actually pay for their drugs, (b) the proportion of the cost supported by stealing, and (c) the exchange value of stolen merchandise.

The total annual cost of heroin to the addicts of Baltimore City ($78,000,000–$156,000,000) was calculated by multiplying the average cost of heroin per addict per year ($13,000) by the estimated number of addicts in the city (6000–12,000). It is assumed that no more than two-thirds of the total cost is supported by stealing, since trading in drugs and family support is known to account for part of the total income.

Stolen merchandise realizes about one-third of its retail value when resold on the street. Therefore in order to make $100 profit on resale, the addict must steal $300 worth of goods.

If two-thirds of the total cost of heroin is covered by the profit realized from the sale of stolen merchandise, then the customers who are, for the most part, members of the nonaddicted population of Baltimore, are paying between $52,260,000 and $104,550,000 a year in return for these goods.

To obtain a more accurate estimate of the actual figures involved these amounts should be reduced by a factor of one-fifth to allow for incarceration, illness, and other times when the addict is out of circulation.

As 100 percent of the amounts received by the addict is paid to dealers in return for drugs, it can be said that the illicit narcotics industry in Baltimore City derives an annual income ranging from $41,000,000 to $84,000,000 (figures rounded) by way of financial contributions from the general public.

DISCUSSION

This interpretation of the economic facts basic to the maintenance and support of the illicit narcotics industry has major implications for programs of treatment and prevention of addiction.

It appears that a self-sustaining economic cycle is maintained intact by complicity between workers in the narcotics industry, drug addicts, and the general public. Participation in this cycle provides benefits and profits for large numbers of people.

While treatment of addicts on a massive scale can be expected to limit the availability of stolen merchandise to the nonaddicted population by reducing the amount of criminal activity engaged in by addicts, it will not in itself, however, effect major changes in the economic equilibrium, as the addict population is increasing at a rate faster than it is being reduced by rehabilitation, incarceration, and attrition. Efforts at prevention must, therefore, be directed at interruption of the cycle at one or all of several points. This is difficult or impossible to achieve because of a widespread vested interest in the maintenance of the status quo.

Interviews with residents in the neighborhood surrounding the Center, which is classified as a poverty area, indicate that the purchase of stolen goods is endemic to the culture. Some of those interviewed were aware of the illegal nature of their activities, others were not. Few saw any wrong in it, and the interviewer had the impression that buying stolen goods at reduced prices was thought to be the privilege of the underprivileged. People admitted to their complicity with a certain sense of satisfaction and glee. So much so, in fact, that the interviewer was reminded of middle- and upper-middle-class people who, at income tax time, proudly proclaim their cleverness in having cheated the Internal Revenue Service out of large amounts of money. The poor people call it "screwing the Man."

The psychological gains accrued from this form of illegal activity must take second place to economic ones. Poor people are daily bombarded with advertising which exhorts them to acquire material goods far beyond their means. The opportunity, therefore, to obtain such goods at one-third the retail price is welcomed.

All manner of merchandise is available. Many people actually place orders for what they want. Mothers on welfare provide their children with much-needed warm clothing for the winter. Elderly persons on Social Security can prevent attacks of pneumonia with a fur coat and an electric blanket, and so on. Chein et al.,[2] Preble and Casey,[3] and Schur[4] have already referred to the contributions of the nonaddicted population to the narcotics industry and have noted that traffic in stolen goods represents a broad avenue through which merchandise

2. Isidor Chein et al., *The Road to H: Narcotics, Delinquency, and Social Policy* Basic Books, New York, 1964.

3. E. Preble & J. J. Casey, "Taking Care of Business—The Heroin User's Life on the Street, *International Journal of the Addictions* 4 (1969): 1–24.

4. E. M. Schur, *Our Criminal Society* (Englewood Cliffs, N.J.: Prentice Hall, 1969).

flows down the affluent society into the indigent strata. This "Secret Domestic Marshall Plan" is perhaps one of the more successful and less well advertised poverty programs of the Great Society.

The illicit narcotics industry can be considered as an example of "capitalism carried to its logical limits." [5] Many authors have pointed out that the industry is a highly organized and successful one, which operates as a close-to-perfect model of the American version of free enterprise.

Recruitment starts at an early age. Stories of 12-year-old addicts are not apocryphal. Anyone who lives or works in a poor neighborhood is familiar with the sight of a distributor, sartorially magnificent in a $500 suit standing proudly tall beside his sky-blue Cadillac as he pauses for a moment to survey his territory. More often than not, he is surrounded by a knot of little lads gazing up in silent adoration. Later, when they drop out of school, we will encourage these same lads to accept jobs as janitors, laborers, and elevator attendants in upper-middle-class apartment buildings.

The operating methods of the industry are surely similar to those of other major industries which use profit and power to ensure their survival. Connections in high places are crucial to success in big business. Is it unreasonable to assume, as Chief Justice Earl Warren[6] has done, that the situation with the narcotics industry is in any way different?

The phenomenal growth and stability of the illicit narcotics industry can be in part attributed to the fact that many classes of people derive material profits from its presence.

The executives and workers in the industry make profits unprecedented in industrial history. The addicts "benefit" because drugs are readily available, albeit at high prices. The nonaddicted population benefits because valuable and desirable merchandise is available at vastly reduced prices. Those who have property stolen from their homes can benefit by lodging inflated claims against the insurance companies who, in turn, raise the cost of premiums to cover their losses. The government benefits indirectly by virtue of the "Secret Domestic Marshall Plan" which provides the poor with merchandise which otherwise might have to be supplied by the authorities. Small appliance manufacturers rejoice in the knowledge that for each article stolen a replacement is purchased at retail price. Burglar alarm manu-

5. G. Witman, Director of Man Alive Research, Inc., Baltimore, Maryland. Seminar entitled "Drug Abuse and the Public Health," Johns Hopkins School of Hygiene and Public Health, January 1971.

6. Chief Justice Earl Warren, Milton S. Eisenhower Symposium, United States in the 1970s: Perspectives on Violence. Johns Hopkins University, 13 November 1970.

facturers and security agencies have never had it so good. Department stores, who budget for "shrinkage" due to shoplifting, manage to side-step disaster by passing on their losses to the customer. Second-hand stores and pawnbrokers would undoubtedly feel the pinch if their supplies of stolen goods were suddenly reduced. Medical institutions everywhere are frantically applying for monies made available by the federal government for drug abuse programs.

There are also those who lose—not only psychologically, but materially and physically too. Losses from street robberies and muggings are often not retrievable. People are wounded and sometimes killed in crimes connected with narcotics.

And then there are the addicts. Sixty-seven of them died from over-doses in Baltimore during 1970.

Beyond that, many of them are emotionally crippled at the age of 25. Skilled only in the art of deception and the practice of crime, they slide into a subculture of unspeakable degradation, where the principal values are those which determine the availability of the next fix. Often, their capacity to relate maturely to another human being is crushed before it has had a chance to develop. Episodes of incarceration entrench their antisocial tendencies. Alienated and bitter, they wage relentless guerilla warfare on the society which has produced them.

But society is well-versed in the art of making profit out of pain. Accordingly, the addict-victim has been put to work as a middleman in an enterprise which principally benefits the nonaddicted population. The maintenance of the economic equilibrium is therefore in the "best" interests of all concerned.

There is considerable evidence to support this view. Drug addiction has reached epidemic proportions. Its causes, however, are endemic. The Establishment, as well as the general public, must accept responsibility for the support and sponsorship of the illicit narcotics industry. Many mechanisms combine to protect the industry from effective intervention. Considered separately, these might not be regarded significantly. When operating in concert, they constitute a formidable bastion behind which the narcotics industry is free to flourish.

For instance, the national hysteria about the evils of marijuana can be viewed as an effective decoy mechanism which distracts attention from the economically more significant traffic in heroin, thereby allowing it to continue operation with relative immunity from interference.

Accurate information about the extent of the drug abuse problem is hard to obtain from official sources. Effective efforts to attack the problem on all fronts—medical, social, psychological, and economic—

are often impeded by a combination of ambivalent attitudes and immovable bureaucracy. Because of raw prejudice, law enforcement and medical approaches are often dichotomized, leading to a reduction in the potential effectiveness of both. Funds appropriated for the investigation and treatment of drug addiction are incomparably less than the amounts lost to the economy by its continuing existence.

The Harrison Act of 1914 was the progenitor of increasingly repressive legislation, which actually affords the industry protection by forcing it to operate underground. Laws designed to prevent crime among addicts have had the effect of increasing it instead. A more rational legal approach to the problem would vastly reduce the incidence of crime among addicts and provide law enforcement agencies with more time and freedom to investigate the problem at source. It would eliminate also, of course, the fantastic amounts of hidden profits which will continue to accrue as long as the illicit narcotics industry remains in good health.

The experience of the individual who attempts to cross the boundary which separates the addicted from the nonaddicted worlds is perhaps the most persuasive evidence of the fact that such a boundary exists and that the Establishment has some vested interest in maintaining it. We refer, of course, to the dilemma of the addict who wishes to be rehabilitated so that he can rejoin society as a productive citizen.

Despite every evidence of his willingness to reform, he is discriminated against more than ever before. Many unions deny him membership and job opportunities are limited because of his criminal record. Personnel policies designed for the straight population are inimical to his needs and have the effect of discouraging him from work. Like the proverbial buck, he is passed around from place to place, never trusted and never believed. He is denied the privileges which are the rights of his brothers, and in general, is made to feel unwanted and unwelcome.

Rendered socially incompetent in the straight world by a life style developed during the long years of addiction, he often surrenders to the overwhelming pressures and returns to drugs, more deeply convinced than ever that there is no hope and no welcome for him in society.

Surely, one might conclude that society has some vested interest in the preservation of his role as addict, criminal, and deviant?

Because of the range of vested interests involved—both economic and sociopsychologic—little change can be expected to occur in the status quo between the narcotics industry and the general public until it is widely accepted that the industry is, in fact, a pillar of the nation's economy, rather than a wedge which threatens to split it apart.

Closer inspection by qualified economists of the hypothesis advanced in this paper might well reveal that a significant percentage of the public investment which constitutes the profits earned by the narcotics industry is not returned to the economy, but instead, is siphoned out of it to be stored for future use at a more propitious time.

Bankers in Switzerland, we understand, continue to grow rich.

7

Taking Care of Business:

The Heroin User's Life

on the Street

Edward Preble and John J. Casey, Jr.

INTRODUCTION

This report is a description of the life and activities of lower-class heroin users in New York City in the context of their street environment. It is concerned exclusively with the heroin users living in slum areas who comprise at least 80 percent of the city's heroin-using population. They are predominantly Negro and Puerto Rican, with some Irish, Italian, and Jewish.

It is often said that the use of heroin provides an escape for the user from his psychological problems and from the responsibilities of social and personal relationships—in short, an escape from life. Clinical descriptions of heroin addicts emphasize the passive, dependent, withdrawn, generally inadequate features of their personality structure and social adjustment. Most sociological studies of heroin users make the same point. Thus Chein et al. (1964) reported that street gang members are not likely to become heroin users because they are resourceful, aggressive, well-integrated boys who are "reality-oriented" in their street environment. They held that it is the passive, anxious, inadequate boy who cannot adapt to street life who is likely to use heroin. Similarly, Cloward and Ohlin (1960) referred to heroin users as "re-

The authors received support and consultation from Dr. Oscar K. Diamond, Director, Manhattan State Hospital; Dr. Calvin A. Michael, Director, Division of Narcotics, New York State Department of Mental Hygiene; and Dr. Esra S. Petursson, Principal Research Scientist, Manhattan State Hospital, Drug Addiction Unit.

treatists" and "double failures" who cannot qualify for either legitimate or illegitimate careers. Unaggressive "mamma's boys" is the usual stereotype these days for the heroin addict, both for the students of narcotic use and the public at large. Experienced researchers and workers in the narcotics field know that there is no such thing as "the heroin addict" or "the addict personality." However, most attempts to generalize—the goal of all scientific investigation—result in some version of the escape theory.

The description which follows of the activities of lower-class heroin users in their adaptation to the social and economic institutions and practices connected with the use of heroin contradicts this widely held belief. Their behavior is anything but an escape from life. They are actively engaged in meaningful activities and relationships seven days a week. The brief moments of euphoria after each administration of a small amount of heroin constitute a small fraction of their daily lives. The rest of the time they are aggressively pursuing a career that is exacting, challenging, adventurous, and rewarding. They are always on the move and must be alert, flexible, and resourceful. The surest way to identify heroin users in a slum neighborhood is to observe the way people walk. The heroin user walks with a fast, purposeful stride, as if he is late for an important appointment—indeed, he is. He is hustling (robbing or stealing), trying to sell stolen goods, avoiding the police, looking for a heroin dealer with a good bag (the street retail unit of heroin), coming back from copping (buying heroin), looking for a safe place to take the drug, or looking for someone who beat (cheated) him—among other things. He is, in short, *taking care of business,* a phrase which is so common with heroin users that they use it in response to words of greeting, such as "how you doing?" and "what's happening?" *Taking care of biz* is the common abbreviation. *Ripping and running* is an older phrase which also refers to their busy lives. For them, if not for their middle- and upper-class counterparts (a small minority of opiate addicts), the quest for heroin is the quest for a meaningful life, not an escape from life. And the meaning does not lie, primarily, in the effects of the drug on their minds and bodies; it lies in the gratification of accomplishing a series of challenging, exciting tasks, every day of the week.

Much of the life of the heroin user on the street centers around the economic institutions of heroin distribution. Therefore, this report features a description of the marketing processes for heroin, from importation to street sales. The cost of heroin today is so high and the quality so poor that the street user must become totally involved in an economic career. A description of typical economic careers of heroin users will be presented. Preceding these two sections is a brief historical account of heroin use in New York City from World War I to the present, in which it will be seen that patterns of heroin use have changed at a pace and in a direction in correspondence with the social changes of the past fifty years. Theories and explanations about heroin use based upon observations of fifty, twenty-five, or even five years ago are inadequate to account for the phenomenon today. It is hoped that this contemporary account of the social setting for heroin use will provide useful data for the modifications of theory and practice which should accompany any dynamic social process.

METHODOLOGY

The data on which this report is based have come from interviews with patients at the Manhattan State Hospital Drug Addiction Unit and from participant-observation and interviews with individuals and groups in four lower-class communities in New York City—East Harlem, Lower East Side, Yorkville, Claremont (Bronx). The communities represent the neighborhoods of approximately 85 percent of the addict patients at Manhattan State Hospital. The anthropologist's role and approach to the heroin-using study informants was in the tradition of Bronislaw Malinowski (1922) and William F. Whyte (1955), which, in Whyte's words, consists of "the observation of interpersonal events." Another dimension was added with the modified use of research techniques introduced by Abraham Kardiner and his collaborators (1939) in their psychosocial studies of primitive and modern cultures. The main feature of this methodology is the life-history interview with individual subjects. Initial and subsequent contacts with the research informants occurred, in all cases, with their voluntary consent and cooperation. The anthropologist had the advantage of twelve years experience of street work and research in the study neighborhoods, and was able to enlist the assistance of long-time acquaintances for this special project. Four major ethnic groups were represented among the approximately 150 informants: Irish, Italian, Negro, and Puerto Rican.

HISTORY OF HEROIN USE IN NEW YORK CITY

The recent history of heroin use in the city can be broken down into six time periods: (1) between World War and World War II, (2) during World War II, (3) 1947 to 1951, (4) 1951 to 1961, and (6) 1961 to the present.

1. Between World War I and World War II

Prior to World War II the use of heroin was limited, for the most part, to people in *the life*—show people, entertainers, and musicians; racketeers and gangsters; thieves and pickpockets; prostitutes and pimps. The major ethnic groups represented among these users were Italian, Irish, Jewish and Negro (mostly those associated with the entertainment life). There were also heroin users among the Chinese, who had a history of opium use. The distribution of heroin by those who controlled the market was limited mostly to these people, and there was little knowledge or publicity about it.

2. During World War II

World War II interrupted the trade routes and distributorships for illicit heroin supplies, which resulted in a five-year hiatus in heroin use.

3. 1947 to 1951

When World War II ended there was a greatly expanded market for heroin in the increased population among Negroes from the South and among migrating Puerto Ricans, who came to New York during the war in response to a manpower shortage. In 1940 the Negro population in New York City was 450,000; in 1960 it was over 1 million. In 1940 the Puerto Rican population was 70,000; in 1960 it was over 600,000. As with all new immigrants in New York, they worked at the lowest economic levels, settled in slum neighborhoods, and were the victims of unemployment, poverty, and discrimination. From 1947 to 1951 the use of heroin spread among lower-class Negro and Puerto Rican people and among other lower class, slum-dwelling people, mainly the Irish and Italians. The increased rate of use was gradual, but steady, and did not attract much attention. Most of the users were young adults in their twenties and thirties. They were more or less circumspect in their drug consumption, which they were able to be because of the relatively low cost and high quality of the heroin.

During this period, heroin was sold in number five capsules (the smallest capsules used for pharmaceutical products). These *caps* could be bought for about one dollar apiece, and two to six persons could get high on the contents of one capsule. Commonly, four persons would contribute one quarter each and *get down on a cap*. There was social cohesion, identification, and ritual among the users of this period. Sometimes as many as twenty people would get together and, in a party atmosphere, share the powder contents of several capsules, which were emptied upon a mirror and divided into columns by means of a razor blade, one column for each participant. The mirror was passed from person to person and each one would inhale his share through the nose by means of a tapered, rolled-up dollar bill which served as a straw, and was called a *quill*. A twenty, fifty, or hundred dollar bill was used on special occasions, when someone wanted to make a show of his affluence. Since heroin was so inexpensive during this time, no addict had to worry about getting his fix; someone was always willing to loan him a dollar or share a part of his drug. The social relationships among these addicts were similar to those found in a neighborhood bar, where there is a friendly mutual concern for the welfare of the regular patrons. The most important economic factor in these early postwar days of heroin use was that heroin users were able to work even at a low-paying job and still support a habit, and many of them did. Relatively little crime was committed in the interest of getting money to buy heroin. A habit could be maintained for a few dollars a day, at little social or economic cost to the community.

4. 1951 to 1957

Around 1951 heroin use started to become popular among younger people on the streets, especially among street gang members who were tired of gang fighting and were looking for a new high. As heroin use had become more common in the latter days of the previous period, the more street-wise teenagers learned about it and prevailed upon the experienced users to introduce them to it. Contrary to popular reports, experimentation with heroin by youths usually began at their initiative and not through proselytism. The stereotype of the dope *pusher* giving out free samples of narcotics to teenagers in school yards and candy stores in order to addict them is one of the most misleading myths about drug use. Also, contrary to professional reports about this development, it was not the weak, withdrawn, unadaptive street boy who first started using heroin, but rather the tough, sophisticated and respected boy, typically a street gang leader. Later, others followed his example, either through indoctrination or emulation. By 1955 heroin use among teenagers on the street had become widespread, resulting, among other things, in the dissolution of fighting gangs. Now the hip boy on the street was not the swaggering, leatherjacketed gang member, but the boy nodding on the corner enjoying his heroin high. He was the new hero model.

As heroin use spread among the young from 1951, the price of heroin began to rise in response to the greater demand, and the greater risks involved in selling to youths. Those who started using heroin as teenagers seldom had work experience or skills, and resorted to crime in order to support their heroin use. They were less circumspect in their drug-using and criminal activity, and soon became a problem to the community, especially to those who were engaged in non-narcotic illegal activities, such as bookmaking, loan-sharking and policy (the gambling game popular among working-class people, in which a correct selection of three numbers pays off at 50 to 1). The activities and behavior of young drug users brought attention and notoriety to the neighborhood which jeopardized racketeer operations. It was not uncommon for a local racketeer to inform the parents of a young heroin user about his activities, hoping that they would take action.

5. 1957 to 1961

In 1957 the criminal organization, or *syndicate*, which had been mainly responsible for heroin distribution (according to law enforcement agencies and government investigation committees), officially withdrew from the market. This resulted from two conditions: the passage of stricter federal laws that included provision for conspiracy convictions, and the related fact that illegal drug use was receiving increased attention from the public and officials, especially as a result of the increased involvement of youth with heroin. The risks had become too great, and the syndicate did not want to endanger the larger and more important sources of revenue such as gambling and loan-sharking. However, the instruction to get out of narcotics was more honored in the breach than in the observance by certain syndicate members. Those who stayed involved in narcotics operated independently. Some made it their primary operation, while others would make only one or two big transactions a year when they needed to recoup quickly from an unexpected financial loss in some other operation. Dealing irregularly in narcotics for this purpose became known as a *fall-back*—a quick and sure way to make money. The syndicate also stayed involved indirectly through loan-shark agreements. In these transactions large sums of money were lent to narcotic dealers for a period of one month at a fixed rate of return. No questions were asked regarding its use. By this means the syndicate avoided some of the undesirable aspects of narcotic distribution and still participated in the profits. The official withdrawal of the syndicate from narcotics created opportunities for independent operators, which resulted in a relatively free market.

6. 1961 to the Present

The next major development in the history of heroin use in the city occurred in November, 1961, when there was a critical shortage of heroin. Known as a *panic,* this development, whatever its cause, had a profound effect on the course of heroin use in the city. The panic lasted only for a few weeks. During this time the demand for the meager supplies of heroin was so great that those who had supplies were able to double and triple their prices and further adulterate the quality, thus realizing sometimes as much as ten times their usual profit. By the time heroin became available again in good supply, the dealers had learned that inferior heroin at inflated prices could find a ready market. Since that time the cost of heroin on the street has continued to climb, through increased prices, further adulteration, and *short counts* (misrepresentation of aggregate weight in a given unit). A few minor panics—about two a year—help bolster the market. Today an average heroin habit costs the user about $20 a day, as compared to $2 twenty years ago. This fact is responsible for a major social disorder in the city today. It has also had important effects on the personal, social, and family relationships of the heroin users themselves. There is no longer social cohesion among addicts. The competition and struggle necessary to support a habit has turned each one into an independent operator who looks out only for himself. Usually, addicts today will associate in pairs (partners), but only for practical purposes: in a criminal effort which requires two people (as when one acts as lookout while the other commits a burglary), to share in the price of a bag of heroin, to assist in case of an overdose of drugs, to share the use of one set of works (the paraphernalia used to inject heroin). There is no longer a subculture of addicts based on social cohesion and emotional identification, but rather a loose association of individuals and parallel couples. Heroin users commonly say, "I have no friends, only associates."

The economic pressures on heroin users today are so great that they prey on each other as well as on their families and on society at large. An addict with money or drugs in his possession runs a good risk of being *taken off* (robbed) by other addicts. An addict who has been robbed or cheated by another addict usually takes his loss philosophically, summed up by the expression, "that's the name of the game." Referring to a fellow addict who had cheated him, one victim said, "he beat me today, I'll beat him tomorrow." Another addict who specializes in robbing other addicts said, "I beat them every chance I get, which is all the time." Sociability even among partners extends no farther than that suggested by the following excerpt: "You might be hanging out with a fellow for a long time, copping together and working as crime partners. You might beat him for a purpose. You might beat him because maybe you bought a bag together and you know it's not going to do both any good, so you beat him for it. But then you try to go and get some money and straighten him out; make it up to him." Another informant summed up the attitude between partners this way: "I'm looking out for myself—I might be sick tomorrow; anyway, he's got something working for him that I don't know about." Sometimes a distinction is made between a hustling partner and a crime partner (*crimey*), where it is suggested that the latter is more dependable; however as one informant put it, "there are larceny-minded crimeys." The causes of these changes in the relationships of heroin users to each other, to family members, and to other members of the community are to be found in the economic practices of heroin distribution.

THE DISTRIBUTION OF HEROIN
IN NEW YORK CITY

Heroin contracted for in Europe at $5000 per kilo (2.2 pounds) will be sold in $5 bags on the street for about one million dollars, after having passed through at least six levels of distribution. The following description of the distribution and marketing of heroin from the time it arrives in New York until it reaches the hands of the heroin user in the street is a consensus derived from informants in the hospital and in the street representing different ethnic and racial groups from different parts of the city. There are many variations to the account given here at all levels of the marketing process. For example, as in the marketing of any product, a quantity purchase can be made at a lower price, and a dealer who makes a rapid turnover of the product for a wholesaler will receive higher benefits for his work. All the way down the line, the *good customer* is the key to a successful operation. He is one who buys regularly, does a good volume of business, does not ask for credit or try to buy short (offer less than the established price) and can be trusted. The following account does not include all the many variations, but can be taken as a paradigm.

Opium produced in Turkey, India, and Iran is processed into heroin in Lebanon, France, and Italy and prepared for shipment to the East Coast of the United States. A United States importer, through a courier, can buy a kilogram of 80 percent heroin in Europe for $5,000. The quality is represented to him in terms of how many cuts it will hold (that is, how many times it can be adulterated). In earlier days, when the marketing of heroin was a more controlled operation, the word of the European seller was accepted. Now, it is customary for the importer to test it, either by means of scientific instruments, or through a reliable tester—an addict who makes experimental cuts, uses the drug and reports on its quality. The importer, who usually never sees the heroin, sells down the line to a highly trusted customer through intermediaries. If it is a syndicate operation, he would only sell to high level, coded men, known as *captains*. These men are major distributors, referred to as *kilo connections* and, generally, as *the people*.

Major Distributors

The *kilo connection* pays $20,000 for the original kilogram (kilo, kee), and gives it a one and one cut (known as *hitting it*), that is, he makes two kilos out of one by adding the common adulterants of milk sugar, mannite (a product from the ash tree used as a mild laxative), and quinine. The proportions of ingredients used for the cutting varies with the preferences of the cutter. One may use 5 parts milk sugar, 2 parts quinine, and 1 part mannite, while another may use 2 parts milk sugar, 3 parts quinine, and 1 part mannite. All three of these products are quickly soluble with heroin. A match lit under the *cooker* (bottle cap) will heat and dissolve the mixture into a clear liquid in a few seconds. The milk sugar contributes the bulk, the mannite inflates the volume—described as *fluffing* it up—and the quinine heightens the sensation of the *rush*, when, upon injection into the vein, the mixture first registers on the nervous system. In the cutting procedure the substance to be cut is placed under a fine sieve, often made from a woman's nylon stocking stretched over a coat hanger. The adulterants are sifted on top of it, then the new mixture is sifted through several more times. After the cut, the kilo connection sells down the line in kilos, half kilos, and quarter kilos, depending upon the resources of his customers. He will get approximately $10,000 per half kilo for the now adulterated heroin.

The customer of the kilo connection is known as *the connection* in its original sense, meaning that he knows *the people*, even though he is not one of them. He may also be called an *ounce man*. He is a highly trusted customer. (One common variation here is that the kilo connection may sell to a third line man, known, if a syndicate operation, as a *soldier* or *button man*. He in turn, will make a one and one cut and sell to the connection.) Assuming that the connection buys directly from a kilo connection, he will probably give the heroin a one and one cut (make two units of each one), divide the total aggregate into ounces, and sell down the line at $700 per ounce. In addition to the adulteration, the aggregate weight of the product is reduced. Known as a *short count*, this procedure occurs at every succeeding level of distribution. At this stage, however, it is called a *good ounce*, despite the adulteration and reduced weight.

The next man is known as a *dealer in weight*, and is probably the most important figure in the line of distribution. He stands midway between the top and the bottom, and is the first one coming down the

line who takes substantial risk of being apprehended by law enforcement officers. He is also the first one who may be a heroin user himself, but usually he is not. He is commonly referred to as one who is
into something and is respected as a big dealer who has put himself
in jeopardy by, as the sayings go, *carrying a felony with him* and
doing the time; that is, if he gets caught he can expect a long jail
sentence. It is said of him that "he let his name go," or "his name gets
kicked around," meaning that his identity is known to people in the
street. This man usually specializes in *cut ounces.* He may give a two
and one cut (make three units of each one) to the good ounce from
the connection and sell the resulting quantity for $500 per ounce. The
aggregate weight is again reduced, and now the unit is called a *piece*
instead of an ounce. Sometimes it is called a *street ounce* or a *vig ounce*
(*vig* is an abbreviation for *vigorish,* which is the term used to designate
the high interest on loans charged by loan sharks). In previous years
twenty-five to thirty level teaspoons were supposed to constitute an
ounce; today it is sixteen to twenty.

The next customer is known as a *street dealer.* He buys the *piece*
for $500, gives it a one and one cut and makes *bundles,* which consist
of twenty-five $5 bags each. He can usually get seven bundles from each
piece, and he sells each bundle for $80. He may also package the heroin
in *half-bundles* (ten $5 bags each), which sell for $40, or he may
package in *half-loads* (fifteen $3 bags), which sell for $30 each. This
man may or may not be a heroin user.

The next distributor is known as a *juggler,* who is the seller from
whom the average street addict buys. He is always a user. He buys
bundles for $80 each and sells the twenty-five bags at about $5 each,
making just enough profit to support his own habit, day by day. He
may or may not make a small cut, known as *tapping the bags.* He is
referred to as someone who is "always high and always short," that is,
he always has enough heroin for his own use and is always looking for
a few dollars to get enough capital to cop again. The following actual
account is typical of a juggler's transactions: He has $25 and needs $5
more to buy a half-load. He meets a user he knows who has $5 and
would like to buy two $3 bags; he is short $1. The juggler tells him
he needs only $5 to cop, and that if he can have his $5, he will buy a
half-load and give him his two $3 bags—$1, in effect, for the use of
the money. When the juggler returns he gives the person his two bags.
In the example here, the person had to wait about two hours for the
juggler's return, and it was raining. For taking the risk of getting beat
for his money by the juggler, for the long wait and the discomfort of
the weather, the juggler was expected to go to the *cooker* with him
(share the use of some of the heroin), with the juggler putting in two
bags to the other person's one bag and sharing equally in the total.

The juggler had his fix and now has eleven bags left. He sells three bags for $9. From the eight bags he has left he uses two himself to get straight—not to get high, but enough to keep from getting sick so that he can finish his business. Now he sells four bags for $12 and has three left. He needs only $7 more to cop again, so he is willing to sell the last three bags for the reduced price, and he can begin a similar cycle all over again. He may do this three or four times a day. The juggler leads a precarious life, both financially and in the risks he takes of getting robbed by fellow addicts or arrested. Most arrests for heroin sales are of the juggler. Financially he is always struggling to stay in the black. If business is a little slow he may start to get sick or impatient and use some of the heroin he needs to sell in order to recop. If he does this he is in the red and temporarily out of business. A juggler is considered to be doing well if he has enough money left over after a transaction for cab fare to where he buys the heroin. One informant defined a juggler as a "nonhustling dope fiend who is always messing the money up."

Table 7.1 summarizes the major features of the distribution transactions.

Other Specialists

There are ancillary services provided by other specialists in the heroin marketing process. They are known as: (1) lieutenants, (2) testers, (3) drop men, (4) salesmen, (5) steerers, (6) taste faces, and (7) accommodators.

1. *lieutenant:* Very often a connection or weight dealer will have in his employ a trusted associate who handles the details of transactions with the street-level dealers. He arranges for deliveries, collects the money, and acts as an enforcer if things go wrong. He may work for a salary or a commission, or both. Sometimes he will be given some *weight* (part of a kilo) to sell on his own as a bonus.

2. *tester:* Heroin dealers down the line are likely to keep a trusted addict around to test the quality of the drug for them. In return for this service he gets all the heroin he needs and pocket money.

3. *drop-man:* This person, often a young, dependable nonuser, is used by sellers to make deliveries. He works for cash and may make as much as $500 for a drop in behalf of a top-level seller. He may also handle the transfer of money in a transac-

TABLE 7.1. THE HEROIN MARKET. CHAIN OF SUPPLY,
ADULTERATION PROCESS, AND PROFIT

Distributor	Type of Cut	Adulteration	% Heroin	Rate of Return on Investment
Importer	—		80%	300%
Kilo Connection	1 & 1		40%	100%
Connection	1 & 1		20%	145%
Weight Dealer	2 & 1		6.7%	114%
Street Dealer	1 & 1		3.3%	124%
Juggler	?	?	?	56%

tion. He is usually a tough, intelligent, trusted street youth who is ambitious to work his way up in the criminal hierarchy.

4. *salesman:* Sometimes the type of person used as a drop-man will be used as a street salesman of heroin for a fairly big dealer. The use of this kind of salesman is growing because of the unreliability of addict jugglers and the desirability of having a tough person who can be trusted and not be easily robbed and cheated by addicts. Sometimes these boys are about 16 to 18 years old and may be going to school. Being young, they usually do not have a police record, and they attract less attention from the police. One informant summed up their attributes this way: "The police won't pay much at-

tention to a kid, but if they do get busted (arrested) they don't talk; they want to be men . . . they (the dealers) trust a guy that don't use it, because they know the guy ain't going to beat him. They got a little gang and nobody is going to get their stuff because they're going to gang up on the guy. In that case they can use a gun in a hurry. The kids that sell the stuff, they don't use it. They buy clothes or whatever they want with the money." They often sell on consignment, starting with a small advance (usually a bundle) and working up to more if they are successful.

5. *steerer:* The steerer is one who in race track parlance would be known as a *tout,* or in a sidewalk sales operation as a *shill.* He is one who tries to persuade users to buy a certain dealer's bag. He may work off and on by appointment with a particular dealer (always a small street dealer or juggler) in return for his daily supply of drugs. Or he may hear that a certain dealer has a good bag and, on a speculative basis, steer customers to him and then go to him later and ask to be taken care of for the service. This is known as *cracking* on a dealer. One of his more subtle selling techniques is to affect an exaggerated looking high, and when asked by a user where he got such a good bag, refer him to the dealer. Usually he is a person who stays in the block all day and is supposed to know what is going on; he is, as they say, *always on the set.*

6. *taste face:* This is a derogatory term given to one who supports his habit by renting out works—loaning the paraphernalia for injecting heroin—in return for a little money or a share of the heroin. Possession of works (hypodermic needle, eyedropper fitted with a baby's pacifier nipple, and bottle cap) is a criminal offense and users do not want to run the extra risk of carrying them; thus they are willing to pay something for the service. Although they perform a useful service, these people are held in contempt by other users. Taste refers to the small amount of heroin he is given (known as a *G shot*) and face is a term applied to anyone on the street who is known as a *creep, flunky,* or *nobody.*

7. *accommodator:* The accommodator is a user who buys at a low level—usually from a juggler—for someone new to the neighborhood who has no connections. These purchases are for small amounts bought by users from other parts of the city or the suburbs. The accommodator receives a little part of the heroin or money for his services. Sometimes he will also cheat the buyer by misrepresenting the price or the amount, or just by not coming back. However, he has to be somewhat

reliable in order to support his habit regularly in this way. Many selling arrests by undercover narcotics police are of these low level accommodators.

THE STREET BAG OF HEROIN

The amount of heroin in the street bag is very small. A generous estimate of the aggregate weight of a $5 bag is ninety milligrams, including the adulterants. Assuming, as in the above account, that the original kilo of 80-percent heroin is adulterated twenty-four times by the time it reaches the street, the amount of heroin would be about three milligrams. There is considerable fluctuation in the amount of heroin in the retail unit, running the range from one to fifteen milligrams, which depends mainly upon the supply available in the market. The important point is that no matter how small the amount, heroin users are never discouraged in their efforts to get it. The consensus figure of three milligrams is a good approximation for an average over a one-year period. This is the average analgesic dosage that is used in those countries such as England where heroin can be prescribed in medical practice. It is a minimal amount, being considered safe for someone who does not use opiates. It is equivalent to about ten milligrams of either morphine or methadone. . . .

In controlled experiments with opiate addicts, as much as sixty milligrams of morphine have been administered four times a day (Martin, personal communication, 1967). Each dosage is equivalent to about twenty milligrams of heroin, which is seven times the amount in the average street bag. In another experiment, it was found that the average heroin addict "recognized" heroin at a minimum level of about fifteen milligrams—five times the amount in the street bag (Sharoff, personal communication, 1967). The average dosage of methadone used in opiate maintenance treatment is one hundred milligrams —about ten times the amount in the street bag. One informant said of the effects of a street bag today: "All it does is turn your stomach over so that you can go out and hustle, and you had better do it fast." Heroin users who are sent to jail report that they are surprised when they do not experience serious withdrawal symptoms after the abrupt cessation of heroine use. Physicians working in the withdrawal wards of narcotic treatment centers refer to the abstinence syndrome among most of their patients today as "subclinical."

The amount of heroin in the street unit has resulted in an institution known as *chasing the bag*. In a community with a high incidence of heroin use there will be two, three, or four competing bags on the street; that is, bags which have come down through different distributorship lines. Because of the low quality of the heroin, users want to get the best one available on a given day. The number of times it has been cut and the ingredients that were used to cut it are the main considerations. The dealer who has the best bag on the street at a given time will sell his merchandise fast and do a big volume of business. A dealer with a good bag who works hard can tell forty to fifty bundles a day. A good bag dealer can sell seventy-five to one hundred bags a day. By keeping the quality relatively high—for example by giving a one and a half cut to a quantity represented as being able to hold two cuts—he makes less profit on each unit. However, this loss can be off-set by the greater volume and the reduced price he gets from his whole-saler as a result of buying more often and in large quantities.

Those with inferior bags on the street do not have a rapid turnover, but they know that sooner or later they can sell their stock, since the demand tends to exceed the supply. There are also other factors oper-ating in their favor. Some users are not known to the dealer of the best bag and cannot buy from him except through the mediation of some-one else. This service costs the prospective buyer something and he has to weigh that consideration against the better bag. Usually, how-ever, if he is sure that one bag is much better than another one, he will find the price to pay for the service to get it; the quality of the bag, not the money, is always the primary consideration.

Another condition favorable to the dealers of inferior bags is that a user who hustles for his drugs is too busy to be around all the time waiting for a particular bag to come on the street. He is usually pressed for time and has to take what is available. If the dealer of the good bag is out recopping, the user cannot afford to wait for what may be a long time. The dealer of an inferior bag whose heroin moves more slowly is reliable, that is, he is always around and can be depended upon. Even in extreme cases where a bag is so bad that the dealer builds up a surplus because of slow business, he knows that sooner or later a temporary shortage of heroin—even for a few days—will insure his selling out. Heroin does not spoil, and can be easily stored for an indefinite period.

Sometimes the dealer of an exceptionally good bag will be ap-proached by his competitors, and they will make a deal whereby he agrees to leave the street on the condition that they buy their bundles from him. In such a deal, those buying the good bundles will *tap the bags* (adulterate them a little more) and put them on the street at the same price. This is one of the many variations in marketing heroin.

It is common practice for a new dealer to come on the street with a good bag and keep it that way until he has most of the customers. Then he will start to adulterate the heroin, knowing that his reputation will carry him for a few days; by that time he has made a good extra profit.

When he starts losing customers in large number, he can build the bag up again. Users are constantly experimenting with the products of different dealers, comparing notes with other users, and attempting to buy the best bag that is around. As one informant put it: "You keep searching. If the guy is weak and you buy from him and it's nothing, then you go to Joe or Tom. Like you get a bag over here now, you run over there about in an hour and get another bag from the other guy, and get another from this other guy after awhile. You just go in a circle to see. You run in different directions." One informant said, "There are no longer dope addicts on the street, only hope addicts." A report on the street that a heroin user died of an overdose of heroin results in a customer rush on his dealer for the same bag.

ECONOMIC CAREERS OF HEROIN USERS

The nature of the economic careers of heroin users on the street is epitomized in the following quote from a research informant: "I believe in work to a certain extent, if it benefits my profit; but I do believe there is more money made otherwise." Another informant, in referring to a fellow user, said: "He just got no heart to be pulling no scores. He can't steal, he don't know how to steal. You can't be an addict that way. I don't know how he's going to make it."

Virtually all heroin users in slum neighborhoods regularly commit crime in order to support their heroin use. In addition to the crimes involving violation of the narcotic laws which are described above, heroin users engage in almost all types of crime for gain, both against property and the person. Because of the greatly inflated price of heroin and because of its poor quality, it is impossible for a heroin user to support even a modest habit for less than $20 a day. Since the typical street user is uneducated, unskilled, and often from a minority racial group, he cannot earn enough money in the legitimate labor market to finance his drug use; he must engage in criminal activity. It is a conservative estimate that heroin users in New York City steal $1 million a day in money, goods, and property. About 70 percent of the inmates in New York City Department of Correction institutions are heroin users whose crimes were directly or indirectly connected with their heroin use.

As with nonaddict criminals, addict criminals tend to specialize in certain activities, depending upon their personalities, skills, and experience. One of the myths derived from the passivity stereotype of the heroin user is that the heroin user avoids crimes of violence, such as robbery, which involves personal confrontation. This no longer seems to be the case. A 1966 New York City Police Department study of the arrests of admitted narcotic (primarily heroin) addicts for selected felonies other than violations of narcoitc laws, showed that 15.1 percent of the arrests were for robbery (New York City Police Department, 1966). This compared with 12.9 percent robbery arrests of all arrests (addict and nonaddict) during the same year. Murder arrests among the addicts amounted to 1 percent of the selected felonies, as compared to 1.4 percent of all arrests in the same categories. The biggest differences between addict arrests and all arrests in the seventeen felony categories selected for study were in the categories of burglary and felonious assault. Among the addicts, 40.9 percent were burglary arrests, compared to 19.7 percent of all arrests; felonious assault constituted 5.6 percent among the addicts, compared to 27.9 percent of all arrests. What these figures reveal is not that heroin users avoid crimes of violence as compared to nonaddicts, but that they avoid crimes not involving financial gain, such as felonious assault. Where financial gain is involved, as in robbery, the risk of violence is taken by heroin users in a higher percentage of cases than with nonaddicts. These statistics confirm the observations and opinions of street informants, both addict and nonaddict. The high percentage of burglaries committed by heroin users is often cited as evidence that, in comparison with nonaddict criminals, they prefer nonviolent crime. What is overlooked here is that burglary, especially of residences, always involves the risk of personal confrontation and violence. Of the 1745 burglary arrests of admitted addicts in 1966, 975 (51 percent) were residence burglaries.

Analysis of the data from the informants for this study showed the following with regard to principal criminal occupations, not including those connected with narcotic laws offenses: burglar—22.7 percent, *flatfooted hustler*—12.2 percent, shoplifter—12.1 percent, robber—9.0 percent. *Flatfooted hustler* is a term used on the street for one who will commit almost any kind of crime for money, depending upon the opportunities. As one self-described flatfooted hustler put it: "I'm capable of doing most things—jostling (picking pockets), boosting shoplifting), con games, burglary, mugging, or stick-ups; wherever I see the opportunity, that's where I'm at." The main advantage of crimes against the person is that the yield is usually money, which does not have to be sold at a discount, as does stolen property. It is easily concealed and can be exchanged directly for heroin. In the case of stolen goods and property, the person has to carry the proceeds of, say, a burglary around with him as he looks for a direct buyer or a fence. . . . This exposes him to extra risk of apprehension. When he does find a buyer, he can only expect to get from 10 percent to 50 percent of the value, the average being about 30 percent, depending upon the item—the more expensive the item, the higher the discount.

The distribution and sales of goods and property stolen by heroin users has become a major economic institution in low-income neighborhoods. Most of the consumers are otherwise ordinary, legitimate members of the community. Housewives will wait on the stoop for specialists in stealing meat (known as *cattle rustlers*) to come by, so that they can get a ham or roast at a 60-percent discount. Owners of small grocery stores buy cartons of cigarettes stolen from the neighborhood supermarket. The owner of an automobile places an order with a heroin user for tires, and the next day he has the tires—with the wheels. At the Easter holidays there is a great demand for clothes, with slum streets looking like the streets of the Garment District.

It has often been noted that retail stores in a slum neighborhood have higher prices than those in more affluent neighborhoods, and this has been attributed to discrimination and profiteering at the expense of poor people with little consumer education and knowledge. Although such charges have some foundation, another major cause of higher prices is the high rate of pilferage by heroin users and others from such stores, the cost of which is passed on to the consumer. One chain store operation which locates exclusively in low-income neighborhoods in New York City is reportedly in bankruptcy due to a 10 percent pilferage rate. This rate compares to about 2 percent citywide.

One economic institution that has resulted directly from the increased criminal activity among heroin users is the *grocery fence*. He is a small, local businessman, such as a candy store owner, bar owner, or beauty parlor owner, who has enough cash to buy stolen goods and property on a small scale and has a place to store them. He then sells the items to his regular customers, both for good will and a profit. He provides a service for the user in providing him with a fast outlet for his goods.

The heroin user is an important figure in the economic life of the slums. In order to support a $20-a-day habit, he has to steal goods and property worth from $50 to $100. Usually he steals outside his neighborhood, not out of community loyalty but because the opportunities are better in the wealthier neighborhoods, and he brings his merchandise back to the neighborhood for sale at high discounts. This results, to some extent, in a redistribution of real income from the richer to the poorer neighborhoods. Although nonaddict residents in the slums may deplore the presence of heroin users, they appreciate and compete for their services as discount salesmen. The user, in turn, experiences satisfaction in being able to make this contribution to the neighborhood.

The type of criminal activity he engages in, and his success at it, determine, to a large extent, the addict's status among fellow addicts and in the community at large. The appellation of *real hustling dope fiend* (a successful burglar, robber, con man, etc.) is a mark of respect and status. Conversely, *nonhustling dope fiend* is a term of denigration applied to users who stay in the neighborhood begging for money or small tastes of heroin, renting out works, or doing small-time juggling. There are also middle status occupations, such as *stealing copper,* where the person specializes in salvaging metal and fixtures from vacant tenement buildings and selling to the local junkman. About the only kinds of illegal activity not open to the heroin user are those connected with organized crime, such as gambling and loan sharking. Users are not considered reliable enough for work in these fields. They may be used as a lookout for a dice game or policy operation, but that is about as close as they can get to organized criminal operations.

Respite from the arduous life they lead comes to heroin users when they go to jail, to a hospital, or, for some, when they take short time employment at resort hotels in the mountains. In the present study it was found that 43 percent of the subjects were in some type of incarceration at any given period of time. In jail they rest, get on a healthy diet, have their medical and dental needs cared for, and engage in relaxed socialization, which centers around the facts and folklore of the heroin user's life on the street.

If a user has been making good money on the street, he eventually builds up a tolerance to heroin which gets to the point where he can no longer finance the habit. He may then enter a hospital for detoxification. If he stays the medically recommended period of time— usually three weeks—he can qualify for Department of Welfare assistance, which eases the economic pressures on him when he resumes his heroin using life on the street. More often than not, however, he will leave the hospital when his tolerance has been significantly lowered, which occurs in about a week.

Some users solve the problems of too much physical and economic pressure, which build up periodically, by getting temporary employment out of the city, usually in the mountain resort hotels. There are employment agencies in the Bowery and similar districts which specialize in hiring drifters, alcoholics, and drug addicts for temporary work. In the summer there is a demand for menial laborers in the kitchens and on the grounds of resort hotels. The agencies are so eager to get help during the vacation season that they go on to the street to solicit workers. Some of them provide a cheap suitcase and clothes for those who need them. One informant reported about a particular agency man this way: "He'll grab you out of the street. He'll say, 'Do you want a job, son? I'll get you a good job. You want to work up in the country and get fat? You'll eat good food and everything.' " The agency charges the worker a substantial fee which is taken out of his first check, and makes extra money by providing private transportation at a price higher than the bus fare. The heroin user usually works through one pay period and returns to the city somewhat more healthy, with a low heroin tolerance, and with a few dollars in his pocket.

It can be seen from the account in this section that the street heroin user is an active, busy person, preoccupied primarily with the economic necessities of maintaining his real income—heroin. A research subject expressed the more mundane gratifications of his life this way:

> When I'm on the way home with the bag safely in my pocket, and I haven't been caught stealing all day, and I didn't get beat and the cops didn't get me—I feel like a working man coming home; he's worked hard, but he knows he done something, even though I know it's not true.

CONCLUSIONS

Heroin use today by lower-class, primarily minority-group, persons does not provide for them a euphoric escape from the psychological and social problems which derive from ghetto life. On the contrary, it provides a motivation and rationale for the pursuit of a meaningful life, albeit a socially deviant one. The activities these individuals engage in and the relationships they have in the course of their quest for heroin are far more important than the minimal analgesic and euphoric effects of the small amount of heroin available to them. If they can be said to be addicted, it is not so much to heroin as to the entire career of a heroin user. The heroin user is, in a way, like the compulsively hardworking business executive whose ostensible goal is the acquisition of money, but whose real satisfaction is in meeting the inordinate challenge he creates for himself. He, too, is driven by a need to find meaning in life which, because of certain deficits and impairments, he cannot find in the normal course of living. A big difference, of course, is that with the street user, the genesis of the deficits and impairments is, to a disproportionate degree, in the social conditions of his life.

In the four communities where this research was conducted, the average median family income is $3500, somewhat less than that of family Welfare Department recipients. Other average population characteristics for the four communities include: public welfare recipients —four times the city rate; unemployment—two times the city rate; substandard housing—two times the city rate; no schooling—two times the city rate; median school years completed—eight years. Neither these few statistics nor an exhaustive list could portray the desperation and hopelessness of life in the slums of New York. In one short block where one of the authors worked, there was an average of one violent death a month over a period of three years—by fire, accident, homicide, and suicide. In Puerto Rican neighborhoods, sidewalk *recordatorios* (temporary shrines at the scenes of tragic deaths) are a regular feature.

Given the social conditions of the slums and their effects on family and individual development, the odds are strongly against the development of a legitimate, nondeviant career that is challenging and rewarding. The most common legitimate career is a menial job, with no future except in the periodic, statutory raises in the minimum wage level. If anyone can be called passive in the slums, it is not the heroin user, but the one who submits to and accepts these conditions.

The career of a heroin user serves a dual purpose for the slum inhabitant; it enables him to escape, not from purposeful activity, but from the monotony of an existence severely limited by social constraints, and at the same time it provides a way for him to gain revenge on society for the injustices and deprivation he has experienced. His exploitation of society is carried out with emotional impunity on the grounds, for the most part illusory, that he is *sick* (needs heroin to relieve physical distress), and any action is justified in the interest of keeping himself well. He is free to act out directly his hostility and at the same time find gratification, both in the use of the drug and in the sense of accomplishment he gets from performing the many acts necessary to support his heroin use. Commenting on the value of narcotic maintenance programs, where addicts are maintained legally and at no cost on a high level of opiate administration, one informant said: "The guy feels that all the fun is out of it. You don't have to outslick the cop and other people. This is a sort of vengeance. This gives you a thrill. It's hiding from them. Where you can go in the drugstore and get a shot, you get high, but it's the same sort of monotony. You are not getting away with anything. The thing is to hide and outslick someone. Drugs is a hell of a game; it gives you a million things to talk about." This informant was not a newcomer to the use of heroin, but a 30-year-old veteran of fifteen years of heroin use on the street. *Soldiers of fortune* is the way another informant summed up the lives of heroin users.

Not all, but certainly a large majority of heroin users are in the category which is the subject of this paper. It is their activities which constitute the social problem which New York City and other urban centers face today. The ultimate solution to the problem, as with all the problems which result from social injustice, lies in the creation of legitimate opportunities for a meaningful life for those who want it. While waiting for the ultimate solution, reparative measures must be taken. There are four major approaches to the treatment and rehabilitation of heroin users. (1) drug treatment (opiate substitutes or antagonists), (2) psychotherapy, (3) existentialist-oriented group self-help

(Synanon prototype), (4) educational and vocational training and placement.

To the extent that the observations and conclusions reported in this paper are valid, a treatment and rehabilitation program emphasizing educational and vocational training is indicated for the large majority of heroin users. At the Manhattan State Hospital Drug Addiction Unit an intensive educational and vocational program supported by psychological and social treatment methods has been created in an effort to prepare the patient for a legitimate career which has a future and is rewarding and satisfying. The three-year program is divided into three parts: (1) eight months of education, vocational training, and therapy in the hospital, (2) one month in the night hospital while working or taking further training in the community during the day, (3) twenty-seven months of aftercare which includes, where needed, further education and training, vocational placement, and psychological and social counseling. With this opportunity for a comprehensive social reparation, those who have not been too severely damaged by society have a second chance for a legitimate, meaningful life.

REFERENCES

CHEIN, ISIDOR, et al. *The Road to H: Narcotics, Delinquency, and Social Policy.* New York: Basic Books, Inc., 1964.

City of New York, Police Department. Statistical Report: *Narcotics*, 1966.

CLOWARD, RICHARD A., & OHLIN, LLOYD E. *Delinquency and Opportunity.* Glencoe, Illinois: The Free Press, 1960.

KARDINER, ARRAM, et al. *The Individual and His Society.* New York: Columbia University Press, 1939.

MALINOWSKI, BRONISLAW. *Argonauts of the Western Pacific.* London: Routledge and Kegan Paul Ltd., 1922.

MARTIN, W. R., Personal Communication, 1967.

SHAROFF, ROBERT, Personal Communication, 1967.

WHYTE, W. F. *Street Corner Society.* Chicago: The University of Chicago Press, 1955.

8

Radical and Racial Perspectives on the Heroin Problem

James H. McMearn

The ideas that I will express here are my own convictions and are based upon several years of pondering the many complexities of heroin abuse in the black community. As a minister in a black church I have been intimately exposed to the problems, despair, frustrations, anger, and feelings that black people live with and express daily.

One section of the drug treatment program in which I am employed uses methadone medication for treatment of long-term heroin addiction. Therefore, I have had personal experience in working with heroin addicts who live in disadvantaged communities. I have also had experience in working with other drug programs throughout the state of Colorado that are attempting to respond to the problems of heroin addiction. I have very strong feelings that the problem of heroin abuse in black and brown communities has been ignored by middle America for too long and that now there must be some realistic and effective responses.

The feelings and attitudes that dominate our disadvantaged black communities are the outgrowth of a nation that turned a deaf ear to cries of poverty, inequality, injustice, alienation, war, racism, and other conditions that are inconsistent with human dignity. My young black brothers and sisters experience these physically and mentally impoverishing conditions in a land where 70 percent of our national budget goes for defense. These young people find their only relief in heroin. The poorest ghetto dwellers keep themselves narcotized to keep from having to face their miserable existence. Tragically, for too many of these dwellers the relief has become a permanent escape.

America has been told for many years that she has a drug problem, but she has been content to ignore the warnings because the drug problem was confined to the ghetto communities. Most of the crimes that relate to drug involvement were committed in the ghettos, at the expense of the people who live there. Therefore, cries from the ghettos that attempted to tell America she had heroin problems were ignored by the white power structure and rationalized by politicians and the situation was allowed to continue. These unheard cries turned into feelings of greater frustration, despair, and anger. Again, it was often heroin that gave comforting, if temporary, relief.

While those in the black ghettos suffered from despair, frustration, and even anger that was a plea for help, white upper- and middle-class America refused to listen. This suggests to us that the white communities suffer from a deeper problem than those voiced in the black ghettos. But because none of those who had the power and resources to effect change would listen, no actions were initiated and no solutions were developed.

Today heroin is no longer confined to the ghetto. There has recently been an upsurge of epidemic proportion of heroin abuse in white upper- and middle-class communities. The horrors of living a life dependent on heroin is now known to leaders of the white power structure. The drug is now claiming their own children. Many of these youth left their homes to become a part of the "Love Generation" and returned heroin addicts. Thousands were sent to Vietnam and returned addicted to heroin. These two phenomena, although very sad, have finally caused America to listen.

Because the cries of agony are now coming from the upper- and middle-class American youth, this country has finally begun to develop programs to try and cope with the problem.

RESPONSE EFFORTS

1. New federal legislation is being introduced and passed to deal with the drug problems. Federal, state, and local drug laws are being reevaluated and revised. Marijuana laws in many states are being changed, enabling first offenders to receive misdemeanor rather than felony charges. Still, penitentiaries are filled with inmates, mostly blacks and browns, who are serving life sentences because possession of marijuana was a felony at the time of their convictions. This suggests to those victims that such an illegal act remains a felony until middle-class America joins you; then that same act becomes a misdemeanor. Think about that!

2. In many public schools throughout the United States, be they

large or small, efforts are being made in drug education. We have just completed the first year of a national effort in drug abuse education. The U.S. Office of Education has appropriated approximately $3 million to implement that effort during the 1970–1971 fiscal year. The Drug Abuse Education Act of 1970, introduced as the Meeds-Mondale Bill, is providing approximately $6 million for drug programs in schools and communities during the 1971–1972 fiscal year.

3. Law enforcement has received the bulk of federal appropriations, because America's first reaction to any social problem is to "lock the misfits up." America admits that this is no solution in itself, but selective enforcement continues to be practiced.

4. Most major businesses, agencies, institutions, and civic groups distribute pamphlets or other printed matter on drug abuse. Attorneys and educators, businessmen and housewives all across the nation are now devising plans of action to deal with the apparently uncontrollable problem.

Yet, as one observes these new responses on the part of America, one immediately sees that they are not designed to include the heroin problems of the black and brown ghettos. Rather, one views large sums of money being poured into law enforcement. One sees appropriations to educational institutions where the major focus is on drug education programs oriented only to the middle class. Comparable amounts of money go to suburban mental health centers oriented towards working on the particular neurotic problems of the middle-class culture. Seldom is education for prevention geared to ghetto youth and funding is rarely provided for treatment programs in those ghetto areas where the problems have existed for years.

Every independent storefront program I know that is located in a disadvantaged community is in need of financial support in order to keep its doors open to addicts. For example, the Crispus Attucks Center in Denver, Colorado, is primarily designed to treat black heroin addicts and is ideally located in the center of their drug community. Crispus Attucks Center treats approximately 200 addicts per week. The program director has submitted some five applications to different funding agencies. He has been waiting since January 1971 for one of those applications to be approved. This black director continues to be optimistic and to hope, chiefly because some agencies say funding is forthcoming. However, this hope will turn to despair—for him and for 200 addicts—when he is finally told, "We have no funds."

Does America really want to respond to the heroin problem in the black ghetto? Certainly she is now aware of the problems and of the need for responses. Following the riots and racial disturbances in 1967, President Johnson appointed his Advisory Commission on Racial Disorders. Their report was not drawn up by militant blacks or ghetto dwellers, but by moderate, responsible professionals within the Establishment. Their report identified and clearly defined the ghetto's problems and proposed solutions. Because of my contacts with people who live in these disadvantaged areas, I can honestly say that if the commission's proposals had become realities in America, not only would they have begun to deal realistically with racial disturbances, but they would also have offered black ghetto people alternatives to heroin abuse.

America is not responding adequately to the heroin problems of disadvantaged blacks and browns. Money continues to be directed toward suburban-bred neuroses, while the recommendations of the Advisory Commission on Civil Disorders are largely ignored; and injustice, inequality, poverty, racism, war, and alienation continue in the black and brown communities.

Let me refer to an article from Medical World News:

> In Washington, D.C., sometimes called the crime capital of the world, narcotic agents don't seem to be able to catch any substantial percentage of the city's friendly neighborhood pushers. But five of their undercover men, all skilled at mimicking the agonies of an addict in withdrawal, found time recently to set up an elaborate trap for Dr. Thomas W. Moore, a general practitioner who feels that medicine shouldn't simply abandon the pushers' victims.
>
> The result: Early last month, agents armed with a search warrant strode into Dr. Moore's office, arrested him, ransacked his files, and confiscated more than 2000 of his patients' records. The charge: five counts of violating the Harrison Act by allegedly prescribing methadone for the five cloak-and-dagger men "without a preliminary medical examination.". . .
>
> After spending the night in jail, Dr. Moore was released on $5,000 bond. A few days later, on his counsel's advice, he reopened his office and resumed his addict detoxification program. . . .[1]

Dr. Moore, one black physician who had the courage to step out and do something about the problem, was now faced with ridicule, physical and mental discomfort, and injustice. I say injustice because our law enforcement agencies never seem able to catch the major suppliers of heroin, yet they are very adept at catching a black physician who is attempting to handle the problem constructively.

Up to this time I have focused mainly on root causes—the radical

1. "Heroin: The Growing Epidemic Doctors Aren't Allowed to Treat," *Medical World News,* 11, no. 15 (April 10, 1970), 31–40.

attitudes in the black and brown disadvantaged communities that can lead one into the abuse of heroin. Let me now focus briefly on current issues that are responsible for prevailing attitudes within the disadvantaged communities.

Heroin and other drugs are seen by some blacks in the ghetto as the white man's way of exercising social control over ghetto dwellers. Every time there has been a major disturbance in a disadvantaged community, heroin has become readily available. Black leaders believe and rigidly accept the idea that the enemy places heroin in the community to prevent them from rising above their situation. The word is spreading that drugs are being placed in the black communities deliberately as a means of genocide. Black leadership has termed this phenomenon the "drug conspiracy."

Since many black leaders view the drug suppliers as enemies and see them as being white, the dwellers' distrust for whites is reinforced. Therefore, when whites, unknown to the community, establish drug treatment programs to treat heroin addiction, blacks and browns will not go to them. Some whites have done and are doing excellent work in these disadvantaged communities, but others have gone in and presented themselves as "do-gooders." Until it can be demonstrated that whites are there to share and relate to the community, for the benefit of the community, distrust will remain a problem.

Today a sense of internal pride has developed in many black disadvantaged communities. That the dreams of some have been realized has reestablished hope. If America is ever to respond effectively to the heroin problems of blacks and browns, *now* is the time.

I will conclude with what I feel to be workable and acceptable recommendations. Although it is a fact that black and brown disadvantaged communities cannot make it alone, much caution must be taken in proposing approaches to assist them. I therefore offer these recommendations:

1. Any whites attempting to work with the black community must first work for acceptance.
2. Any program lending support to these communities should involve community dwellers in initial planning stages. This ensures goals and objectives that are relevant and also eliminates reasons for distrust.
3. Meaningful employment for the community dwellers should be a major consideration in these programs.
4. Trust and responsibility should be delegated to black program directors, black administrators, and so forth.
5. Financial resources must be opened with as little red tape as possible.

6. Those who dwell in the community—physicians, legislators, agencies, and other resourceful people—should share in achieving the program's goals.

White America must become just as concerned about the heroin problem in the black and brown communities as she is with the heroin problems in Vietnam and among upper- and middle-class young people. Even though the disadvantaged communities have been ignored in the past, black and brown leaders must now take advantage of opportunities to save the youth of these communities so that they may have a chance.

It will be interesting to observe America get behind a common problem with all of her resources for the benefit of all her people. This will only be accomplished when we stop seeing problems as black and white problems, young and old problems, rich and poor problems, and see instead only *people problems*. Let us therefore endeavor to effect total societal change by working together.

9

Needle Sharing in the Haight:
Some Social and Psychological Functions

Jan Howard and Phillip Borges

DATA COLLECTION

During the summer and fall of 1968 we interviewed fifty persons in the Haight-Ashbury district who at one time or another had injected drugs for the purpose of "expanding their minds or feeling high." The interviewer, a senior dental student, generally sat on the curb of a parking lot near Shrader and Haight Streets and approached subjects as they walked by. Those who appeared to be members of the straight community, tourists, or "teeny-boppers" were bypassed, but others were asked if they lived in the immediate area or in San Francisco. If they said "yes" (and almost all did), the interviewer explained he was from the University of California Medical Center and was conducting a survey on hepatitis that could ultimately help in controlling the problem. The subject was asked to participate.

Most responded affirmatively and sat down. Since we were only interested in questioning needle users, the subject was then asked if he shot drugs. Some said "no" and were excused. Because we were particularly interested in needle sharing, the respondents were also asked if they had ever shared needles, and those who said "no" were generally excused. However, a few nonsharers were interviewed for purposes of comparison.

CHARACTERISTICS OF THE SAMPLE

We chose twenty-six women and twenty-four men. Most of the respondents were in their late teens or early twenties. The median age

of the males (20.5) was one and one-half years older than that for
females. The education level of the subjects reflected their youth and
the "dropout" character of their social existence. Only one person
had finished college, and only fifteen (30 percent) had any college
training at all. Fourteen more, for a total of 58 percent, had completed
high school. All the subjects were white.

We classified occupation of father into five socioeconomic levels
according to a scheme used by the Public Health Service.[1] About 40
percent of the subjects' fathers had Class III occupations (clerical,
sales, and skilled workers). Only a few fell into Class I (professional
workers), and only 30 percent fell into Classes I and II (technical,
administrative, and managerial workers). The rest were semiskilled or
unskilled laborers.

SHARING THE NEEDLE

Perceived Consequences of Sharing

Our data strongly suggest that shooters know the negative consequences of sharing needles. All but four people (92 percent of the
sample) mentioned the risk of disease as a disadvantage of needle sharing. In addition to hepatitis, they feared venereal disease, diabetes,
malaria, leukemia, lockjaw abscesses, damage to the circulatory system,
and allergic reactions to a different blood type. Eighteen subjects (36
percent of the sample) mentioned the disadvantage of dull, barbed,
broken, or bent points; 22 percent mentioned clogged needles; 22 percent referred to the anxiety of waiting for dope in a sharing situation;
and 10 percent disliked the "dirt." As one female phrased it: "When
you are sharing, everyone gets nervous to get hit. As soon as the spoon
is brought out, there is tension in the room. Especially with smack and
speed. If you have your own fit, there is no tension of waiting."

When asked what sort of person they wanted to share a needle with,
nine respondents (18 percent) said "a healthy person"; 12 percent
mentioned a clean person; and 6 percent wanted people with clean
outfits. Fifteen respondents (30 percent of the sample) said they would
not want to share a needle with "diseased persons" (hepatitics or
syphilitics); 14 percent said dirty people; and 4 percent mentioned
people who use dirty needles.

In comparing the sharing of needles with solo shooting in a group
context, two respondents mentioned other disadvantages of sharing:

1. L. Guralnick, "Mortality by Occupation Level and Cause of Death Among Men
20 to 64 Years of Age: United States, 1950," *Vital Statistics*, Special Report no. 53,
1963.

the hassle over who goes first and the difficulty of "doing your own thing" in a sharing context.

When asked specifically if they made any effort to clean their fits and points between passes, the subjects mentioned a number of different techniques: rinsing with alcohol, rinsing with water, rinsing and boiling, and boiling or soaking in alcohol. Only seven respondents (14 percent of the sample) said they did not clean their points and fits, and another three did not know whether the needles they used were cleaned or not. Between periods of shooting the subjects also attempted to clean their paraphernalia. They mentioned a variety of techniques similar to those used between passes, but none of the methods, except perhaps lengthy boiling, would be sufficient to kill the hepatitis virus.

Eleven respondents (22 percent of the sample) had hepatitis at the time of the interview or had had it at some time in the past, and almost everyone was negatively disposed toward the disease. Everyone was asked to estimate in light of his shooting habits the likelihood of his getting hepatitis within a year. Approximately 25 percent of the respondents thought their chance was 50/50 or greater. Those who felt it was greater than zero (62 percent of the sample) were asked why they continued to share needles. The most usual answer was they "dug dope" more than they feared hepatitis; thirteen subjects (26 percent of the sample) gave this type of reply. The following comments were common:

> "I didn't care at the time. I wanted the experience of the drug." "You get a better rush with needles. You put it out of your mind at the time." "Anyone injecting drugs into their body does not care about their body. Shooting is one of the most effective screens against awareness." "Hepatitis really did not matter that much. I knew if I got it I could get rid of it."

Another group of subjects expressed a strong need for drugs:

> "My husband would not get me a new point. The only way I can get the dope is by sharing with him." "Speed really felt good to me. I was copping out of everything." "I don't share needles. But I know it [hepatitis] will recur if I keep shooting speed. I keep shooting speed because I don't want to give it up." "I didn't want to come down—there's too much of a brain mess when you come down."

When asked if they would share a needle with someone they knew had hepatitis, almost all the subjects said "no." A few equivocated with answers like the following:

> "No, not if I could help it. I don't want hepatitis—yes, if there were no other needles." "No, I am not strung out so I don't need to. If I was, I would share with anyone."

Six respondents (12 percent) were less reserved in their willingness to share with hepatitics:

> "Yes, I would share, but I would boil it before I used it." "Yes, if there were no other fits around I would not have a choice. I was really strung out." "Yes, I already got it; so it doesn't make any difference." "Yes, I think I am that stupid."

If cancer were the disease transmitted instead of hepatitis, 33 percent of the subjects thought they would still continue to share their points. Their reasons included:

> "You don't understand. I need the shit [dope]." "I smoke and know the dangers." "If you take precautions you make it; if not. . . ." "I wouldn't care at all. Shooting drugs is a life or death thing anyway." "I would only share with my husband in that circumstance, and I would boil the needle more." "It would be the same. I would just avoid people with obvious cancer."

SOCIAL AND PSYCHOLOGICAL FUNCTIONS OF NEEDLE SHARING

Needle sharing in the Haight survives in spite of awareness of its link to hepatitis. It obviously serves certain social and psychological functions for participants. Our subjects gave us clues to the nature of these functions.

Pragmatic Considerations

In California everyone must have a prescription to purchase a hypodermic syringe or needle except persons with special authorization (e.g., diabetics and asthmatics.) It is therefore not surprising that a shortage of points and fits was most often mentioned as an advantage of needle sharing.

A further consideration, according to several of our respondents, is the thought that carrying a needle makes one more vulnerable to arrest. Sharing reduces the likelihood of being busted. It is also viewed as economically expedient because it saves the cost of outfits and because sharing needles can be tantamount to sharing drugs.

Sharing for the Sake of Sharing

It is commonly believed that sharing is an important norm and behavior pattern of the hippie subculture.[2] The pervasiveness and in-

2. F. Davis & L. Munoz, "Heads and Freaks: Patterns and Meanings of Drug Use Among Hippies," *Journal of Health and Social Behavior* 9 (1968), 156–64.

tensity of this ethic are unknown, but food and lodging are often shared, and at least for some sharing needles and drugs is not simply expedient but also an end in itself. As one female put it, "In some circles there's a social stigma if you don't share."

A number of respondents said they would share needles with "anyone who shoots or turns on," and two people said they would share with anyone who needs a shot or wants a high.

A Sense of Fraternity

When we first considered the functions of needle sharing, we hypothesized that it gave many people a feeling of closeness and brotherliness. Responses to a number of our questions are relevant.

When asked the advantages of sharing needles, only three respondents spoke of the social aspect of sharing—that it brings people closer together. But when they were asked to compare sharing needles and shooting in a group situation with each person using his own fit, ten people (20 percent of the sample) mentioned a feeling of closeness in sharing:

> "It's sort of a permitted thing. A feeling of fraternity even though an irrational way of doing it." "It might give one more of a feeling of belonging by passing it around. Some individuals like to leave some blood in the point. This gives them a sense of brotherliness. They get the idea from the Indians of blood brothers." "I would fear screwing up when shooting if I were alone. I feel very attached when someone is shooting for me. I like the close feeling." "It made it more of a family thing."

The similarity to passing a joint was mentioned by one respondent, but two others indicated that sharing a joint gave them more of a communal feeling than sharing needles.

Comments regarding the type of person with whom they would want to share a needle were also suggestive. Approximately one-third of each sex mentioned a close or intimate friend or just a friend, and one person spoke of "someone with my philosophy who is able to express the truth and finds love in everything I see and touch."

In describing whom they actually shared needles with, all but one respondent mentioned friends or intimates. A large proportion of each sex said that strangers had been present in one or another sharing situation, but half of those mentioning strangers indicated that their presence was rare and a number specified that they never shot with strangers or that strangers made them "paranoid."

Everyone was asked to compare solo and group shooting. Although the answers are not directly applicable to sharing needles, they high-light the communal aspect of shooting in a group. Ten people (20 percent of the sample) mentioned the importance of relating to others and feeling a sense of community:

> "You get a sense of community to do with people. People take drugs in the first place to relate to others—that's the whole thing. I don't like it alone at all." "Shooting alone is like masturbating. In a group it is more like an orgy. I prefer an orgy to masturbating." "I don't like to shoot alone. With people, I like to look at the peace in others' eyes."

Group shooting also lets one rap with others and share experiences.[3] Sixteen respondents (32 percent of the sample) mentioned this advantage:

> "It's a lot better when in a group. It's good to rap to someone. When I'm alone, I just sit back and look at the walls. I don't dig this." "It's much more enjoyable when I'm not alone. Something you can share. I like people and like to rap. I have dropped acid alone and felt super alone. More alone than I really was."

For some people, shooting alone has certain advantages. It permits more introspection than a group setting. No one bugs or jostles you or limits your high. You can get things done—like painting or writing poetry. You can relax and avoid the rushed, tense atmosphere of the group, the stares of others, and the painful ego games that people play. Thus, we have the following comments:

> "Everyone was paranoid in New York. I preferred to be alone." "When you are alone, you get to yourself a little better. You don't have to worry about other people. You get a better perspective on yourself." "I get higher with psychedelics when I'm by myself. Then I can let myself go. People around can limit the high. When I smoke grass, I like to be around people." "When alone you get into yourself more. It's much more religious and less inhibited. When we were with others we pretended to share but actually we were alone. Everyone was on his own special trip. We thought we were a community but we were not."

A Means of Socialization

Most of the females in our sample (65 percent) had never shot alone and the majority of those questioned on the subject shared

3. J. T. Carey & J. Mandel, "A San Francisco Bay Area 'Speed' Scene," *Journal of Health and Social Behavior* 9 (1968), 164–74.

needles 100 percent of the time. One-fourth of the males had never shot alone and 17 percent had always shared needles.

Our data suggest that the sharing process is a means of socialization to the needle culture. In specifying with whom they would want to share needles, two males said, "A person starting, a chick," and three females commented: "Someone cool, not addicts, someone who knows the drug scene"; "Someone who can hit me well"; "Someone who knows what he is doing, who is not strung out."

When we asked our subjects to describe the mechanics of the shooting procedure, they revealed some important sex differences relevant to socialization. Approximately half the girls were being tied off and hit by someone else, but this was true for only 5 percent of the males. ("Tying off" means applying a tourniquet to the arm so the vein will be easier to hit. "Hitting" means injecting the dope.) And whereas 47 percent of the males were tying off and shooting themselves, this was true for only 21 percent of the females. More females than males (21 percent versus 5 percent) tied themselves off but were hit by others, and more males than females (11 percent versus 4 percent) were tied off by others but hit themselves. To summarize the situation, 68 percent of the males compared to 29 percent of the females had at one time or another hit themselves.

A number of respondents described the transitional nature of the "who-shoots-whom" process. At first others hit them, but later they learned to shoot themselves:

"The first ten times my chick hit me. I tied my own self off. Now I do it all myself." "When I started, someone else hit me. After a few times, I began to hit myself." "If I can, I have someone else hit me. I'm not an old hand at it." "I started with some guy hitting me. But I learned quite fast. Now I tie myself off and hit myself."

A Means of Protection

When we asked our subjects to distinguish between sharing needles and shooting in a group with their own fits, several of the males spoke of a sense of security in having others present, but they seemed to blur the concepts of needle sharing and group shooting. Thus, one respondent said he felt safer in a group because someone was there to help him if he took too much. He once shot in a bathtub and did not get out for two days.

In commenting on the positive and negative aspects of solo and group shooting seven females and two males (18 percent of the sample) mentioned the feeling of security and protection provided by the group. There was less chance of flipping out or of overintrospection.

A Means of Achieving Status

When questioned about status attributes among shooters, the respondents mentioned a wide variety of behavior patterns and symbols. Twenty-eight percent of each sex said the amount of dope a person can shoot in a given amount of time confers status, and 39 percent of each sex mentioned tracks or bruises as prestige symbols.

A few comments suggest that mastering certain aspects of the needle-sharing ritual also confers status on participants. Thus, one person said:

> "Guys who can shoot themselves well and shoot chicks' veins (that is a hard job) are admired by me."

Another said:

> "Who shot the most in a certain period of time. Who can turn the most people on to it [the drug]. Who gives the most drug away."

In discussing the shooting scene as an ego trip, one person commented:

> "The whole scene is a cult. There's a lot of ritual in the practice of needle use (doing up, tying off, boiling the dope, etc.)."

To some extent, then, needle sharing seems to be self-perpetuating. Excelling in the ritual is a means of gaining prestige among shooters, so in one way or another the scene is probably manipulated to provide opportunities for status striving.

A Substitute for Sex

It seemed quite possible that sharing needles might have sexual implications beyond the feeling of closeness or brotherhood mentioned by some respondents, so we directly questioned thirty-six of our subjects on the sexual connotations of needles.

Most respondents (64 percent of the subsample) said there were sexual overtones to needle use, either for them personally or for others. A wide variety of connotations were mentioned. Six people (17 percent) described the rush as orgastic,[4] and seven (19 percent) drew an analogy between penetration of a needle and penetration of a penis. Other ideas mentioned were the following: guys dig chicks hitting them and vice versa; needle use is a substitute for sex; the needle is a phallic

4. *Ibid.*

symbol; using needles and having intercourse release one for self-realization; boosting (letting blood in and out of the needle) is like masturbating; shooting a chick makes her seem submissive.

Some actual comments were:

"There's no need to go into Freudian symbolism. Guys dig chicks hitting them and vice versa. One chick that hit me up would play around with the blood awhile before injecting it. I usually hit myself. It's a sexual thing to me to have a chick hit me." "Having a person stick something in you is very sexual. Girls particularly like to be injected by boys." "Using needles is like screwing your arm. I have observed this while stoned on acid, and it is very clear to me." "It seems to be a sexual substitute for guys. Their own insecurity and paranoia can't let them become involved with anyone else. Thus, they can't have sex and turn to the needle as a sexual substitute. I knew this play junky whose whole trip was doing up other cats."

Gratification in Self-destruction

Almost everyone we asked felt that continued shooting would result in self-destruction, especially for those on speed. As in the case of heroin addicts, interaction with other shooters can provide daily concrete models of what life may be like in later years as a consequence of continued use of drugs.[5] Eighteen of the thirty-six respondents questioned on the subject mentioned both the physical and mental deterioration that follows from shooting. The rest spoke of one or the other effect or of self-destruction in general. Prototype comments were as follows:

"They won't live too long. If they don't die physically, they become so mentally screwed up they may kill themselves." "Definitely, I won't be around much longer." "Once on it a person wants to kill himself. When I was shooting, I just wanted to shoot and shoot until I died. When you come down, you are very depressed." "I have heard of this. A guy who ruined his body. His teeth fell out and he talks real slowly."

Our data suggest that for many people needle use is not only self-destructive but masochistic (that is, purposely self-destructive). This would help explain why needle sharing is so prevalent in spite of its known relationship to disease.

About one-half of the eighteen males and two-thirds of the eighteen

---

5. M. B. Ray, "The Cycle of Abstinence and Relapse among Heroin Addicts," in *The Other Side: Perspectives on Deviance,* ed. H. S. Becker (New York: Free Press, 1964), pp. 163–77. Ray also discusses self-concepts of heroin users based on values of the larger society and the addict subculture.

females questioned on the subject said that the shooting experience was masochistic. The following comments were typical:

> "Some people say I like the rush because it burns my brain cells up. Some individuals take up blood and shoot it out and continue this." "Especially with smack. There's a lot of self-hatred. They shoot up and say, 'Man, am I fucked up.' They use that feeling to feel down." "Some people definitely. I have known people who abscess on purpose." "I myself feel mad at times. Then I run for the needle and inject it into myself. I shot once for eight hours straight. I must have stuck the needle into my arm several hundred times."

These statements convey the idea that many needle users enjoy the experience of self-inflicted pain. It is not simply that they have accommodated themselves to an "occupational" risk of physical and mental disease. They talk as though self-punishment were pleasure. Perhaps this is a response to guilt, an indication that they have not totally accepted the new roles they have defined for themselves but are still tied to the larger culture from which they came. This perspective appears to differ from the emancipated outlook of marijuana users which has been described elsewhere.[6]

Instead of bragging about the joys of shooting, our subjects debase themselves and paint a picture of people locked in a treadmill of inevitable self-destruction. It is not surprising that they would share needles and risk hepatitis. The consequences of this disease are fairly well known and the probability of disaster is slight. The prospect of burning up one's brain cells is much more ominous and self-destructive. To tempt that kind of fate a person has to be really stupid or unworthy, and there is every indication that the respondents conceive of themselves in this light.

Under the veneer of excitement, pleasure, and love is a negative opinion of the shooting scene. When we asked thirty-six of the subjects what they thought of that scene, half of them had an entirely negative view. Only one person took a positive stance. The rest were equivocal or refused to judge. Among the negative comments were the following:

> "It's really a sad scene. These people aren't happy. They haven't enough love."

> "These are people escaping from reality. Speed gives you a tremendous ego. I have seen too many nice people go bad. Especially smack people get violent. I have seen people rob."

6. Davis & Munoz, "Heads and Freaks"; and H. S. Becker, *Outsiders: Studies in the Sociology of Deviance* (New York: Free Press, 1963), pp. 41–78.

"It's a bad scene. Hepatitis collapses the veins. Usually these people turn into needle freaks."

IMPLICATIONS FOR FURTHER RESEARCH

Our research lays the groundwork for more extensive and intensive studies of a number of questions with implications beyond drug abuse and hepatitis per se. Some avenues for further inquiry are:

1. *Sharing patterns among other populations of drug users:* It would be important to know how typical or atypical our sample is of shooters in general. Is sharing as popular elsewhere as it appears to be in the Haight? Is the social context of sharing (number of people present, mechanics of the shooting procedure, and so forth) the same in different places? Does the type of drug used affect the sharing pattern?

2. *Processes of alienation from the larger social order:* In some respects the drug scene we studied appears to be a microcosm of the larger culture. Sex roles in shooting were rather clearly differentiated in predictable ways. The males shot the females, and novice girls turned their heads in fright. Instead of bragging about their life style, our respondents verbalized a harsher contempt for the physical and mental consequences of drug abuse than the straight world would probably express. This raises a number of questions for further inquiry: Does the type of drug used (speed, heroin, marijuana) influence the perception of consequences? Are there various stages in the definition of the situation that indicate more or less separation from the larger moral order? Do background characteristics (such as family experiences, social class, and education) influence the process of alienation?

3. *Sharing as a transitional stage in deviant behavior:* Our findings indicate that needle sharing is a means of socializing newcomers to the drug subculture. Perhaps "social shooting," like "social drinking," is only a stage in a process that eventuates in more individualistic ("loner") behavior. What factors besides inexperience distinguish those who shoot in a group setting from solitary users? Are some shooters always loners? What types of people shoot in a group context but refuse to share their needles?

4. *Necessary and sufficient conditions for needle sharing:* According to our data, needle sharing serves a number of functions for shooters. But the relative importance of the various possi-

ble motives for sharing is yet to be determined. Are there alternatives to sharing that will satisfy the motivations behind it but reduce the risk of disease? What kind of people are likely to be nonsharers?

5. *Social control of illness-producing behavior:* Needle sharing is related to hepatitis as smoking is related to cancer and sexual promiscuity to gonorrhea. Certain forms of socially induced behavior increase the risk of disease. Do shooters accurately perceive the consequences of shooting and sharing? Does the fear of consequences decrease over time? Do factors such as education influence fear? Does drug use itself make participants oblivious to consequences? Research on these questions may shed light on possible means of disease control in these situations.

10

Psychological Aspects of Heroin and Other Drug Dependence

Stephen M. Pittel, Ph.D.

Previous papers that have grown out of the Haight-Ashbury Research Project suggest that there are certain similarities in the background and personality organization of young drug users, even though they may differ considerably in the nature of their drug use and in their pattern of involvement in the San Francisco drug culture.[1] The allegedly healthy and Utopian hippies who first came to the Haight-Ashbury neighborhood are in fact quite similar in personality organization to the more heavily committed users of psychedelic drugs who remained in the area after the demise of the hippie experiment. Both of these groups show the same type of character pathology seen among

This is a revised version of a paper presented at the National Heroin Symposium, San Francisco, California, 19 June 1971.

This research was supported largely by National Institutes of Mental Health grant MH-15737 to Robert S. Wallerstein and Stephen M. Pittel for studies of psychological factors in drug abuse. Additional support was provided by the Chapman Research Fund and by Mount Zion Hospital and Medical Center.

I particularly want to thank the Heroin Section of the Haight-Ashbury Free Medical Clinic and David K. Wellisch, George R. Gay, and Steve Lerner of that institution.

I would also like to thank the staff of the Langley-Porter Neuropsychiatric Institute Youth Drug Study Unit for their cooperation in providing MMPI data for this study and to acknowledge my debt to Richard F. Kendall for data analysis and to the entire staff of the Haight-Ashbury Research Project for their contributions to the ideas presented here.

1. R. F. Kendall & S. M. Pittel, "Three Portraits of the Young Drug User: Comparison of MMPI Group Profiles," *Journal of Psychedelic Drugs* 3, no. 2 (1971): 63–66; and S. M. Pittel & R. Hofer, "The Transition to Amphetamine Abuse," in *Current Concepts of Amphetamine Abuse,* ed. E. Ellinwood (Washington, D.C.; Government Printing Office, in press).

ambulatory amphetamine users and psychedelic users requiring inpatient psychiatric care.

Here we will extend these earlier findings to include a sample of
heroin addicts who have sought treatment at the Haight-Ashbury
Free Medical Clinic. We will compare Minnesota Multiphasic Personality Inventory group profiles obtained from thirty-seven male
and twenty-five female heroin addicts seen at the Haight-Ashbury
Free Medical Clinic Detoxification Unit to those obtained from one
hundred males and seventy-three females who served as volunteer
subjects for the Haight-Ashbury Research Project.

The MMPI profile that is generally indicative of character pathology
was common among both the heroin addicts and the psychedelic users.
Male addicts had significantly higher scores on scales measuring concern over body functioning and depression; female addicts ranked
high on these scales and on others measuring hysterical, psychopathic,
paranoid, and schizophrenic tendencies. These findings are consistent
with the assumption that the addicts are more overtly disturbed and
that they have experienced a greater degree of psychic and physical
suffering. The overall similarity of profiles suggests (1) that heroin
addicts who seek treatment closely resemble psychedelic users who
seek treatment and (2) that both of these more overtly disturbed groups
are comparable in basic personality organization to volunteer subjects who are deeply involved in the psychedelic drug culture.

Although it is possible that the MMPI is simply insensitive to the important differences between addicts and heavy users of psychedelic
drugs, there is still good reason to explore further the possibility that
these groups are psychologically similar. It is likely that methodological
and practical considerations have caused us to avoid this issue in the
past. Also, most drug researchers have recognized the eagerness of the
public and the press to accept simple generalizations about drug users;
they have fought hard to demonstrate that all drug users do not fit the
stereotype of the heroin addict. Psychedelic users have often been characterized as seekers of beauty and truth, amphetamine users as seekers
of energy and power, and opiate users as seekers of uphoria and oblit-
eration of pain. Since these characterizations correspond in general to
the subjective experiences of users during acute drug intoxication, it is
tempting to accept the notion that more differences than similarities
exist among users of different drugs. It is clear that the initial drug
involvement of most users is determined by social background and
ideological orientation, but, regardless of their expressed motives for
particular subjective effects, some percentage of casual experimenters
do go on to use and abuse other, more dangerous drugs. For example,
a recent paper based on the same population of heroin addicts sampled
for this research, reports that over 40 percent of those addicted since

1967 were heavy users of psychedelic drugs prior to using heroin.[2] Similarly, the continuing longitudinal investigations of the Haight-Ashbury Research Project are revealing an increasing number of former psychedelic users who have made a transition to the concomitant or exclusive use of amphetamines, barbiturates, alcohol, or opiates.

There are, then, two distinct lines of reasoning: the first emphasizes similarities among users of different drugs and, at least implicitly, suggests the existence of a single underlying personality constellation common to all drug dependence. Although little research evidence is available to support this view, the ability of some users to derive gratification from a variety of different drugs or to shift preferences from one drug to another both point to the notion of a drug-dependent personality type.

The second line of reasoning emphasizes differences among users of different drugs and suggests that unique personality constellations and/or social factors are associated with the use of each. This notion has become increasingly popular since the recent emergence of a largely white, middle-class population of young drug users whose preference for mind-altering drugs did not appear to be comparable to the more familiar use of opiates and whose drug use could not be accounted for easily as a consequence of social deprivation, constitutional weakness, or inadequate motivation.

We found that psychedelic drug users and heroin addicts with varying degrees of overt psychopathology show a personality organization that is neither primarily neurotic nor psychotic. They are relatively immature, lack impulse control, and are more or less incapable of maintaining intimate and enduring relationships, except perhaps to gratify their own narcissistic desires. This general picture is consistent with clinical evidence concerning heroin addicts.[3] Some recent studies have found that it also applies to chronic psychedelic drug users.[4]

Various neurotic or psychotic *signs* are common among regular users of many drugs, but the well-organized and relatively stable *symptom syndromes* of such pathology are not.

2. C. W. Sheppard, G. R. Gay, & D. E. Smith, "The Changing Patterns of Heroin Addiction in the Haight-Ashbury Subculture," *Journal of Psychedelic Drugs* 3, no. 2 (1971): 22–30.

3. Isidor Chein et al., *The Road to H: Narcotics, Delinquency, and Social Policy* (New York: Basic Books, 1964).

4. S. P. Barron, P. Lowinger, & E. Ebner, "A Clinical Examination of Chronic LSD Use in the Community," *Comprehensive Psychiatry* 11, no. 1 (1970): 69–79; V. Calef, R. B. Gryler, L. Hilles, R. Hofer, P. Kempner, S. M. Pittel, & R. S. Wallerstein, "Impairments of Ego Functions in Psychedelic Drug Users," paper presented at the Conference on Drug Use and Drug Subcultures, Asilomar, California, February 1970; and D. Welpton, "Psychodynamics of Chronic Lysergic Acid Diethylamide Use: A Clinical Study of Ten Voluntary Subjects," *Journal of Nervous and Mental Disease* 147, no. 4 (1968): 377–385.

Drug dependence seems most likely among individuals who lack the *psychological resources* to deal adequately with inner conflicts or environmental frustrations—those whose psychological development has been disrupted early in childhood by emotional deprivations, inordinate exposure to stress, severe trauma, or the cumulative impact of any combination of these elements. Such individuals suffer from an impaired development of ego functions that limits their ability to master inner conflict and that precludes the development of *any* stable personality organization (including those resulting in neurotic or psychotic symptomatology). The same may occur among those whose egos are too weak to handle inordinate amounts of stimulation from within or without. The Haight-Ashbury Research Project has observed some psychedelic users who apparently began using drugs because of their inability to handle an unusually rich and overwhelming abundance of sensory experience and intellectual challenge.

Finally, some individuals appear to become dependent on drugs, despite a reasonable degree of personality organization, when they are subjected to unusually severe situational stress, chronic pain, or anxiety. This is especially prevalent among early adolescents who must deal with unusual stresses in addition to the normal social and biological burdens of puberty. The normal child undergoes massive personality reorganization at this time, so the preadolescent ego is particularly vulnerable to any additional assaults. The early adolescent who finds that drugs can compensate for temporary ego weakness might well become drug dependent without ever testing his own resources. Just as the superego is said to dissolve in alcohol, it is likely that other personality structures are weakened by a continual reliance on chemical rather than psychological means of dealing with anxiety.

By emphasizing impairment in ego functions as the basis for drug dependency, we are, of course, suggesting that neither intrapsychic conflict nor environmental stress plays any necessary role in leading to drug abuse. Instead, ego deficits are themselves the source of considerable anxiety. Drugs are sought to compensate for the absence of inner structure. To the extent that any drug serves to stabilize an individual, he will become dependent upon it.

Consequently, which drugs are used and even the extent of their use can be reduced to questions of the nature and extent of ego impairment. Persons with few or minor ego impairments (in relation to demands) are likely to show specific drug preferences. The choice of preferred drug will vary as a function of their particular ego strengths and weaknesses. Those with many or with relatively severe ego impairments are likely either to show a pattern of multiple drug use (concomitant, cyclical, or episodic) or to be truly dependent on or addicted to a particular drug.

By and large, moderate psychedelic users appear to have certain well-developed ego capacities and to get along well without their preferred drug. They frequently perform well in school and on the job and many have relatively stable social relationships. They are more likely to benefit from psychotherapy or from other relatively unstructured forms of treatment than are heroin addicts. All of this is consistent with the stereotype of the typical psychedelic user as coming from a more or less privileged background and as having had the opportunity to develop at least some of the skills, interests, coping mechanisms, and defensive structures that provide a modicum of inner stability.

The stereotype of the heroin addict contrasts sharply with that of the psychedelic user in almost all respects. Without belaboring the point, let me merely remind you of the typical failure of psychotherapy with addicts and the extremely high recidivism rates in programs that rely on the addict's ability to deal with stress or frustration. The relative success of highly structured and often authoritarian programs in treating addicts further suggests that they rely on external rather than internal structures.

To the extent that chronic drug use implies the absence of internalized structure, the search for common personality traits either within or between groups of drug users is fruitless. Attention should be focused on the processes of personality rather than on fixed trait structure.

Second, even though the heroin addicts' problems in handling sexual and aggressive drives appear to be similar to the conflicts of neurotics, they do not necessarily result from the work of inner conflict and defense. A failure to recognize this fact has led to the proliferation of therapeutic approaches based on talking about problems, gaining insight and understanding, and the like, all of which are doomed to failure because they ignore the actual basis of the patients' problems. Therapy for these patients should be geared to their need for structure and stability and to the gradual building of ego functions that have never developed fully.

Finally, I would like to emphasize that heroin addiction results from the needs of individuals—not from the properties of a drug. Unless a person needs the drug to compensate for long-standing ego deficits, the probability of his becoming drug dependent is slight. Normal individuals may find drugs pleasurable or not, but they will not use them regularly. Even if a tissue dependency should result from repeated analgesic use of drugs for chronic pain, psychologically healthy individuals will not become dependent on them and will not crave them following detoxification. If we assume that many of the GIs who become addicted in Vietnam do so because they use high-grade heroin in response to situational stress, it follows that their addiction can be stopped by detoxification alone. Labeling them as addicts or treating them as if they shared the psychological problems of those who become addicted gradually in the absence of extreme stress places them in great social and psychological jeopardy.

11

End of the Road:

A Case Study

John Luce

Ed was raised in the Richmond district of San Francisco, but he visited the Haight-Ashbury often as a child. His mother was depressed and disoriented during those days. She also drank heavily after her husband, a plumbing contractor, left home. Yet she still had relatively lucid moments in which her bitterness was tempered by maternal feelings. So, when the weather matched her mental state, she would dress her son in short pants, shop with him on Haight Street, and take him to the Haight Theater for Saturday matinees.

Ed loved sitting in the ancient movie palace. He felt secured by the thought that life could be stable, relaxed by the celluloid sensations that enveloped him. But this ease was shattered shortly after his fourteenth birthday, when his mother died. Ed then moved in with his grandmother, a religious fundamentalist who resented having to take care of him. He went to high school, began dating, and grew to his present six-foot height. "But I always felt like some part of me was missing," he says. "I couldn't make it with the other kids. I was angry, guilty about my mother, full of these weird sexual feelings. I couldn't concentrate. I tried to keep myself together with booze."

Aided by alcohol, Ed finished high school in the middle of his class. He then left his grandmother, spent six months in the Army, and married "a naive chick whose ideals are pretty blown now." He also entered City College, where he majored in dramatics, worked in the registrar's office, and joined the antiwar movement. But Ed was not equipped for academia or activist politics. As his anxiety mounted, he sedated himself with marijuana and succumbed to the psychedelic messiahs in San Francisco who hoped to alter themselves and society with LSD.

"I really blossomed behind acid," Ed remembers:

> Before I was just maintaining, but LSD turned life into a circus; suddenly it all made sense to me. I dug on peace and love, like we are all one. So I started dropping acid pretty regular, man, and I knew there was just no point to school. The only problem was, my old lady was down on drugs. I got a job at the post office, but she wanted me to finish up at City and get into some status game. We had our son by then; I had ideas for that kid, but she just couldn't see.

Ed's wife saw him through the summer of 1966, when he became involved in the new alternative community that rock musicians and other young people were trying to create in the Flatlands near Haight Street. He asked her to join him, but she told him either to see a psychiatrist or give her a divorce. A month later, Ed was notified that his army reserve unit might be reactivated. He panicked and ran to the only oasis of his youth: Haight-Ashbury.

His first refuge was a flat on Cole Street, which he rented with a dozen other persons who shared their meager resources and established elaborate rituals to heighten their hallucinogenic drug experiences. His second was the Haight, now Straight, Theater, which a hippie tribe was converting into a dance hall and sensorium. Ed worked as a carpenter at the theater during the fall and gave away acid at the Human-Be-In in January 1967. He spent the spring hanging around the Psychedelic Shop, witnessing the birth of the Haight-Ashbury Free Medical Clinic and waiting for the Summer of Love.

Ed survived the summer, but his dream of peace and love perished in July. The death occurred during an STP trip which unearthed frightening feelings. "Everything fell apart," Ed says about his experience. "Walking on the street, I freaked on all the tourists and gangsters there. I got paranoid, started flashing on my wife and kid, what a lousy father I'd been. I wanted to kill myself. Some shrink at the clinic put me straight, but I was never the same after. It all goes back to that bummer with STP."

More bad trips followed, forcing Ed to renounce hallucinogens. Haight Street also became more chaotic, as its summer influx turned the circus atmosphere of the new community into a horror show. In September the Free Clinic closed for a month to raise funds, staff members, and medication; in October the hippies held a symbolic funeral near the bankrupt Psychedelic Shop and then left town. Ed joined them in the country temporarily, but depression, inner confusion, and STP-precipitated flashbacks drove him back to the Haight. "I tried yoga and meditation. Then somebody turned me on to uppers, and pretty soon I was crashing in this crystal palace on Clayton. I spent more time on the street, but instead of shopping there like I used to with my mother, I started shooting and dealing speed."

In 1968 amphetamines helped Ed endure the Haight-Ashbury. So did the clinic physicians, who tried to keep him eating and stitched his head after it was cracked open during a flurry with the police. But as he increased his speed intake, Ed started to pay the price for self-medication. His euphoric highs led to agonizing lows; his paranoia intensified; he lost three teeth to pyorrhea and, to malnutrition, forty pounds. After the July riots on Haight Street, he began injecting barbiturates to insulate himself from his environment and to ease his agitation. By September, when the clinic closed again for lack of medicine and money, he was strung out on barbs.

The clinic reopened in January 1969 and helped Ed get into Mendocino State Hospital for three months to heal his abcesses and curb his addiction. He then returned to the Haight, hoping to find something there to do. But the Straight Theater had closed by this point; the rock musicians had abandoned the district; and the new community had been overrun by a new population made up of desperate runaways, grizzled winos, burnt-out speed freaks, barbiturate and heroin addicts from New York and other cities, and blacks from the Flatlands and the Fillmore district nearby. Ed mingled with the street people, looking for an old lady. When President Nixon's Operation Intercept cut the flow of marijuana across the Mexican border in September, he found heroin.

"Smack is the greatest," he says today:

> . . . the mellowest downer of all. You get none of the side effects of speed and barbs. After you fix, you feel the rush, like an orgasm if it's good dope. Then you float for about four hours; nothing positive, just a normal feeling, nowhere. It's like being half asleep, like watching a movie; nothing gets through to you, you're safe and warm. The big thing is, you don't hurt. You can walk around with rotting teeth and a busted appendix and not feel it. You don't need sex, you don't need food, you don't need people, you don't care. It's like death without permanence, life without pain.
>
> For me, the only hard part is keeping in H, paying my connection, man. I know these rich cats who can get good smack and shoot it for years and nothing happens, but me, you know, it's a hustle to stay alive. I run about a $100-, $150-a-day habit, so I have to cop twice that much to keep my fence happy. I was driving cab in 1970; I'd stage these robberies and keep the receipts. Now, me and my partner are into burglary; no strongarm stuff—you feel quiet on dope—just boosting TV sets from houses where we know the people are away. And I do a skin flick once in a while. But it's a hassle, believe me. Everybody on the street wants to rip you off; you can get burned from

pushers who try and sell you sugar or rat poison. Then there's always the threat of the law.

Ed's biggest danger, though, is himself. He often feels suicidal and, because his tolerance has been set by the low-quality smack solid on Haight Street, he is also subject to accidental overdose from injections of more potent heroin. Ed O.D.'d once in 1970 and once in 1971. The first time he was saved by companions who administered stimulants after his breathing was depressed. The second time he was taken to the clinic and given Nalline, a narcotic antagonist. The Nalline countered the effects of heroin in his body but plunged him into severe withdrawal.

Ed has also voluntarily undergone cold turkey to kick heroin. But he fears abstinence, knowing that it will leave him anxious, hungry for his next intravenous meal. His eyes and nose start to water when he misses a scheduled dose of smack; his muscles twitch without the pain-killer in his system; and his bowels churn after months of chemically induced constipation. He has lived through these comparatively mild symptoms several times, in part because his supply of drugs is so inconsistent. Yet physical withdrawal always leaves him with an even more torturous insomnia and psychological bereavement, as if he had lost his mother once again.

Pain is one reason he has stayed addicted. Another is the lack of programs that can or will assist him. Establishment medicine has little stomach for the addict and the San Francisco Public Health Department, like its counterparts in so many cities, offers only hospitalization for those who seek withdrawal. One hope is methadone, the long-acting and orally active synthetic that eliminates the hunger for other narcotics and is used to ease addicts off heroin and maintain them on a productive level of functioning. Methadone is employed with remarkable success in some states, but its use, until quite recently, was limited to research purposes in California.[1] Although San Francisco is known to have from 12,000 to 15,000 resident addicts, only 200 patients can receive treatment at its Center for Special Problems on Van Ness Avenue.

Not being one of the 200, Ed remains in the Haight, on heroin. At night, when he is not stealing to support his habit, he shoots up with his partner-roommate. "We don't play games—our only ritual is deciding who's going first." By day, he wanders through the fog of Haight Street, slouches against the boarded-up entrance of the Straight Theater, stands with the other junkies and alcoholics alongside the screened windows of a liquor store at the corner of Haight and Clayton,

1. [In September 1970, California State law was changed to allow methadone maintenance projects to expand as primary treatment agencies.]

or climbs the steps leading to the clinic's Heroin Detoxification Section at 529 Clayton Street, a half-block away.

Ed gets sedatives and tranquilizers at the clinic, along with non-narcotic analgesics to assuage his pain. He also receives personal contact from his physician, Dr. George "Skip" Gay. A bearded, sad-eyed man who has worked with over 2,000 addicts since 1969, Dr. Gay knows that periodically detoxifying Ed is not enough; his patient must find an involvement other than drugs that will make him want to live again. With this in mind, Dr. Gay is training Ed as a counselor for younger heroin abusers and trying to keep up his sagging spirits. But Haight-Ashbury has taken a heavy toll of Ed and he walks the street with stooped shoulders, as if his 28-year-old body will soon break under its burden of gloom.

"I never really belonged in this world," Ed says today as he tries to talk himself unconscious:

> I've seen lots of scenes, man, but I've never been part of one. People have treated me like an animal as long as I can remember. Dope meant hope once, and Skip and the kids at the Clinic treat me right; I think I can make it if they can find me a job there. But, you know, my head is really hurting. Sometimes I think it'd be better for everyone if I just overdosed and died.

12

Treatment Methods for Heroin Addicts:
A Review

Edward C. Senay, M.D. and Pierre F. Renault, M.D.

INTRODUCTION

Recent developments in the field of heroin addiction form another chapter in the history of science illustrating the essential humanism in adopting an analytic rather than a theological or moral stance toward a major problem for social, legal, and psychiatric perspectives on heroin addiction have changed remarkably in the last two decades. Where there was only apathy and hopelessness there is now a feeling of meaningful movement. The effective catalyst seems to have been the realization that heroin addiction should be regarded as a disease and not as a crime or a moral affliction. The pioneering work of Dole and Nyswander,[1] who demonstrated that methadone may be used to rehabilitate chronic heroin users together with the work of Charles Diderich, who developed the first therapeutic community, gave tremendous impetus to such a point of view and it is now formalized in law in many states. Currently methadone is used in the treatment of heroin users in most major urban areas in the country and the therapeutic community model is also widely used.

Repeated evaluations of Dole and Nyswander's work have corroborated the essential findings: methadone if combined with a program of rehabilitation can be effective in aiding large numbers of addicts:

1. To abolish or to decrease greatly the use of narcotics.
2. To work at a legitimate job.

1. V. P. Dole and M. Nyswander, "A Medical Treatment for Diacetylmorphine Addiction," *Journal of the American Medical Association* 193 (1965), 646–50. (N4.M44)

3. To abolish or to decrease greatly the need for engaging in criminal behavior.
4. To relate to spouse and children in more desirable ways.
5. To experience a real increase in self esteem and in the esteem in which they are held by other people.

Controversy still surrounds the use of methadone despite the general acceptance in the medical world of Dole and Nyswander's approach. There is also controversy regarding the effectiveness and the role of therapeutic communities in treatment programs. In this paper we will examine the major methods of treating heroin addiction, review controversial issues and attempt to indicate the present status and future directions for each of the treatment methods considered.

The reader should bear in mind that despite the repeated efforts of competent and experienced specialists in the field no satisfactory definition of addiction has been created. The World Health Organization and the American Psychiatric Association have decided on the simple phrase Drug Dependence—Heroin to describe what some experts (Jaffe,[2] for example) prefer to think of as a "psychosocial pattern of compulsive drug use." We want to emphasize that the vantage point of the observer determines what definition is useful. The public health official or researcher may do well with the term Drug Dependence—Heroin. The person responsible for treatment may find it more useful to be reminded by his definition than under most circumstances the use of heroin is compulsive, i.e., the patient cannot easily elect or in many instances may not have any degree of choice in deciding to seek or not to seek heroin. Ideally the definition for the student should help him bear in mind that the reasons for beginning heroin addiction are quite different from the reasons for maintaining the pattern. In general we subscribe to the view that the compulsion experienced by the addict is substantially but not solely determined by real or anticipated withdrawal symptoms. However, the fact that psychological and social factors are always relevant in drug related behavior cannot be repeated often enough. Beecher's statement that 70 percent of the analgesic effect of morphine is pharmacologic and 30 percent due to psychological factors illustrates the point well. It should be clear from the following review that the definition of the problem is by no means an academic matter; who to call a patient, how to identify him or her, and what constitutes success or failure in treatment are matters of real import.

2. J. H. Jaffe, personal communication.

METHADONE

1. Methadone Maintenance

Methadone is useful in rehabilitating heroin addicts because it suppresses withdrawal symptoms and reduces or eliminates narcotic hunger; it can be taken orally, its effects last a whole day, it does not usually produce euphoria or lassitude, and it wholly or partly, depending on dose, blocks the effects of heroin. In contrast, heroin:

1. Usually is taken intravenously thereby creating danger of infection (most addicts have abnormal liver function as a consequence of use of unsterile needles).
2. Suppresses narcotic hunger for only a period of hours (most addicts "shoot" three or four times a day if they can).
3. Sometimes produces a high or a "nodding" state in which motivation for work and/or relating to other people is decreased or abolished.

There are no serious side effects from using oral methadone; if patients do have side effects they generally have one or more of the following: sleepiness, constipation, excessive sweating, and change in libido—usually a decrease but occasionally an increase. Patients who have taken methadone for many years have not developed major difficulties so that it appears that the drug is safe for both short- and long-term use even if patients take "high" doses, i.e., in excess of 100 milligrams per day. The approach under consideration in these paragraphs is termed Methadone Maintenance because an open-ended therapeutic contract is created with a patient in which it is understood that he will be given daily methadone, i.e., be "maintained" until some unspecified future time. At present such therapeutic contracts can extend over periods of many years.

The pharmacologic advantages of methadone would not have been realized if there had not been a reassessment of what treatment goals are desirable and possible for chronic heroin abusers. The experience in federal hospitals[3] is well documented and indicates that immediate and sustained abstinence for the addict seeking treatment is simply not a realizable goal; while the addict may "clean up" for a period of weeks or months in the hospital, when he goes back to his community his return to drug abuse has a 95 percent probability attached to it.

3. G. E. Vaillant, "A Twelve Year Follow-up Study of New York Narcotic Addicts," *American Journal of Psychiatry*, 122 (1966), 727–37. (N4.M1)

When the goals of treatment programs changed from excessive pre-occupation with drugs to a concern for the person treatment results began to improve. Given a patient's psychological realities and pharma-cologic state what are achieveable next steps for him or for her was and is the "right" question for most of the effective treatment methods for chronic heroin addicts today is a function of the fact that treat-ment efforts are not drug centered.

Treatment goals generating effective results in conjunction with the use of methadone are as follows:

1. Return to legitimate employment.
2. Cessation or substantial reduction in criminal behavior.
3. Simple reduction of the amount of time an addict must think about drugs and a reduction in the amount of time spent in drug seeking behaviors.
4. Involvement with a social system in which there is a positive reinforcement for relating to people—particularly family and other addicts in various stages of readjustment.
5. Furnishing an impetus for living by internalized goals which many addicts who seek treatment generally feel substantial guilt about having abandoned.

Not all of these goals can be reached by every patient seeking help; for some legitimate employment is not a relevant goal because of major medical disability, advanced age, or need for training in ac-quiring marketable skills.

The use of methadone obviates the need for large sums of money to purchase heroin; therefore a patient can—and is usually relieved to be able to—decrease his involvement in criminal activity. Most ad-dicts do not derive pleasure or thrills from crime; almost without ex-ception they report extreme fatigue from the seven-day-a-week neces-sity of having "to get out and hustle." Occasionally one sees an addict who appears to want to be jailed so that he may escape the feeling of being "imprisoned" in the need for crime. It is a common misconcep-tion that various poor minority groups have incorporated a different set of values than is seen in middle-class populations. Prohibitions against stealing, promiscuity and/or prostitution, dishonesty in inter-personal relations, etc., are internalized in these groups exactly as they are internalized in other groups. Stated differently, the values by which self-esteem is determined are not substantially different from one social class to another; from a clinician's point of view there is as much variance within as between classes.

Many poor addicts have had fundamentalist religious orientations and have strict superegos, a situation which insures that coincident with dishonesty and criminal behavior there is guilt and low self-esteem. The feeling tone is apparent to the observer who notes that the most frequent complaint of the addict patient is applying for treatment is "I'm tired," "I'm sick of it," referring to the enervating, depressing cycle of crime and drug seeking, which when established as a pattern is without pleasure and is often without feelings of any kind except fatigue. Drug abuse generally is associated with a decrease in social relatedness of all kinds and, in particular, sexual drives are suppressed. Some addicts will report that long periods in their lives— weeks, months, years, even decades—were "empty" of anything except "hustling."

These observations help to explain a problem which frequently emerges during the early phase of treatment with methadone. Since it is no longer necessary to use his energies in drug seeking, the addict begins to have time and energy enough to realize that he has not the kinds of relationships with other people which he now finds he wants. Establishing or reestablishing friendships and love relationships in this period is necessary for successful rehabilitation. Unfortunately, for many it is difficult. Help for the problem of relatedness and how to achieve it can be obtained through the group experience which is an integral part of effective rehabilitation programs for heroin abusers. Currently most experts feel that it is methadone, with its unique pharmacoloigc properties in combination with rehabilitation efforts which accounts for the successes achieved in treatment. Methadone alone or rehabilitation efforts alone do not appear to have anywhere near the impact of the combination.

In addition to methadone and group therapy, legal counseling, vocational rehabilitation, and social services are elements in the major programs successful in treating chronic heroin addicts. Monitoring urine for narcotics and other drugs is also an integral part of current treatment programs, for such testing discourages the patient from attempting to fool himself and his counselors about his real behavior; thus an honest basis is created for relationships both with himself and with those treating him. The frequency with which urine is tested varies in different programs and it varies with the stage of treatment. Early in therapy urine may be collected two to three times per week— later when a patient has established trust only spot checks may be employed.

Dose levels of methadone vary widely in methadone maintenance programs. Dole and Nyswander have used levels in excess of 100 milligrams per day. They feel that such dose levels are useful because complete blockade of the effect of administered heroin is achieved. Since positive reinforcement for heroin use is thereby abolished, the behavior should diminish in frequency. Jaffe (1969,[4] 1970) however feels that further studies are needed to establish optimal dose level, for he has data indicating that differences between high- and low-dose study groups are not great.

Contrasting the methadone maintenance approach with the so-called English system may serve to sharpen the picture of both. In England a physician writes out a prescription for narcotics which the addict takes to a drug store. The addict then fills the prescription and can regulate his dose and the frequency of drug administration. He is free to give away or to sell the drug if he chooses. Urine monitoring is not employed. In methadone maintenance programs, as noted above, urine monitoring is basic; the patient takes his medication under the direct observation of addiction rehabilitation counselors—at least until he has established a pattern of attendance in treatment and has "clean" urines for a number of weeks and/or other evidence for motivation.

Illicit sale of medication is much more difficult in methadone maintenance programs than in the English system and the amount of support given to a patient is of course greater in programs in this country. Most experts feel that our treatment approach is superior but it is important to keep in mind that our programs for the most part deal with voluntary patients. It may well be that the English system will be useful in dealing with the large population of addicts who do not want the kinds of treatment being offered at present.

Criteria for admission into methadone treatment programs are under review at this time. Earlier because of the experimental nature of methadone, patients had to be over 18, could not be psychotic or pregnant, and had to have a history of failure in some form of treatment. Most clinicians feel that none of these criteria are beneficial in any way. They point out that the requirement of prior failure in treatment means that a patient has increased probability of arrest and imprisonment or overdose and death as a condition for involvement with an effective program. Pregnancy and psychosis if combined with heroin abuse increases rather than decreases the need for treatment. Preliminary work with adolescent heroin abusers suggest that the combination of methadone and rehabilitation may be beneficial for some patients in this population. It is clear however that the young heroin user with relatively recent onset of his or her abuse pattern constitutes a quite different problem from the older patient population presently deriving benefit from Methadone Maintenance. Younger patients tend to be much more mobile socially and geographically; they tend to

---

4. J. H. Jaffe, M. S. Zaks, and E. N. Washington, "Experience with the Use of Methadone in a Multi-Modality Program for the Treatment of Narcotic Users," *International Journal of the Addictions,* 4 (September, 1969), 481–90.

abuse many more drugs and their identity is not settled in the sense in which identity is settled for the population in Methadone Maintenance programs. All of which makes for new problems in treating these patients.

Treatment results in major methadone programs suggest that there is approximately a two in three chance of success in treating voluntary patients, the criteria for success in treatment being those described above. Some of the patients included in the category of successful treatment are dropouts who return to treatment and are then able to rehabilitate themselves. The dropouts who do not return to treatment or who return only to fail again constitute a substantial problem without a known solution. The ability to rehabilitate many addicts where this was once impossible has been such a striking advance that it has occupied the attention of all concerned. Now however there is enough energy to begin to look at the enormous problems that lie ahead. The virtues and the limitations of methadone are coming into sharper focus and the stage hopefully is being set for new approaches.

Controversy over methadone maintenance continues because of the uncertain nature of its effects over a number of years. Although it appears that methadone can be administered safely for at least seven or eight years, we do not have definite studies demonstrating that this is true also of years nine, ten, etc. Without any particular rationale, critics object to the necessity for sanctioning the administration of an addictive drug over a decade or more. Some feel that methadone has subtle tranquilizing effects and that long-term use of such an agent might interfere with psychological growth. We have not seen this effect in our clinical experience probably because it has occurred in a program where "low" doses of methadone are employed.

Other critics feel that illegal redistribution of methadone may constitute a significant social problem in itself. Addicts have registered in more than one program thereby obtaining extra medication which they can sell; it is also possible for sociopathic addicts to establish themselves as "good" patients, to secure privileges of taking home several doses of methadone, and then to decrease their habit by slow adjustment, thus creating a steady supply of drug for illicit sale. At entrance to treatment it is necessary to have criteria to identify who is an addict; the control of sociopathic behavior by addicts with multiple registration in different treatment programs, together with FDS requirements, dictate that criteria have to be set up. Urine monitoring for the presence of opiates, needle tracks, the physical signs of acute use of heroin, e.g., pinpoint pupils, and corroboration by staff that the prospective patient has used heroin are the basic criteria usually employed. In the instance of addicts who emerge from hospitals or jails "clean" but who know that they cannot remain that way and want methadone urine testing is, of course, without value. Clinical judgment is utilized in such cases.

Experience is limited with detoxification of patients who have been on methadone maintenance for years. Patients detoxified for disciplinary reasons have the same high rates of readdiction as was the case with hospital-based treatment. From clinical experience it appears that detoxification on a voluntary basis probably carries a little higher chance of success than disciplinary detoxification, but results of voluntary detoxification do not look promising from the perspective of applicability to large numbers of patients.

Because epidemiologic studies are so uncertain in the problem of heroin addiction, we have no sound idea of how many heroin addicts there are and therefore no idea of what proportion are amenable to treatment. It is certain that substantial numbers of addicts—it may be that more are not reachable by known techniques than are—do not want and/or cannot use present methods of rehabilitation.

Before turning to other approaches it should be noted that Jaffe has demonstrated that all the major successful treatment methods can be combined in one program so that it is possible to apply what appears to be the most appropriate treatment for any given case. For example, the addict of long standing who is married, has children and a legitimate job is probably better served by Methadone Maintenance than by referral to a therapeutic community. When the modalities are varied, treatment results should be improved. Jaffe also has experimented with the concept of methadone pretreatment in which patients are given methadone and a minimum of clinical "input" prior to acceptance into crowded "regular" treatment facilities. The approach appears to be quite feasible. Final results however are not in. The best summary statement one can make about Methadone Maintenance is that it appears to be preferred by most addicts who are offered a choice between various treatment modalities and of course it offers a two in three chance of successful rehabilitation for voluntary patients. Until some breakthrough occurs, Methadone Maintenance will probably be the most important therapy for heroin addicts.

OTHER TREATMENT METHODS UTILIZING METHADONE

2. Detoxification and Abstinence

In this method of treatment the patient is placed on methadone and then slowly withdrawn over a period of days or weeks with the idea of achieving and maintaining abstinence. Clinically one does not usually attempt the withdrawal outside a hospital ward or residential setting, but a few patients have been "detoxed" "on the street" with success. It is clear from the Lexington experience that success in the detoxification-abstinence method necessitates involvement—probably on an open-ended basis—in a therapy program with all the services legal, vocational, etc., and guidelines, e.g., urine testing, as are employed in Methadone Maintenance. Additionally, we know now that the treatment program must be based in the addict's community.

At present this approach does not have the general effectivenses of Methadone Maintenance, but clinical experience suggests that for at least a few patients it may be useful. It must be emphasized that engagement in a program is the keystone of this approach and that it also requires rehabilitation over a period of years. Additionally the treatment system should be able to offer a rapid response for crises, because patients who under most circumstances may be able to function independently may under stress need intensive short-term help if they are not going to relapse.

This approach has not received the attention it deserves. However, it is being tried and we can look for research reports on it in the near future. One of the drawbacks in this approach is that it requires more staff and a greater psychological "input" to the patient than Methadone Maintenance. There may not be enough funds to support this as a basic treatment method applicable to large numbers of addicts even if further studies should show that it can be effective.

A METHADONE CONGENER: ALPHA-ACETYLMETHADOL

Alpha-acetylmethadol, a congener of methadone, has the same set of effects as methadone, differing only in that methadol is effective in relieving narcotic hunger and suppressing withdrawal symptoms for a two to three day period—in contrast to the twenty-four-hour relief afforded by methadone. Preliminary testing indicates that methadol is safe and cannot be distinguished from methadone by patients or physicians blind to the medication being administered to a particular patient. If further testing confirms the results of prior studies, methadol may be a significant addition to the clinician's armamentarium, for it is probably desirable to suppress narcotic hunger for two to three days in many if not most patients in current treatment programs.

Methadol may furnish the means to study the role of the addictive aspects of the medication in maintenance programs. Some critics feel that one of the reasons, if not the most important reason, for the success of methadone programs is that patients become addicted to methadone and that their motivation for involvement with the treatment program is largely a function of the fact of physiologic dependence.

Some clinicans would dispute such an analysis. Motivation for therapy is a function of the fact that many patients have a genuine desire for maturation. Most addicts report a substantial degree of ambivalence toward their habit at all stages in the development of the pattern. Their involvement with treatment appears to be continuation of the —at least intermittent—struggle to be free of the necessity to live by drugs. While physiologic dependence may be a factor in the holding power of methadone programs it does not appear to be the predominant reason for therapeutic success. However, this important question can be settled only by research and methadol, by virtue of its long duration of action, may be a tool by which such research may be accomplished. Since most of the effects useful in treating narcotic addicts are attributable to the l isomer of the alpha-acetylmethadol, racemate research is being conducted on the pure l form. Methadol can be substituted for methadone and vice versa. It is now possible therefore to create more flexible pharmacologic regimens than has been the case heretofore.

Narcotic Antagonists

Narcotic addiction can be explained by the principles of classical and instrumental conditioning. Viewed from such a theoretical vantage point, drug-seeking behavior is reinforced positively by self-administration of narcotics. It follows therefore that if the effects of self-administered narcotics can be blocked, drug-seeking behavior should be extinguished. To date two drugs—cyclazocine and naloxone—have been found to have the capacity to block the effects of administered heroin. In addition to the blockade of subjective effects, they prevent the development of physiologic dependence and afford protection from death by overdose. Their usefulness now has been assessed in many clinical centers. The present consensus on both of these agents is that they have limited value; clearly they do not have the general applicability of the methadone maintenance approach.

Clinical trials have been more extensive with cyclazocine than with naloxone and it will be considered first. At this writing approximately 450 patients have been studied with cyclazocine. Experience with these patients suggest that cyclazocine is useful for relatively short-term administration. Patients do not appear to continue to take it for years, for only 20 of the 450 patients were still taking cyclazocine after three years. This finding is probably explained by the fact that many patients find the subjective effects of cyclazocine unpleasant.

A daily dose range of 4–8 milligrams of cyclazocine is needed to block the effects of heroin. This dose level cannot be instituted immediately, however. The drug must be given first in low doses and the dosage then increased slowly over a period of weeks. If the dose is increased too rapidly, patients have experiences of feeling unreal. Lightning flashes in the head are reported by some and insomnia, irritability, and tension by others. Still others may report a "high like marihuana" or effects "like LSD." These side effects can be countered without difficulty by dose adjustments and/or the use of tranquilizers.

Cyclazocine does not reduce narcotic craving, so that in the case where it may have therapeutic benefit the patient experiences narcotic hunger as usual but the reinforcement from "shooting" heroin is lost because of the blockade. In addition to the drawback that many patients experience cyclazocine negatively, it is necessary to withdraw patients from all narcotics before building up cyclazocine dosage. Cyclazocine can precipitate severe withdrawal syndromes—some believe these can be lethal—if administered to a patient not free from narcotics.

Withdrawal from cyclazocine itself can be accomplished by muscle aches, rhinitis, and subjective discomfort. The clinical utility of this drug is limited by all the foregoing factors, but there are patients seeking help in achieving immediate abstinence who will continue to take the drug and who appear to derive benefit. Whether drug effects or motivation effects (inherent in the fact that patients must volunteer to take the drug) can account for treatment success remains to be settled by controlled experiments. The agonist effects of cyclazocine give it an abuse potential. Such a consideration may have relevance if, for example, one were choosing between this and some other drug without "agonist" effects.

Compared with cyclazocine, naloxone has the advantage of being free from unpleasant subjective effects but it has the disadvantages of being of short duration and of variable potency when taken orally. There is no physiologic dependence induced by naloxone. As in the case with Antabuse in treating alcoholics, daily administration of naloxone is necessary. This means close supervision or strong and continuing motivation for success in treatment. Naloxone is quite expensive at present. It is in short supply and it appears that in its present form it has limited usefulness, primarily because of its short duration of action. Its relative lack of subjective effects gives it a low abuse potential.

Experts in the field feel that there are hundreds of potential narcotic antagonists of value. Currently, cyclorphan and n-allyl opiate derivatives are receiving the closest attention. Additionally, long-acting antagonist depot vehicles are either being considered for investigation or, in the instance of silastic (a material made from silicone and rubber), are under active investigation. The successful invention of such delivery system could be of major importance for treatment programs.

THERAPEUTIC COMMUNITIES

Whatever the past record is or whatever the future role of therapeutic communities turns out to be, one fact is clear: "graduates" of these institutions are the cadre par excellence of current drug abuse programs. The chief drawback of therapeutic communities is that they do not constitute a treatment applicable to large numbers of addicts. A look at what they require may serve to explain why. The expectation on entering a therapeutic community is prompt and complete renunciation of heroin. Traditionally this meant "cold turkey," but many current therapeutic communities have "relaxed" or "loosened up" in their treatment ideology to the point of allowing a detoxification with methadone over the first five or seven days of treatment.

A remarkable aspect of the detoxification occurring in the setting of a therapeutic community is the relatively benign nature of the withdrawal syndrome. In jails and in hospitals—indeed in any psychosocial setting which permits passivity and regression on the part of the patient, the withdrawal syndrome can be severe. Passivity and regression, however, are not encouraged in the setting of the therapeutic community; the patient is called upon to perform routine housekeeping chores and to participate actively in social relating. Under such circumstances, the withdrawal syndrome is frequently mild and occasionally may hardly be experienced by patients. As noted above, psychological set and psychosocial reinforcement or the lack of it are always relevant variables in drug-related behavior.

A prospective patient must be able to live in the therapeutic community and to do so for one to two years of twenty-four-hour-a-day, seven-days-a-week involvement with the "dynamic" of the house. All relationships—past, present, and future—are subject to group inspection and evaluation. A patient is viewed as having to prove his ability to be independent, for central to the treatment philosophy of therapeutic communities is the view that the heroin addict is a dependent child who has not the ability to be honest about property or feelings. Treatment is seen as a resocialization process in which direct honest communication is practiced with respect to all aspects of the addict's new life. If the addict can adjust to the experience—and it is clear that many cannot—he or she experiences tremendous support from his membership in the group.

Humor, tenderness, and affirmation begin to be felt experiences in relation to other live human beings; the addict learns that negative feelings do not necessarily destroy the possibility of future warmth and he begins to learn that affective and social experience can be positive and not fresh confirmation for the depressive position and/or a stimulus for drug seeking. Those who become successfully involved in the "dynamic" evaluate their new status as being much more desirable than the monotonic affective experience they knew from the drug scene. "Graduates" of such experiences possess valuable skills. Their sensitivity to the feelings of others, their ability to communicate, their understanding of group process, their particular appreciation of the ordeal of change makes them ideally suited for helping addicts in any kind of treatment setting.

On the negative side, rigid allegiance to the abstinence ideology sometimes creates problems in adjusting to what is now a fact; namely, that many people can be helped significantly even though they continue to take a drug such as methadone. Many former patients emerging from therapeutic communities resisted the idea of methadone maintenance, feeling that it was bound to fail because people had not "cleaned up really."

Most experts in the field of drug abuse today feel that therapeutic communities are of unquestioned value for some patients but, as noted above, they do not constitute an approach which is applicable to large numbers of patients. Charles Diderich, the creator of the first therapeutic community, is reported to have said that his method was suitable for one out of ten addicts seeking help. From a clinical point of view, this still seems a fair statement. Patients in therapeutic communities tend to be younger on the average than those on methadone maintenance; as might be anticipated from the therapeutic contact described above, they tend to be more mobile socially and geographically. The addict who is married with children and who has a steady job is usually not disposed to want or to accept treatment in therapeutic communities. The single, usually younger, addict is of course much more liable to do so.

Most therapeutic communities are organized around more or less identifiable steps in which increments of trust, status, and power in the group are acquired. These steps can be thought of as roughly similar to the various rites (e.g., confirmation or Bar Mitzvah) utilized by social groups in the "straight" world to mark various stages of maturation. Therapeutic communities have not institutionalized these basic steps but the underlying process is the same.

To date the style and general purpose of the group experiences in therapeutic communities have been transformed to the group therapy offered as an integral element of methadone maintenance programs. In brief, the value reinforced by the group is honesty in communication with direct confrontation being the vehicle to achieve the desired result. There has not been enough time to evaluate different group methods either in therapeutic communities or in methadone maintenance programs. The confrontation group works well enough but perhaps more conventional styles of group interaction may be more effective. From a psychiatric point of view, honesty in communication is certainly basic and desirable; however, exclusive preoccupation with the value of honesty ignores the genuine difficulty people have in labeling many of their feelings and their real need for defense against many psychological problems. The prospect is for the continued multiplication of therapeutic communities. It is likely that further experimentation will produce experiences appropriate for different problems. The adolescent poly-drug abuser, for example, will probably do better with a less demanding and less authoritarian social structure.

OTHER APPROACHES

The methods sketched briefly above are those with the most support among clinicians and researchers at the present time. Other methods, e.g., the "use of rational authority," "Civil commitment," or engaging in standard types of individual or group psychotherapy with a clinical psychologist, psychiatrist, or psychoanalyst, counseling with a clergyman or priest, and the so-called English system have not received more than passing reference because these approaches have not found widespread acceptance. The failure to focus on these approaches implies only that they have not been employed effectively to the present time. Given the basic change in the cultural ambience which has occurred in the past two decades, some of these methods may yet prove to be worthwhile. For example, if a general psychiatrist works in a community setting in which addicts are given the status of rehabilitable human beings and if he has the facilities for urine monitoring and if he is permitted to use methadone or cyclazocine, he may be able to service substantial numbers of addicts. It appears likely that new approaches will be found and added to those already of proven value so that in the future almost every heroin addict seeking help can find a suitable and effective treatment modality.

SUMMARY

Methadone maintenance and therapeutic communities are the major treatment methods for heroin addicts today. Methadone has been found to be safe and it offers a two in three chance of helping a voluntary addict patient substantially to reduce his need for and abuse of narcotics while he resumes legitimate employment, decreases or ceases criminal activity and begins to relate to his family and friends in more mutually rewarding ways than was the case when he was taking drugs.

The long-term outcome of methadone maintenance is not yet known; while there is no reason for anxiety, critics have seized on the uncertainty. Newer forms of methadone, such as the methadols, promise more flexible treatment regimens than has been possible in the past. The use of methadone in a relatively rapid transition from heroin abuse to an abstinence pattern has been little tried but may have promise.

Therapeutic communities are effective in the treatment of heroin addicts but there is question about the applicability of this method to large numbers of patients. The graduates of therapeutic communities are outstanding workers in rehabilitation programs.

The narcotic antagonists—cyclazocine and naloxone—have limited value to date, appearing to be chiefly utilized by the addict seeking abstinence. The many problems with these agents—agonist effects in the instance of cyclazocine and variable potency when given orally in the instance of naloxone—remain to be solved. The potential therapeutic value of narcotic antagonists, however, is enormous. It is likely that the real achievements of the last two decades will be extended and supplemented in the decades to come, for we have now a scientific and medical base from which to view these problems in place of the theological-punitive-legal stance of the past.

13

Treatment Techniques
for Narcotic Withdrawal

Donald R. Wesson, M.D., George R. Gay, M.D.,
and David E. Smith, M.D.

For the individual who has become physically as well as psychologically dependent on heroin or barbiturates, abruptly stopping or decreasing the daily amount taken may produce symptoms of withdrawal. We distinguish two classes of acute withdrawal syndromes: the *narcotic withdrawal syndrome,* produced by the abstinence of heroin, morphine, meperidine (Demerol), and methadone; and the *depressant withdrawal syndrome,* produced by the abstinence of barbiturates, meprobamate, and a variety of other tranquilizers, sedative-hypnotics, and alcohol. This division in to two classes is based on similarities of the withdrawal syndrome and the ability of a drug within a class to suppress the manifestations of physical dependence of other drugs wihin the same class. For example, methadone will completely suppress the withdrawal symtoms of heroin or morphine, but not the withdrawal symptoms of barbiturates. Alcohol is included in the depressant class because of partial cross tolerance to other sedative-hypnotics. Alcohol will not, however, completely suppress all symptoms of barbiturate withdrawal. Individuals who abuse *both* depressants and narcotics simultaneously may develop physical dependence on both. This dual dependence is referred to as a "mixed addiction."

As physicians, we are prone to overrate the importance of withdrawal in the overall treatment of addiction because it fits well into the traditional illness-treatment model and its management involves dispensing medications. Withdrawal or detoxification is a step that is necessary at some point during treatment, but singly, in itself, it is very rarely adequate treatment for the drug-dependent individual. To avoid a predictable and rapid recidivism, the life style associated with the drug abuse must be modified in some other way.

For psychological reasons, some individuals who are dependent upon heroin prefer to withdraw "cold turkey." Wikler offers the explanation that experiencing withdrawal symptoms serves as atonement for the guilt over having received prior pleasure from drugs.[1] For heroin addicts on the West Coast, withdrawing abruptly poses no medical threat, as the heroin here is relatively expensive but of monumentally poor quality. Abruptly stopping barbiturates, on the other hand, is more dangerous and should be done only under close medical supervision, (in a hospital if possible).

HEROIN WITHDRAWAL

The onset of heroin withdrawal symptoms begins six to eight hours after the last fix. The symptoms produced are similar to a bad case of the flu: runny nose, stomach cramps, diarrhea, vomiting, muscle cramps, shaking chills or profuse sweating, "gooseflesh" skin, insomnia, and general irritability or jitteriness. The maximum severity of symptoms develops within twenty-four to seventy-two hours after the last dose of heroin and the more dramatic symptoms subside in five to seven days, even without treatment. More subtle withdrawal symptoms, however, such as irritability and difficulty with sleeping, may last much longer. Methadone, meperidine (Demerol), and other narcotics can produce similar withdrawal symptoms, but differ primarily in time, course, and severity (for example, methadone withdrawal symptoms are more prolonged but milder than those of heroin withdrawal).

Although the physiological basis of these withdrawal symptoms is well established and is primarily subcortical in origin,[2] psychological factors modify to a great extent how the symptoms are perceived and interpreted.

TREATMENT WITH METHADONE

Trying to determine the amount of a heroin habit with accuracy is all but impossible. The purity of heroin varies greatly and the addict, hoping for more potent medication from his doctor, frequently exaggerates the magnitude of his addiction on initial history.

1. M. Nyswander, *The Drug Addict as a Patient* (New York: Grune & Stratton, 1956), p. 68.
2. Ibid., p. 53.

Fortunately ten milligrams of methadone given orally four times a day will suppress the withdrawal symptoms of most habits. One workable method of withdrawal is to substitute a fixed amount of methadone (forty milligrams per day) for the heroin habit. Two days are then allowed for making the transition from heroin to methadone. After this stabilization period, the methadone is withdrawn five milligrams a day in a stepwise fashion.

NONNARCOTIC TECHNIQUE OF HEROIN WITHDRAWAL

Nonnarcotic withdrawal involves treating withdrawal symptoms with a variety of symptomatic nonnarcotic medications. The suppression of withdrawal symptoms is rarely complete, however, and at the Haight-Ashbury Free Medical Clinic less than 20 percent of individuals beginning narcotic withdrawal in this manner complete the process.[3]

Strong and continued psychological support from peers, exercise, a *change in environment, luck,* and strong motivation for quitting are all important ingredients required to complete an outpatient withdrawal from narcotics.

3. D. E. Smith, G. R. Gay & B. S. Ramer, "Adolescent Heroin Abuse in San Francisco," paper presented at the Third National Conference on Methadone Treatment, New York, November 1970. See also G. R. Gay, A. D. Matzger, W. Bathurst, and D. E. Smith, "Short-Term Heroin Detoxification on an Outpatient Basis," *International Journal of the Addictions* 6, no. 2 (1971): 241–64.

14

The Heroin Addict in a Therapeutic Community for Adolescents: A Cultural Rip-off

Sheil Salasnek, M.D. and Fariborz Amini, M.D.

In July of 1967 the Youth Drug Unit at the Langley Porter Neuro-psychiatric Institute opened its doors to the burgeoning number of young people having difficulty with drugs. It was the "Summer of Love" in Haight-Ashbury, three blocks away, and we cut our thera-peutic eyeteeth on starry-eyed acid visionaries and Ph.D. dropouts. Marijuana, psychedelics, and amphetamines were the drugs of abuse. Heroin, still hidden in the deepest recesses of the ghetto communities, was virtually unknown among our patient population. Our four-year history has seen many changes in the patient population and in the patterns of drug abuse. Today's patient is younger, possesses fewer social skills, and instead of starry-eyed visions is more likely to have the glazed stupor of the barbiturate or narcotic user.

In a book published in 1868, H. B. Day remarked that there was no agreement in the medical profession as to the proper treatment of opium disease.[1] If he had written his book three years later, we could be celebrating the centennial anniversary of his comment by under-scoring it again. Today there still exists significant disagreement in the medical community as to what constitutes appropriate treatment for heroin addiction. Not until the 1930s did the medical profession in this country even begin to address itself to anything beyond the

Presented at the National Heroin Symposium at the University of California, San Francisco, 20 June 1971.

1. H. B. Day, *The Opium Habit, with Suggestions as to Remedy* (New York: Harper & Brothers, 1868).

problem of the treatment of opiate withdrawal. After the Harrison Narcotics Act of 1914, addicts were lawbreakers. The development of the Public Health Service Hospitals in Lexington, Kentucky, and Fort Worth, Texas, in 1935 and 1938 respectively, were early attempts to treat the longer-term problems of addiction, based on an understanding of the mental and emotional underpinnings of the disease. The Narcotic Addict Rehabilitation Act of 1966 seems to leave the addict in a legal limbo between the world of the criminal and that of the medical patient.

In 1969 James Maddux, Director of the Public Health Service Hospital in Fort Worth, Texas, identified six features of the varying approaches to the problem of treatment:

1. Continuity of treatment: an ongoing treatment program stretching through prehospital, hospital, and posthospital course.
2. Civil commitment via Title I, II, or III of the Narcotic Addict Rehabilitation Act.
3. Methadone maintenance.
4. Narcotic antagonists.
5. Mutual help organizations.
6. Religious experience.[2]

Our concept of the therapeutic community represents a synthesis between two of Maddux's approaches. The feature of continuity of treatment through prehospital, hospital, and posthospital periods would apply to us, since we exist in a medical setting. The unique features of a therapeutic community, when compared to the more standard psychiatric inpatient settings, put us also in the category of the mutual help organizations.

The aim of the therapeutic community is as old as the idea that man is a product of his environment and that creating a more perfect environment will produce a more perfect man. Henry Brill, at the research conference of the therapeutic community in 1960 traced the idea back to the *Republic* of Plato:

> When any of the citizens experience good or evil the whole state will make his case their own—rejoice or sorrow with him. . . . And is not that the best ordered state which most nearly approaches to the condition of the individual; as in the body, when but a finger of one of us is hurt, the whole frame . . . feels the hurt and sympathizes all together with the part affected.

2. James F. Maddux, M.D., "Current Approaches to the Treatment of Narcotic Addiction," *Journal of the National Medical Association* 61 (1967): 248–254.

Past Plato the concept was traced through Sir Thomas Moore's *Utopia,* Francis Bacon's *New Atlantis,* and Wells' *A Modern Utopia.* Brill defined efforts like the Oneida Community and Mormonism as attempts at implementing the theory of the more perfect environment and at applying directly the principles of group action, individual freedom, democratic self-government, and the value of productive work.[3]

The modern therapeutic community as an offshoot of the psychiatric inpatient service got its start at the end of World War II in England. Maxwell Jones, an English psychiatrist, remains the grandfather of all such communities. Keeping in mind that the therapeutic community was developed for a wide variety of psychiatric inpatients, we would like to underline four points in his definition:

1. The unit is oriented to productive work and a quick return to society.
2. The unit uses educational techniques, group dynamics, and group pressures for constructive purposes.
3. There is a marked diffusion of authority from personnel to patients so that there is decision-making machinery at all levels and everyone is identified with the aims, successes, and failures of the unit.
4. The unit must establish open, two-way communication involving, as far as possible, all personnel, both patients and staff.[4]

In bringing the broader concept of the therapeutic community closer to the subject of this symposium, we want to refine it in two ways. In the first place, we want to consider how the therapeutic community can be applied to the particular symptom of drug abuse and addiction. In the second place, because of our particular experience, we wish to further refine this to the question of applying the therapeutic community principles to a group of adolescents.

ADOLESCENCE, DRUGS, AND THERAPEUTIC COMMUNITIES

Adolescence offers a particularly rich medium for the development of the symptom of drug abuse. As the prepubertal youngster is unceremoniously tossed into the matrix of anxiety, depression, and physical discomfort that we label the adolescent process,

3. Herman Denber, C. B., ed., *Research Conference on Therapeutic Community* (New York: Thomas, 1960).
4. Maxwell Jones, *Beyond the Therapeutic Community* (New Haven: Yale University Press, 1968).

the regressive reappearance of magical thinking reinvests the concept of drugs with the seductive promise of relief without the need for active mastery and adaptation. . . . The dominant conscious motive is not the seeking of "kicks," but the wish to produce pharmacologically a reduction in distress that the individual cannot as easily achieve by his own conscious efforts.[5]

In comparison with his adult compatriot, the adolescent addict is more in need of habilitation than of rehabilitation. He presents an across-the-board picture of emotional, educational, and vocational underdevelopment.[6]

Boyd, who worked with adolescent heroin addicts in England, defined seven reasons that adolescents were attracted to drugs:

1. Like alcohol in adults, drugs provide an easy way of getting instant pleasure in a social setting.
2. Drugs allow them to engage in something secret and special to themselves.
3. Drugs offer a special challenge—like the game of "chicken."
4. Drugs appeal to the magical thinking of adolescence—a journey beyond the confines of the mind.
5. Drugs bolster an adolescent's identity at a time of uncertainty.
6. Drugs offer an avenue of escape when stress is overwhelming.
7. Drugs destroy something unwanted within the self.[7]

The first four of these reasons appear in all drug experimenters, but Boyd felt that as the drugs began to be used for the last three reasons the result was more likely to be addiction.

Boyd and his coworkers ran a threapeutic community in England for adolescent heroin addicts. The major differences between their program and the one we run are in their exclusive commitment to the treatment of their heroin addict and in their liberal use of methadone as a regular part of their treatment. In the first year of their program eighty-seven addicts were admitted. Of these eighty-seven, thirty-nine were no longer there at the time of the review. These were program failures and were lost to follow-up. Of the forty-eight addicts remaining in the program, eight were off all drugs (17 percent). The others were on methadone.[8] Boyd's conclusions and the questions he

5. Herbert Weider & Eugene Kaplan, "Drug Use in Adolescents: Psychodynamic Meaning and Pharmacogenic Effect," *The Psychoanalytic Study of the Child* (New York: International Universities Press, Inc., 1969) Vol. XXIV.

6. David Laskowitz, "Psychological Characteristics of the Adolescent Addict," in *Drug Addiction in Youth,* ed. Ernest Harms (New York: Pergamon Press, 1965), pp. 67–86.

7. Philip Boyd, "Heroin Addiction in Adolescents," *Journal of Psychosomatic Research* 14 (1970): 295–301.

8. Boyd, "Heroin Addiction in Adolescents," p. 301.

raises are similar to those of our Youth Drug Unit, and before considering them we would like to pass on to a description of the operation of the Langley Porter Youth Drug Unit and report on some of our results.

THE LANGLEY PORTER YOUTH DRUG UNIT

Since July of 1967 the Youth Drug Unit has tried to provide some neutral territory where young people having trouble with drugs can reexamine their directions. Our staff is made up of professionals and an occasional ex-patient, all of whom are interested in helping others understand and gain better mastery over themselves and their lives. Each member of the community participates in the ongoing process of self-evaluation and examination of his and others' interactions.

We are open to adolescents and young adults. Historically, our patients have been involved primarily in the abuse of hallucinogens, sedatives, and stimulants. The past year, however, has seen a larger number of heroin abusers admitted into our program. For the last year 25 percent of our patients have been heroin abusers. We have generally not accepted the acutely psychotic and have required that detoxification be performed elsewhere. Patients are admitted "clean."

We function as a therapeutic community and patient-staff roles often become blurred. Each member of the community is expected to share in defining the operation of the program. Our treatment program includes community meetings, small-group therapy, individual therapy, family therapy, an individualized school program with a teacher who is a full-time member of the community, and the use of videotape. In addition, there is an outside vocational rehabilitation counselor who works closely with our ward. All of these therapies and services require of a patient that he invest much of his time and energy into the program.

After a patient is accepted into the program he is expected to live in on a twenty-four-hour basis. Our door is not locked and patients are free to come and go as long as they abide by their commitments to the program. The length of stay is not fixed, but four to six months seems to be best for optimum results. Plans for discharge are discussed throughout a patient's stay and he is helped to leave the hospital with realistic vocational and educational counseling. Social functioning has a high value in the ward culture.

The rules are kept as simple as possible. Patients must attend all required meetings; there is no use of drugs or alcohol, no physical violence, no sexual contact with other members of the community;

the patients must abide by curfew and participate in Unit Ecology (clean up their own mess).

If a patient breaks the rules, it is handled either in the community meetings or in an evaluation with a team of patients and staff. In the evaluation an attempt is made to understand why the patient is having difficulty with the rules. Every effort is made to make it possible for a patient to stay, but if he can make no attempt at understanding and changing his behavior and if he repeatedly breaks the rules, he is discharged from the unit.

The emotional climate of our unit is as variable as the people who come there. Each new patient or staff member has an effect on the mood of the group. We function best as a group of people who are trying to understand our interactions with one another. Optimally, we share a willingness to struggle toward an honest and open evaluation of our thoughts, feelings, and behavior. In our four years of existence we have had to learn and relearn that not everyone can benefit from our community, but anyone with a desire to make changes in himself and a capacity for self-examination is given a chance in the program.

THE YOUTH DRUG UNIT—POPULATION AND RESULTS

As we have already mentioned, the Youth Drug Unit historically has not been interested in heroin abusers. Our official policy still maintains that those primarily addicted to opiates are not accepted into the program. In comparing the 25 percent figure for the past eleven months to the 2–3 percent of heroin abusers seen in our first three years, it would seem that we are changing our practice and that our policy will soon have to comply. In view of the changes in what drugs are popular at various times, we don't think this increase is surprising and we would predict an even higher rate of increase over the next twelve months. Of the last forty-four patients discharged from our unit, eleven were heroin addicts. Of these eleven, six were asked to leave and five were considered "graduates." All of the six who were asked to leave have become reinvolved with heroin. Of the five graduates, two have remained drug-free—one for at least eleven months and another for seven. The other three have become readdicted to heroin. Comparing our heroin patients with those abusing other drugs, we find that approximately half of both groups did not finish the program. Several of the heroin addicts were found to have severe underlying psychoses and other treatment programs were recommended. The others are equally divided between those who were kicked out for various reasons and those who chose to leave. Of the nineteen others who have completed the program, only one is known to have gone back to using drugs. Eleven are known to be drug-free. Seven others have not yet been recontacted. Even without counting the seven who have not been contacted, we have a "cure" rate of at least 60 percent of those who have finished the program. To be sure, these are short-term follow-ups, but they nevertheless give us some reason for optimism in a field where dismal failure has been the rule.

It surprised us, in going over our discharges and contacting ex-patients, to discover that we have done about as well with heroin abusers as we have with those using other classes of drugs. If we could somehow sharpen our judgment at the time of admission as to who is likely to stick with the program, we would have more impressive results. In using such small numbers, it is hard to make any statements about percentages and statistical significance that would hold up on critical analysis.

PHARMACODYNAMIC CONSIDERATIONS

We have a general impression, as yet not validated statistically, that two categories of drug patients have been the most difficult to treat in our program. One is the heroin addict and the other the barbiturate abuser. With both of these patients we usually have the vague discomfort that there is no real alliance, no desire to work together for change. Some consideration of the pharmacodynamic similarity of the drugs is worthwhile. Heroin and barbiturates, as compared to marijuana, psychedelics, and amphetamines, are affect diminishes. They provide a blunting of affects and the chronic user is usually someone who will go to any lengths to turn himself off and avoid coming to terms with his psychological disequilibrium. His goal is a state of nothingness— the best feeling is no feeling. Marijuana, psychedelics, and even amphetamines, on the other hand, are abused more often by people seeking an increase in affective states. These people are more interested in exploring the meaning behind their drug fantasies. These patients have tended to be more psychologically minded and can be more readily helped to develop controls over their feelings and to discover that intense interpersonal relationships can provide gratifications similar to those they are obtaining from the drug, but on a much richer level.

It seems that the abuser's drug of choice is not solely the product of his environment. Although experimentation with any drug might be understood only in terms of social factors, when we get to chronic abuse, the drug of choice appears to have more to do with intrapsychic factors.

We don't think this contradicts the data presented by Dr. Pittel at this conference. Our patients have generally not been the poly-drug addicts that he described, heroin addicts who had an extensive earlier history of experimentation with psychedelics. Our eleven heroin addicts had little or no history of earlier experimentation with psychedelic drugs. The concept of the poly-drug addict having more gross ego deficits than the patient who chooses a specific drug of abuse seems reasonable.

In our population we are dealing with drug users who make specific choices between the "down" side of alcohol-barbiturates-heroin and the "up" side of psychedelics-amphetamines.

HEROIN ADDICTS AND THE CULTURAL RIP-OFF

It is in these differences that we come up against the cultural rip-off mentioned in the title of this paper. As was already noted, the culture in a therapeutic community must stress the importance of open two-way communication. In a culture where young people are being invited to share their inner struggles, it is the development of trust that facilitates emotional growth. In a group of young people who view the outside world with open hostility, this trust and openness is tenuous at best, but it seems the heroin addicts and barbiturate abusers are more resistant to open, honest communication than are the other patients.

Although it is not possible to make absolute distinctions between the abusers of different drugs on a psychological basis, it nevertheless seems clear that the heroin and barbiturate abusers use certain defenses or safeguarding devices that are extremely destructive to our culture. Laskowitz defined these as

1. Isolation (depersonalization)—they disown behavior magically. They feel that they can do anything—as long as no one finds out, no faith has been violated.
2. Desensitization—they behave as though social involvement and emotional participation are excessively stressful and they render themselves invulnerable to emotional encroachments.
3. Environmental manipulation—they are always trying to protect themselves by creating a surrounding where their self-system is inviolate. They try to pit staff against staff or to get staff involved in personal indiscretions.
4. Counterphobic attitude—they need to prove they can use heroin without getting hooked. A need to prove their behavioral potency.[9]

9. Laskowitz, "Psychological Characteristics of the Adolescent Addicts," p. 80–81.

These factors are found to some extent in all adolescent drug abusers, but there seems to be an increase in the investment in these defenses when we compare the heroin and barbiturate abusers to others.

Because of the investment in this sort of defensive system, these people usually make a mockery of any attempt at shared openness and two-way communication. Empirically, our ward has developed a double standard that we think underlies whatever success we have with heroin abusers. When most people come into the program, there is a general acceptance of their verbal position and an emphathic reaching out on the part of all members of the community. The response to the heroin addict stands in stark contrast to this. The immediate assumption is that whatever he says is a lie and that his only concern is in protecting himself from exposure and feelings. This double standard is right out front and is usually spelled out clearly to the new patient in his first community meeting. The heroin addict has to prove himself far beyond what is expected from any other member of the community. As distasteful as this seems, it developed out of ongoing experience with heroin addicts and barbiturate abusers. It became a matter of survival of our culture. Having started with the flower children of Haight-Ashbury in 1967, we were not prepared for what seems to be the more delinquent psychology behind the heroin addict.

We were accustomed to psychological defenses, but not to overt lying from a patient who just walked in the door asking for help in changing his life. After the first few blackened spoons were found in the bathroom and after watching one or two patients pass out in meetings while vehemently denying to their last conscious breath that they had used drugs, we began to come to terms in our community with lying, cheating, and stealing as regular personality attributes of some of our members.

The tenuous commitment that the patient culture has toward improvement and moving toward a nondrug life style was destroyed by the first few heroin addicts we took into the program. The adolescent environment is an exciting one. We find ourselves surrounded by young people struggling with the basic issues of human identity and who are only too willing to share their struggles and their doubts with any compassionate listener. These people are at a crucial time in their development—all the conflicts of early childhood that had been temporarily patched up and resolved are reopened like old wounds under the stress of puberty. The amount of scarring that will be the end result is very much a product of how this time in their lives is handled. The excitement of this community also has a sense of fragility to it and the feeling of closeness and openness exist in precarious balance—even at best these qualities fluctuate between extremes. The addition of the heroin addict to this culture heavily weighs the odds in favor of distrust and chaos.

THERAPEUTIC COMMUNITIES VERSUS NONMEDICAL COMMUNITIES

It is in trying to work with the heroin addict that it seems we can learn from the harsher reality of nonmedical community approaches. Hopefully, we are not too far afield in what we understand the nonmedical community approach to be. Many of the lessons that we have learned through painful experience this year seem to have been basic assumptions by Synanon: the idea that distrust rather than trust is the basic premise with addicts; the realization that the major problem is in aftercare and stressing the importance of long-term commitment to the program (two-year minimum in Synanon); the recognition of the need to substitute a meaningful way of life for the opiates; and the recognition of the importance of offering ongoing contact—a "life line" similar to the emotional resources of the family.[10]

Those outside the medical community seem to expect us to still operate as the old authoritarian "bug-house" à la Ken Kesey's *One Flew over the Cuckoo's Nest*. In our community everyone participates and everyone is a potential "patient." Our business is understanding ourselves and our interactions and none of us is exempt. No one tries to direct the community from above. To whatever degree some of us are above and have more power, that power and position are used to facilitate community interaction and decision making. We work together—not against.

We feel no need to make apologies for our professional credentials or for the knowledge that they represent. It seems to us that one place where we offer a clear advantage over a nonmedical community approach like that of Synanon is that we offer individual psychotherapy. This seems to have allowed a greater percentage of our patients to remain in the program and make use of the social therapies that we offer.

Many of our young people are not able to participate immediately in the intense emotional work of the group meetings. It is through the use of individual psychotherapy that these people are helped in a more protected setting to get a glimpse at their defensive systems and to begin to repair some of their ego deficits.

It seems to us that the nonmedical community, in taking an appropriate step away from the rigid professionalism of the classic psy-

10. Elliott L. Markoff, "Synanon in Drug Addiction," *Current Psychiatric Therapies* 9 (1969): 261–272.

chiatric inpatient setting, has stepped too far away and is making a stranger out of what could be an appropriate ally. In our experience the combination of individual psychotherapy and the social therapies of the community fit together hand in glove. The often too-sterile setting of the psychotherapeutic situation is given new vitality in an environment where the patient is constantly invited to try out his new insights and restructured defenses. By individual psychotherapy the harsh reality of the group setting is rendered tolerable to some of those young people who would have had to run from this encounter as they have run every time earlier in their lives.

The major obstacle that we see for the use of the therapeutic community in treating the heroin addict is an economic one and it is here that the nonmedical community approach has the advantage. We exist in a hospital and have a large staff of highly trained professionals. The cost is $86.50 per day for each patient in our program. In agreeing with Synanon that long-term treatment is a necessity, we quickly price ourselves out of any large-scale involvement. Synanon, with its industrial programs and business interests, manages to support itself from within, through the initiative of its members.

It is worth wondering what we are entitled to expect from the larger society in terms of financial commitment and also to raise the question as to whether the availability of a lot of long-term treatment centers and the promise of "being cared for" doesn't play into the seductiveness of heroin in the potential addict.

HOW DO WE PREVENT THE FAILURES?

What happens to the young addict who isn't motivated enough to get into our program on the Youth Drug Unit, or to the man that Synanon refuses, or the one who is turned down for methadone maintenance? After years of arguing with the police to turn the problem of addiction over to us, what should be now suggest be done with our failures? Do we take some small percentage off the top that we feel we can help and then hand our failures back to the police, wringing our humanitarian hands in despair? Whatever we do, let us not ignore the fact that we do fail in all too many cases.

In no other place is prevention as important as it is in heroin addiction. In this instance, an ounce of prevention is worth literally a thousand pounds of our best cure. For prevention, education and threats of incarceration seem to hold limited promise. To the modern American nihilist death is an amusing toy to be played with. As the youngster risks death with each shot, any of society's threats is an impotent joke.

Listen to the words of Alice Cooper's current hit:

> Lines fall on my face and hands
> Lines fall from the ups and downs
> I'm in the middle without any plans
> I'm a boy and I'm a man
> I'm eighteen
> And I don't know what I want
> Eighteen
> I just don't know what I want
> Eighteen
> I've got to get away.

In an article in the *Village Voice* (14 June 1971) called "The Return to Cool" the author uses the song to reflect on the current street drug problem of pills and heroin:

> Eighteen is a low down raunchy death-wish celebration of being eighteen in 1971. The word "eighteen" appears throughout the song in adolescent foghorn shouts of agony and despair. The rest of the words are half-sung, half-moaned, to the accompaniment of guitars that are slapped around, not played. It is not a profound song. It's a hit. The song is a simplistic, ugly, magical masterpiece that affords the careful listener a crystal insight into the abscessed scene among teen-agers today.

As we reflect on the importance of self-motivation for the drug user who is going to be helped by our therapeutic program, we must wonder about the hopeless, tragic kids who haven't got enough of anything going for them to get into any of our "treatment programs." The kid listening to that song stoned on pills or heroin not only doesn't know what he wants, today he doesn't care either.

It is here that our hope goes out to the many community programs that are in operation. They may well be our best hope for prevention. It is in these programs that the youngster can be handled by a group of his local peers and have a chance to taste something of emotional intimacy. Local groups would offer psychological testing grounds— relatively safe settings where the young adolescent could explore his new feelings and come to terms with the fact that he may not be as isolated as he imagines and that it is not necessary to be constantly flexing his muscles to hide his feelings of impotence.

Local clinics like that in Haight-Ashbury or organizations like Synanon or Fort Help could be applied prophylactically. Synanon is already doing this. They offer their "games" to anyone interested and drug problems are not a prerequisite to participation. We could begin before there are drug problems to help young people see that they *can* make it and that there are at least some people out there that are worth relating to. We could turn them on to emotional intimacy in a supportive setting.

It is a sad commentary on our country and our times that this has become necessary. It is a job that has been handled for centuries by the family structure. Our experience on the Youth Drug Unit makes it apparent that we can no longer look to the family to provide the emotional supports needed by the growing youngster. Mom and Dad have, as often as not, changed partners two or three times already, thus validating the adolescent's feeling that it is useless to count on anyone outside of himself. In families where there is no commitment, the child never experiences intimacy. For these children drugs can either offer the illusion of human intimacy or blunt the pain of their isolation and loneliness. As a goal we would like to suggest a return to a more realistic emotional climate in our society. We would suggest working toward a society where we can drop some of the burden of pretense. Let us work toward a revaluation of strength—not any more in terms of mass, wealth, and the other qualities that make the modern American hero some kind of unfeeling rich psychopath. It is time to reach out for one another again—this time not with the drug-blurred vision of ecstatic union, but with the realistic knowledge that getting close to another person is hard work and takes time and commitment.

15

Methadone: Some Myths and Hypotheses

Edward C. Senay, M.D.

The growing use of methadone in the past five years has led to an exaggerated—sometimes hysterical—claim that the heroin problem is finally solved. Two problems have been generated, first the assessment of the real effectiveness of methadone and second the combatting of anger and disbelief stimulated by medal seekers grooving on the early and still uncertain success of the drug.

Most people are repelled by the dishonesty of the hustler—whether he is an M.D. touting a still unproven method or whether he is of the street variety. Their response in this context, however, may confuse the drug with the hawker. The real issue—whether the drug is useful to people—remains only partially solved. As a clinician, this writer believes that methadone is definitely useful, but as a physician committed to research—he has to recognize that the status of methadone remains uncertain, that is, it has not been studied under fully controlled conditions. The discrepancy between the clinical and research points of view can be confusing, particularly for nonprofessionals. For example, a highly respected worker in the field of addiction, speaking at the Second National Methadone Maintenance Conference in 1969, stated:

> Further, it is regrettable that none of the treatment results reported at this meeting have been statistically compared to an appropriate control group. In the pilot studies of methadone maintenance, this was a necessary and excusable deficit. Now that the programs are achieving dimensions of hundreds of patients, it is not.[1]

These remarks are as applicable today as they were at the time they were spoken. We have not carried out the studies suggested by

1. Stanley Einstein, ed., *Methadone Maintenance* (New York: Marcel Dekker, Inc. 1971), p. 203.

Dr. Martin partly because of the politics of the medical establishment and also because of the difficulty of carrying out such studies with methadone. Patients tend to disappear from control groups and it is impossible to withhold a therapy for long when one believes that the consequences are severe. When eminent authorities point out such facts, many can find confirmation for their fears about the drug and may reject methadone entirely. To do so would be an error.

To place the situation in perspective, the general reader should be aware that few of the drugs he might receive from his physician have been studied under "fully controlled" conditions. Indeed, only in the past two or three decades have we learned how to test treatment methods of any kind. We cannot damn methadone or its present use because it has not been studied under completely controlled conditions. One can ask, however, why haven't all the stops been pulled in testing this potentially important drug?

Most of the current problems with methadone are related to the fact that methadone is new to everyone: patients are not sure what its effects are and the physicians involved are often equally uncertain. For example, many treatment programs using methadone do not tell patients anything about the medication or anything about the basic contract—how long they might be on the drug, the conditions under which they will stop, and so forth. Patients left with such uncertainty are, of course, highly susceptible to rumor: they may hear that methadone is like insulin and, since there is some general familiarity with insulin and diabetes, reduced their anxiety by comparing methadone treatment with a known situation.

Most patients, however, even if told explicitly what methadone is and why it is useful, will remain anxious about the drug and its meaning for them. This will be true even though they report and apparently enjoy substantial benefits from being in a methadone treatment program.

Patients taking methadone for two to three years have reported a belief that methadone is a worse habit to get rid of than heroin. These patients may or may not subscribe to the common belief that withdrawal from methadone is easier than withdrawal from heroin (which appears to be the case for some, but not for others). What these patients refer to, however, is not related to ease or difficulty in withdrawal, but to the relationship between dependence on methadone and their new life style. By comparison, they see their old life style as having been not quite as dependent on heroin. Professional uncertainty is thereby reflected in the psychology of patients. Many patients also voice the conviction that methadone "gets in your bones" or similar ideas that express the feeling that methadone becomes a part of a person in a way that heroin does not. Scientifically, there appears to be no basis for such convictions; rather, they appear to be related to the fear generated by the uncertainty and novelty of methadone.

The long-term contract with patients is uncertain because we simply do not know if a substantial number of patients being maintained on methadone can be detoxified and retain their psychosocial gains. We owe it to patients to tell them that we are uncertain. Many feel that methadone could be withdrawn from stabilized patients if the same intensity of clinical input could be devoted to the process of withdrawal that is devoted to the initial phase of the treatment process. With long waiting lists, however, one usually elects to allocate resources to getting new patients stabilized rather than to the still uncertain withdrawal question. This seems best because people on waiting lists appear to die, to go to jail, and to get sick with far greater frequency than those on methadone maintenance.

Withdrawal remains one of the most urgent questions in the field. Patients who have been taking methadone for a decade, however, have not suffered from serious side effects; it may be that such long-term use, with its attendant psychological dependence, will turn out to have been unnecessary. However, until sufficient resources are available to find out what is possible, indefinite maintenance appears to be safe and to be far preferable to ripping and running, hustling, shooting up, and so forth. And this preference emanates from patients themselves. The reader who doubts should talk with the patients involved.

Because methadone is white, Establishment medicine, there is a completely understandable fear and suspicion of it in the ghettos and barrios. Some fear that methadone is a new form of social control—a substitute for facing the basic problems of racism and poverty and, consequently, another copout on the part of the Establishment to avoid change. If the ghetto or barrio is pacified with methadone, submission is assured. Fears like these receive massive reinforcement from the media, which portray the problem in its most concrete erotic aspects, like the glossy color photograph of the high school kid shooting up. Such pictures may sell magazines, but in so doing they further complicate the problem by failing to project a true picture of the economic causes or the destructive consequences of addiction. To the disadvantaged addict, it certainly appears that people are capitalizing on his problem and also that people who should be his allies do not in fact understand how banal addiction really is.

Many in the drug abuse field express the belief that drug abuse programs began when middle- and upper-class whites turned to drugs. Although roughly coincident historically, there probably was not the causal relationship that is so frequently assumed. Drug abuse programs

—identical in effort, if not in name—have been launched throughout the past five decades. The reason for their recent proliferation is simply that, until recently, such successful methods of treatment as methadone facilitation and Synanon were not known.

One need not be a champion of the Establishment to remember that millions of dollars were spent on unsuccessful ventures like the Government Hospital at Lexington or that almost all drug abuse money is currently allocated to treating minority-group drug problems and that money for middle-class soft-drug or poly-drug abuse is hard to come by.

In any large-scale treatment effort, errors are inevitable. A few patients without substantial habits are bound to find their way into treatment, and in so doing, to acquire their first real habit. These are usually patients who have been buying material with little or no heroin in it—their problem has been termed "pseudo-heroinism." Such patients have habits of short duration, but their urines may be positive for metabolites of heroin.

Such pseudo-addicts create a dilemma: extensive screening efforts can exhaust resources and the attempt to prevent one ill can result in the inability to deliber services to those who want and can benefit from them. Discussion of individual instances is impossible, however, because rules for deciding when a given individual was, in fact, a pseudo-addict are impossible to describe. Experienced observers agree that such cases occur, but no one knows how to identify them and prevent them from getting into treatment. A situation so difficult to know yet so provocative of intense feelings is likely to cause contention between treatment agencies and minority groups. In fact, this occurs frequently, as could be anticipated. The only solution is to deliver the highest quality of service possible and to hope that this will help resolve the fears that arise around such issues.

Another myth that intrudes itself and sometimes makes understanding difficult is that the pharmaceutical companies are making large amounts of money from methadone. This is not true; most drug companies do not want to manufacture methadone because there is *no* profit in it. Drug companies may make large profits in many areas, but not in this one.

Many liberal intellectuals are truculent about methadone because of their contempt for "picking up the pieces." What they mean is that anyone genuinely concerned for the welfare of people will work on changing the social conditions that almost all agree are major factors in causing addiction. What they fail to recognize is that it is probably best for those who want to change (patients) to be treated by people who are oriented toward dealing with problems on a one-to-one or small-group level. If the treating person is oriented toward political activity and toward changing the system, he may not be available when the patient is in acute need. Then we may have a spectacle similar to one recently observed, when a prominent psychiatrist on his way to a political convention literally ran by his suicidal patient.

Role confusion, of course, can be avoided and there is no reason why the treatment role and the political role need to conflict. It is just difficult to do both at the same time. For many reasons those closest to patient care are precisely those who should be active politically, for they are most in tune with patient needs. But it is just such people who have the least time for such activities. To try to help people get themselves together appears useful because people are much more liable to be agents for change when they are alert and have self-esteem than when they are compromised by heroin. After all, the only breakthroughs in the field of addiction have been made by Dole and Nyswander and Diderich. Their work has meant more for addicts that that of all the lobbyists and politicians in and out of Washington put together.

On the basis of available data, the most compelling current hypothesis is that methadone facilitates therapy. This hypothesis holds that dispensing methadone is not synonymous with treatment; rather, it is methadone plus an institutional or organizational transference that is responsible for the success of methadone maintenance programs. Institutional or organizational transference can be defined as the sense of relatedness a person acquires through his or her experiences with a set of people and a particular place or set of places associated with them. It should be contrasted with the transference phenomena occurring in sustained one-to-one pairs. It should be clear that probably both kinds of transference can be and frequently are involved, but the basic formula for a successful methadone maintenance program probably requires only the simpler and easier of the two, namely, institutional or organizational transference.

The role of methadone, then, is that of an important element in a whole, but it is a major error to confuse the element with the whole. Critics are quite justified in expressing contempt for "handing out methadone to junkies." Indeed, if no more than methadone is being offered to patients, then we cannot speak of treatment or a program. Unfortunately, there are physicians who make precisely that mistake.

Because the basic formula of methadone and institutional transference can define a treatment, we make a possibly serious error in assuming that it should. Significant results from therapy—something in the neighborhood of one in two or two in three—can derive benefit from such a formula, but it may well be that methadone plus individual transference can further increase the number of patients who can be helped; some patients may do better with the least expensive therapy—methadone plus institutional transference—while others require more. Only future research can give answers to these questions.

16

The Journey beyond Trips:
Alternatives to Drugs

Allan Y. Cohen, Ph.D.

> Interviewer: *Why do you use drugs?*
> User: *Why not?*
> Interviewer: *How could someone convince you to stop?*
> User: *Show me something better.*

Of all the dialogues between clinical and research interviewers and their subjects, ones like the above, though terse, are incredibly significant.

Governments, social institutions, and private individuals have been forced to respond to what is popularly known as "the drug epidemic." Total social response to the fact of drug use has been neither successful nor appropriate; one might say it has been badly botched. Intentions have been good, sometimes truly compassionate; but execution has missed the mark. But, "no blame"—the fault is due less to incompetence than to misconception.

It is the purpose of this paper, humbly conceived though opinionated, to outline some major misconceptions about the causes and solutions of the American drug problem, to offer a simple motivational model of drug use and to suggest a positive orientation which is relevant and applicable.

THE MYTHS

Some obvious myths and stereotypes about drugs have been exposed adequately by previous commentators. Let us investigate more subtle myths, ones which have sprung up from initial public attitudes about drugs and "addicts," nurtured by well-intentioned research and analysis, and rendered inappropriate by the phenomenal growth of drug experimentation. It is my contention that such questionable assumptions have implied strategies doomed to ineffectiveness in the control, treatment, prevention, and amelioration of the drug crisis.

Those Weird Drug Users

One widespread notion is that drug "users" are a certain "breed" of people or social group. (To simplify language, "users" is taken to cover the broad range from "experimenters" to "drug dependers," unless specifically modified below.) Predictably, many studies have abounded with conclusions about personality and sociocultural correlates of drug use. The object of such research, aside from pure science, is to understand "what makes drug users tick," extrapolating the implications to prevention or to education.

But *is* there a certain type using drugs? Can one ever "predict" individuals predisposed to drug use? More importantly, does it help to talk in such terms . . . I think not. I say this because behind the common personality-social research lies an assumption which is now very suspect—that drug experimentation and use is a *minority* phenomenon, that study of this special group will generate practical insights.

On the contrary, the apparent survey and interview evidence suggests that drug use has become a *majority* phenomenon, not only among the young. Even excluding alcohol, coffee, and cigarettes, it is now safe to estimate that over 50 percent of the total American population over 13 years of age has at least tried some powerful mind-altering drug via prescription or on the illicit market. Rare is the urban school using authentic survey data which reports that less than 50 percent of their secondary students have used amphetamines, psychedelics, barbiturates, cannabis products, and like drugs within the last twelve months. No figures can be given on overall *regular* use, but scores of spot interviews indicate that the high school "dopers" peer culture is challenging the size of the "straights." In the adult world, one recent survey found that 25 percent of all American women over 30 were currently under prescription for amphetamines, barbiturates, or tranquilizers, the percentage going up to 40 percent for ladies of higher-income families.[1]

All things considered, it is my contention that drug use must now be admitted as the social *norm*. We must realize that our chemical culture has produced an atmosphere leading to the naturalness of using drugs —no matter what the underlying complaint or need. Failure to com-

1. Data relayed in a 1970 speech by Professor Joseph Maloney, University of Louisville, Louisville, Kentucky.

prehend this cultural reality leads to dysfunctional priorities. Popular now is the notion that drug users are necessarily deviant or pathological. Drug use, too many surmise indicates something terribly wrong with the person, either morally ("send 'em to jail") or psychologically ("send 'em to a mental hospital"). But we know better. Drug users may not necessarily show lack of morality or personality disturbance, at least not more than many nonusers. Indeed, the *nonuser* may be "deviant" in the purely statistical sense. It may well be that the primary question among youth presented with the opportunity for experimentation is no longer "Why?" but "Why not?" A basic inadequacy in this "deviance-minority" model is that it tends to focus emphasis on *symptoms* rather than *causes*. It produces a philosophy of social intervention which is essentially *reactive* and *negative*. Perhaps we might be able to come up with another kind of conceptual model, a more useful one, based on logic, common sense, and our accumulated knowledge of the drug scene.

THE MOTIVES

In this conceptual model, which leads to an ultimate emphasis on alternatives to drugs, we begin with a simple formulation of the most basic motivational forces leading to drug use:

Principle I. People take drugs because they want to.

Principle II. People *use* drugs to "feel better" or to "get high." Individuals *experiment* with drugs out of curiosity or hope that using drugs can make them feel better.

Principle III. People have been taught by cultural example, media, etc. that drugs *are* an effective way to make them feel better.

Principle IV. "Feeling better" encompasses a huge range of mood or consciousness change, including such aspects as oblivion-sleep, emotion shift, energy modification, and visions of the Divine, etc.

Principle V. With many mind or mood-altering drugs, taken principally for that purpose, individuals may temporarily feel better. However, drugs have substantial short- and long-term disadvantages related to the motive for their use. These include possible physiological damage, psychological deterioration, and cognitive breakdown. Drugs also tend to be temporary, relatively devoid of satisfying translation to the ordinary nondrug state of life, and siphon off energy for long-term constructive growth.

Principle VI. Basically, individuals do not stop using drugs until they discover "something better."

Principle VII. The key to meeting problems of drug abuse is to focus on the "something better," and maximize opportunities for experiencing satisfying nonchemical alternatives. The same key can be used to discourage experimentation or, more likely, keep experimentation from progressing to dependency.

This model may seem simplistic, but I find it valuable. If I admit to the logic that people use drugs because they *want* to, I also have been forced to realize that people will only stop drug use *when* they *want* to.

THE ALTERNATIVES

I shall call this kind of formulation the "Alternatives Model." While the above assumptions are most relevantly applied to the common psychotropic substances, they might even be extended to common medicinal drugs (i.e., if we gave as much attention to the natural prevention of the common cold as to cold remedies, we would all be healthier).

The Alternatives Model emphasizes *causes;* and mandates increased attention to the development and communication of alternative attitudes, strategies, techniques, institutional changes, and life styles which could diminish the desire for using drugs to attain legitimate personal aspirations. "Alternative" is *not* just a synonym for "substitute" since it implies an orientation which is *more effective* than drugs for giving the person real satisfaction.

Considering its logical importance, the literature on alternatives to drug use is very sparse, although the situation seems to be improving.[2] Ironically, there is a huge store of literature and wisdom about possible alternatives, but this material has not been specifically applied to drug use education and research.

Once we presume that "alternatives" are important, we must expand the model to fit complex variables in all phases of the drug scene. We face questions like: "Which alternative for which drug?"—

2. *Articles:* A. V. Dohner, "Mood-Altering Agent Use in America: Why Drugs?" *Rocky Mountain Medical Journal* (February 1970); A. Chanin, "Understanding Teenagers: Alternatives to Drug Abuse," *Clinical Pediatrics* 8 (January 1969): 6–10; P. Townshend, "In Love with Meher Baba," *Rolling Stone* 71 (26 November 1970): 25–27. *Books:* R. Gustatis, *Turning On* (New York: Macmillan, 1969); J. Needleman, *The New Religions* (New York: Doubleday, 1970); P. Marin & A. Y. Cohen, *Understanding Drug Use: An Adult's Guide to Drugs and the Young* (New York: Harper & Row, 1971); B. Payne, *Getting There without Drugs* (New York: Viking Press, in Press).

"Which alternative for which motive?"—"Which alternative for which person?" At this point, I wish to share a list of categories which has assisted me in thinking about applying alternatives. It was obvious to me that motives and relevant alternatives were intimately connected, and that one way of conceptualizing the relationship was in terms of different "levels of experience." Thus, as an illustration rather than an ultimate formulation, I have included Table 16.1. Each level of experience pertains to certain types of motives leading to drug use or experimentation, examples of which are listed in the table. Across from each level-motive category are examples of types of alternatives which might replace, ameliorate or prevent drug abuse. I expect the reader will come up with many more motives and an almost infinite addition of alternatives. Of course, there are other ways to conceptualize the different kinds of alternatives—again, this table is intended to serve only as an example and stimulant. Needless to say, several levels of experience may operate within a particular individual or subgroup, so categories and motives may be related across levels and should not be taken as mutually exclusive.

There is one alternative not mentioned in the table because it is so obvious. Yet it deserves some comment. A growing viable alternative to using drugs is *not to use drugs* or *discontinuing drug use.* Many long-term users move away from drugs because they feel better *not* using them. For some, being "straight" or "clean" is a refreshing change in itself from being stoned or hooked. Often this response is out of negativity, e.g., fright from a bad trip, the agony of being strung out, the realization of personal self-destruction, the boredom of being stoned all the time, etc. The preexperimenter who avoids drugs may also be acting from a flight from negativity—in this case, an avoidance of anticipated hurtful results. It may be, however, that most non-experimenters have already found an alternative so positive that there is no felt need for drugs or a reluctance to risk something perceived as valuable. Preliminary research[3] tends to confirm this supposition— that young nonusers of common illicit drugs avoid them more because of satisfaction gained in exploring positive alternatives, rather than from a fear of consequent harm.

Thus, *not using drugs* only becomes a viable alternative in one of two cases: (1) when a drug user is suffering, and realizes the suffering is drug-related; or, (2) when a preuser has so much going for him that perceived drug-related risks threaten present satisfaction.

3. Survey conducted by students, Pacific High School, San Leandro, California. In response to an essay question: "If you do not use drugs, what has been the biggest deterrent for not using them?" 39.8 percent said there was "no need" (or "life is fine, I'm happy," "turn on other ways," etc.) This contrasts with 7.1 percent who mentioned laws or "getting busted" (study conducted in 1968–1969).

TABLE 16.1

Level of Experience	Corresponding Motives (Examples)	Possible Alternatives (Examples)
Physical	Desire for physical satisfaction; physical relaxation; relief from sickness; desire for more energy; maintenance of physical dependency.	Athletics; dance; exercise; hiking; diet; health training; carpentry or outdoor work.
Sensory	Desire to stimulate sight, sound, touch, taste; need for sensual-sexual stimulation; desire to magnify sensorium.	Sensory awareness training; sky diving; experiencing sensory beauty of nature.
Emotional	Relief from psychological pain; attempt to solve personal perplexities; relief from bad mood; escape from anxiety; desire for emotional insight; liberation of feeling; emotional relaxation.	Competent individual counseling; well-run group therapy; instruction in psychology of personal development.
Interpersonal	To gain peer acceptance; to break through interpersonal barriers; to "communicate," especially nonverbally; defiance of authority figures; cement two-person relationships; relaxation of interpersonal inhibition; solve interpersonal hangups.	Expertly managed sensitivity and encounter groups; well-run group therapy; instruction in social customs; confidence training; social-interpersonal counseling; emphasis on assisting others in distress via education; marriage.
Social (including Sociocultural & Environmental)	To promote social change; to find identifiable subculture; to tune out intolerable environmental conditions, e.g., poverty; changing awareness of the "masses."	Social service; community action in positive social change; helping the poor, aged infirm, young, tutoring handicapped; ecology action.
Political	To promote political change; to identify with antiestablishment subgroup; to change drug legislation; out of desperation with the social-political order; to gain wealth or affluence or power.	Political service; political action; nonpartisan projects such as ecological lobbying; field work with politicians and public officials.
Intellectual	To escape mental boredom; out of intellectual curiosity; to solve cognitive problems; to gain new understanding in the world of ideas; to study better; to research one's own awareness; for science.	Intellectual excitement through reading; through discussion; creative games and puzzles; self-hypnosis; training in concentration; synectics—training in intellectual breakthroughs; memory training.

TABLE 16.1 *continued*

Level of Experience	Corresponding Motives (Examples)	Possible Alternatives (Examples)
Creative-Aesthetic	To improve creativity in the arts; to enhance enjoyment of art already produced, e.g., music; to enjoy imaginative mental productions.	Nongraded instruction in producing and/or appreciating art, music, drama, crafts, handiwork, cooking, sewing, gardening, writing, singing, etc.
Philosophical	To discover meaningful values; to grasp the nature of the universe; to find meaning in life; to help establish personal identity; to organize a belief structure.	Discussions, seminars, courses in the meaning of life; study of ethics, morality, the nature of reality; relevant philosophical literature; guided exploration of value systems.
Spiritual-Mystical	To transcend orthodox religion; to develop spiritual insights; to reach higher levels of consciousness; to have Divine Visions; to communicate with God; to augment yogic practices; to get a spiritual shortcut; to attain enlightenment; to attain spiritual powers.	Exposure to nonchemical methods of spiritual development; study of world religions; introduction to applied mysticism, meditation; yogic techniques.
Miscellaneous	Adventure, risk drama, "kicks," unexpressed motives; prodrug general attitudes, etc.	"Outward Bound" survival training; combinations of alternatives above; pronaturalness attitudes; brain-wave training; meaningful employment, etc.

Referring back to the table, the alternatives model was originally developed around the issue of psychedelic drugs and cannabis. However, this type of categorization allows us to consider all types of psychopharmacological intervention, from the case of the heroin addict to the "housewife junkie" on diet pills; from the fourth-grader sniffing airplane glue to the middle-aged alcoholic.

We are aware that an expressed motive may be different from the "real" underlying motive, and we should be alert to basic motives, no matter what is expressed. We should also remember that certain drugs may be most associated with certain kinds of motives. For example, heroin is likely to be more associated with the classic "escape" motives because of its consciousness-benumbing effect, whereas LSD might be used more to try to satisfy aspirations on the creative, philosophical, or spiritual level of experience.

IMPLEMENTING ALTERNATIVES: GENERAL PRINCIPLES

The alternatives model can be very helpful in assigning priorities to social action for the control, treatment, and prevention of drug abuse. Clearly, punitive control has severe limits upon its effectiveness because it does not respond with viable alternatives to the predisposing motives, and its fear-generating capacity is not an adequate deterrent.

In rehabilitation and treatment, sequences of intervention should parallel priorities in the level of experience category. For example, in treating heroin addiction, methadone represents a viable alternative to the physical component of the addict's needs, but the eventual treatment program must aim at providing more permanent fulfillment of deeper psychosocial needs. The existence or nonexistence of these deeper aspirations will determine whether the addict can resist temptation after withdrawal from methadone. As a parallel case, the "freak-out" victim of strong psychedelics is best first treated on the emotional and perhaps interpersonal levels to return him to ordinary consciousness. But, after that, adequate rehabilitation programs must respond to the things which got him hung up in the first place.

Perhaps the most powerful application of the alternative model lies in the field of drug education. There is still a powerful premise circulating among educators that individuals, especially children, can be *frightened* away from drugs with "proper information about dangers." In all frankness, this hope is a utopian fantasy. Before anyone gets optimistically excited about "dynamic, hard-hitting facts" in a drug abuse curriculum, he should give careful thought to the remarkable staying power of cigarettes in the mature adult population. The case against smoking cigarettes could hardly be much stronger (in view of the demonstrated dangers) and yet widespread antismoking publicity has made only a remarkably small dent in the smoking habits of those most "responsible" citizens.

In view of such a fact, does it seem reasonable to expect a "scare" campaign to be decisive? Of course not. The young are more non-rational, risk-oriented, and unbelieving. Further, the effects of the most-used drugs have not been accurately delineated, and the credibility of authority figures is very strained. (One young pothead told me that he would not believe any research unless the study was conducted in Switzerland! Neutrality equals objectivity, he guessed.)

Reliance on fear motivation can produce the instructor's ultimate frustration in the older age groups. He succeeds in persuading students that drugs have bad effects. But the students reason that they live in a dangerous world (bad air, chemicals in food, possibility of war, etc.) and that the dangers of drugs do not outweigh the pleasure they can give in return. Once again, the educator has paid the price of the "deviance" theory, i.e., that reasonable people will not want to use drugs, and that education regarding the dangers will weed out all those pre-experimenters except the mentally ill or criminally inclined.

I do not wish to downgrade the real value of accurate information about drug effects—such information can be a significant help in the decision-making process. Further, it may serve to bolster the intuitive guess that drugs are harmful and may help some youths to justify to their peers the adoption of nonchemical alternatives. Educational honesty and credibility must be maximized in the same way that legislators should make drug use a public health and not a criminal concern. But the real promise in education would seem to involve educating about alternatives. There is no higher priority; and there are few other ways to give such a powerful assist to the minimization of drug abuse.

It is my contention that education about nonchemical alternatives for each level of experience is the best mode of "prevention." It is also the method of choice for moderate experimenters. And finally, the alternatives model is the treatment of choice for heavy users (here much stress would be put on the alternative of *not using*). In the application of the alternatives model, it must be realized that there is no one pat alternative for everyone, just as there is no one motive responsible for all drug use. Also, it should be noted that the alternatives of best application are those which are *incompatible* with being high. For example, "listening to recorded music" is not an alternative unless it precludes being stoned while listening. In this particular case, techniques or ways of listening must be sufficiently taught so that chemically altered awareness gets in the way of the experience. In general, extremely *passive* alternatives must be utilized with a bit more care than alternatives necessitating *action* or work with one's resources. The more active and demanding alternatives are those which clearly interfere with a drug-taking life style.

IMPLEMENTATION OF ALTERNATIVES: A SPECIFIC EXAMPLE

To give one small specific instance in which the alternatives model may be applied to institutional action, let us take the case of the public schools. It has been argued that many of our public school systems, through rigidity, misassessed priorities, and lack of relevance, have contributed to the dissatisfactions which lead children toward drugs. It seems indisputable that the "Art of Living" has become a critically important skill for young people, one not reflected in course curricula. The schools have become expert at transmitting information and training intellectual skills, but this is partially lost if the young are preoccupied and are not motivated to learn what the schools want them to learn.

The issue of educational reform is far too broad to treat in this paper, but let us offer one small suggestion based on the alternatives model. Most schools offer course experiences in nonintellective areas, but emasculate antichemical possibilities by assigning grades to such courses. I am referring to subjects like music, art, homemaking, drama, physical education, manual training, family life education, and the like. All of these subject areas *could* pertain to the motive levels discussed previously. They *could* get children so personally involved that drugs would not be so inviting. Usually they do not. The arbitrary grading process infuses anxiety and competition into just those areas which might provide creative relief. Students deliberately avoid electives in alternatives areas for fear of lowering their academic average. Only the best students in nonintellective areas are really encouraged to go on developing nonintellective resources, and even they are prey to "evaluation anxiety"—that fear of failure which makes neurotics out of prospective artists.

The abolition of grades in alternatives subjects would be a powerful stroke in turning kids on to a "natural high," with little if any monetary outflow. Parents might object to a lack of competitive evaluation, but they should be reminded that one of the pulls to the drug scene is that no one gets an "F" for turning on. Logically related steps could include the expansion of subject hours in alternatives areas, invitations to community members who could share what turns them on nonchemically, time outside the walls to taste social involvement and service, a philosophical admission of the importance of interpersonal as well as intellectual skills. These are the kinds of steps which might come to mind when focusing on the necessity of alternatives.

TOWARD A NEWER HUMANITY

When proposing a large scale turn towards the alternatives model, some might respond skeptically and ask for research findings which have demonstrated the model's effectiveness. Long-term research simply has not yet been done in the alternatives area. However, survey and interview studies have amply suggested that most users stop (or would stop) because of a preferable alternative.[4]

Perhaps the most exciting aspect of the alternatives models is that it can be applied to any level of action or reaction to drug use. It is limited only by the imagination and wisdom of the implementor. The positive possibilities seem limitless; while obsession with drug-related symptoms and dangers appears an endless pit of futility.

There are other advantages to the alternatives model. Application of provided alternatives to drug use simultaneously provides alternatives to other forms of human difficulties. After all, truly effective solutions to the "problem of drugs" are the effective solutions to the "problem of people" and the "problem of life." Very possibly, deterioration may be shifted to harmony. Those solutions, applied to every level of experience could make man's abuse of himself and others fade into a historical remembrance of a thankfully transcended cultural psychosis.

4. A. Y. Cohen, "Relieving Acid Indigestion: Psychological and Social Dynamics Related to Hallucinogenic Drug Abuse," final report submitted to the Bureau of Drug Abuse Control under Research Contract 67-25 (1968). (Now possibly available through the Bureau of Narcotics and Dangerous Drugs, Washington, D.C.)

Glossary

"A." Amphetamines; speed.

Acid. Lysergic acid diethylamide 25 (LSD).

Addict. Person with physical dependence on a drug.

Amped. High on stimulants, usually amphetamines.

Angel Dust. PCP (Phencyclidine, or "Sernyl," an animal tranquilizer; in pill form called "Peace Pill," "hog," or "elephant") that is smoked, inhaled, or swallowed in a powdered form (mixed with marijuana or oregano).

Apomorphine. A morphine alkaloid derivative, used as an emetic. (William Burroughs claimed he was cured of heroin addiction by using apomorphine.)

Are you holding? Do you have any dope?

Asshole. Stupid person; person one does not like; distal end of alimentary tract.

Baby. Small heroin habit (just getting started).

Backwards. Tranquilizers or barbiturates; to get a habit again; travelling backwards; backsliding.

Bad. Really good. "Bad" dope would be strong, good dope. (Vietnamese heroin, 95 percent pure, is "bad.")

Bad Ass. Someone who is really tough.

Bad Scene. Uncomfortable or unfriendly surroundings; a bad situation; ugly vibrations.

Bag. Ten to twenty-five dollars' worth of heroin; category one fits into: "My bag is smoking weed."

Ball. A good time; sexual intercourse.

Balloon. A bag of heroin actually sold in a rubber balloon.

Barbs. Barbiturates; jagged edges on a used hypodermic needle.

1. These terms were compiled by addicts, ex-addicts and "street people" in the San Francisco area. Editing was minimal and only to correct pharmacologic errors.

Benny. Benzedrine.

Bernice. Cocaine.

Bhang. A drink made in India of the flowering tops, stems, and leaves of cannabis. Produces mild hallucinogenic effects.

Black Beauty. Biphetamine.

Blind Munchies. Overwhelming desire for something to eat, usually after smoking marijuana.

Blood. Black person; Black "brother" or "sister."

Blow it. Bungle a situation; lose control; become very angry; lose one's "cool"; lose face.

Blow the vein. Cause a vein to collapse by overusing it or by injecting something caustic.

Blow your mind. Lose control of your mind; be extremely surprised, either pleasantly or otherwise.

Blue Heaven. Sodium Amytal.

Blue. Overdosed; cyanotic from inadequate respiration.

Blues. Numorphan; also, depression.

Bogart. Monopolize, not pass, a joint.

Boo. Marijuana.

Boot. To release pressure on the pacifier ("outfit"), causing blood to rush back and to inject drug a little at a time (also called "Jacking off").

Boot and Shoot. Heroin addict who supports his habit by stealing.

Boy. Heroin.

Bread. Money.

Bring Down. Something or someone unpleasant. Having to work is a "bring down."

Brother. A male of any race, but usually black or Chicano; also, heroin.

Brown. Heroin from Mexico, usually light brown in color (may be due to dilution with powdered coffee).

Bummer. Unpleasant experience of any nature (especially bad LSD experience producing paranoia and sometimes later "flashbacks").

Bum Rap. Unfair accusation or arrest.

Bunk. Bad dope.

Burn. To sell some other substance, such as sugar, for dope; very bad dope.

Burn Artist. Someone who makes his living selling phony or heavily adulterated dope. (Has short life expectancy.)

Burn out. To use so much dope it destroys your mind; someone who has "burned out"; also, someone who has "outgrown" or "matured out" of his habit.

Bush. Marijuana; female pubic hair.

Bust. Arrest.

Cap. Capsule of drugs.

Carry. To possess drugs; *see* Holding.

Cartwheels. Amphetamine tablets scored crossways (reportedly handed out by medics in Vietnam for night flights or patrols to achieve greater efficiency). Repeated and prolonged use may lead to amphetamine psychosis; paranoia, inappropriate violence.

Cat. Any male; also heroin.

Chasing the Bag. Trying to get dope (heroin).

Chick. Any female; cocaine.

Chillum. A conical shaped pipe used to smoke hashish.

China White. Good quality white heroin.

Chip. To use heroin occasionally so as not to get addicted: "I'm not strung out, I'm just chipping." Often done in social situations.

Chloral. Chloral hydrate (sedative hypnotic); mild "sleeper."

Christmas Trees. Dexamyl Spansules (long-acting amphetamine plus amytal).

Cibas. Doriden (sedative hypnotic with high abuse potential).

Clean. Not using drugs: "I've been clean for a week"; also, not carrying any dope, not having warrants out or being wanted by the police.

Coasting. Feeling good after shooting heroin; also, taking it easy.

Coke. Cocaine.

Cold Turkey, Cold. Coming down from heroin without medication: "He didn't want to kick cold." (Refers to "gooseflesh" or the appearance of a cold turkey.)

Cold Shot. A bad deal; a "dirty trick."

Collar. Strip of paper around the end of an eyedropper to make the needle fit tight on an "outfit."

Come down. To stop using; also, an emotional depression or a disappointment.

Come on. The way someone acts on first meeting, e.g., "He comes on strong."

Connection. Person from whom one gets dope.

Contact. Same as connection.

Contact High. Psychological "sympatico"; feeling of being high merely from being around a person who is high, usually on psychedelics, speed, or marijuana.

Cookin'. Having a really good time.

Cook up. To prepare heroin for injection by heating the powder in a spoon with a small amount of water.

Cooker. A spoon or bottle cap used to prepare heroin for injection.

Cool. Trustworthy, safe, careful; having controlled emotions.

Cop. To get anything; to buy dope.

Cop an Attitude. Be obnoxious, have a chip on one's shoulder.

Cop out. Succumb to the establishment; to lose one's cool; also, to inform the police.

Cop to. Admit to.

Cope. Be able to deal with the situation (usually a difficult one) whether on dope or not.

Co-Pilot. Dexedrine; also a guide for a psychedelic experience.

Count. The amount of dope or drug purchased.

Cottons. The small pieces of cotton used to strain the dissolved and heated heroin before shooting it. Small traces of the drug remain in the cotton, so addicts save the cottons against the day when they have no heroin and then put them all in a spoon, add a little more water, and try to get a shot out of that.

Cotton Fever. Severe chills and fever from using old cottons. May be due to allergic response or actual septicemia.

Crank. Amphetamines.

Crash. Sleep, pass out from drugs; also, spend the night: "Can I crash here for the night?"

Crib. Where one lives (may be a "shooting gallery"), q.v.; *see* Pad.

Crutch. Device used to hold the last part of a marijuana cigarette, so that it can all be smoked without burning the fingers; also called "Roach Clip," q.v.

Crystal. Methamphetamine; *see* Speed.

Crossroads. See Cartwheels.

Cut. To dilute a drug by adding some other substance, such as milk, sugar, quinine; also, to stab someone.

Cut out. To leave, split the scene.

Deal. Sell drugs.

Desoxyn. Dexsoxy-Amphetamine.

Dexies. Dexedrine, Dexamyl.

Dig. Enjoy, like; also, understand.

Dillies. Dilaudid.

Dime. Ten dollars.

Dirty. Using drugs, especially heroin; "hooked."

Dollar. One hundred dollars.

Dollies. Dolophine (Methadone).

Dope. To a heroin user, dope is heroin; to marijuana smokers, dope is anything used to get high.

Do Up. Shoot or inject a drug.

Downer. Barbiturate; any depressant; *see also* Bummer.

Drag. See Bummer.

Drag Queen. A male homosexual dressed up like a woman: "To be dressed in full drag."

Dripper. Eyedropper for shooting dope.

Drop. To swallow (a pill).

Drop a dime. To phone police, turn someone in.

Drop it. To hide dope.

Dry up. To stop using for a while; also, to dry out (viz. the alcoholic).

Dubie. A joint, or marijuana cigarette.

Dude. A male; *see* Cat.

Dugee. Heroin.

Duster. Heroin cigarette (prevalent now in Vietnam).

Dyke. Lesbian.

Dynamite. Unusually good or strong dope.

Easy. Anything that moves smoothly.

Ease off. Get through the door.

Ease on in. Move slowly, so no one knows what you're doing.

Elephant. See Angel Dust.

Fag, Faggot. Male homosexual.

Fall out. Pass out; go to sleep.

Farfetched. See Far Out.

Far Out, Far-Fucking-Out. Very good; also, strange or unusual.

FEDS. Federal police; "narcs."

Fine. An extravagant compliment; very good.

Fit. A syringe or eyedropper and pacifier, and a needle; equipment for injecting drugs.

Fix. To inject drugs; also, one dose of a drug.

Flash. A strong, pleasurable sensation; also, a sudden realization. Also, to regurgitate on heroin.

Flipped out. Crazy; *see* Far Out.

Flow. "Don't fight it"; "flow with" the effect of a drug.

Fluff. To chop up dope (usually heroin or cocaine); to make it bulkier and more even in consistency.

Fours. Codeine pills.

Foxy. Looking good (especially a female).

Freak. Long-hair, noncomformist; dope smoker; also, sexual deviant.

Freak out. Become agitated, distraught, upset or irrational and unable to cope with the immediate situation; may be hysterical.

Freebie. Something for nothing.

Freeze. When a connection cuts you off completely.

Fresh and Sweet. Just out of the penitentiary; new to the dope scene.

Fuck. To have sexual intercourse; also to "blow it": "He can really fuck up a scene."

Fucked up. High on heroin (sometimes other drugs): "He was so fucked up he couldn't even drive a car"; messed up, has problems; also, fucked over, fucked around, and just plain fucked.

Funky. Dirty, low down; may refer to types of music; also, earthy, in general.

Geeze. Inject drugs.

Get down. Shoot heroin.

Get down to it. Get to the basics or what's important.

Get off. Take any drug; also, to feel the effects of a drug: "That dope was no good. I shot a whole bag and didn't get off."

Girl. Cocaine.

Give up. To inform someone; to stop looking; to let anything go.

Goofers. Barbiturates, hypnotics, sedatives; *see* Downers.

Gow. Heroin.

Grass. Marijuana.

Groovy. Good, nice, beautiful; happy or pleasant connotation in general.

Gross out. Totally repulsive.

Gun. *See* Fit. Narcotics paraphernalia; something you kill someone with.

Gutter. Veins inside elbow.

Gutter junkie. Addict who steals from anyone to support his habit, usually transient, habituates shooting galleries, q.v., because he has no place of his own.

Hang in. Keep trying.

Hang it up. Leave a situation; quit.

Hang loose. Take it easy; relax.

Hang out. Do nothing in particular.

Hang up. Anything that takes up time; a bother.

Hard on. An obnoxious attitude; also, an erection.

Hash. Hashish.

Hassle. An inconvenience; a worry or bother; to give or introduce trouble.

Head. Someone who uses drugs, or any particular drug: "He's a juice head."

Heat. Police.

Heater. Gun.

Heavy. Important, serious; also, hard narcotics.

High. An altered state of consciousness which generally makes one feel better while in that state.

Hip. Aware; turned on; conscious of the scene.

Hit. A shot of dope, a puff, a snort of anything.

Hog. *See* Angel Dust.

Holding. Having a drug in your possession.

Honda Hogs. Division of San Francisco Tactical Squad that rides little Honda motorcycles; esp. in Golden Gate Park.

Hooked. Physically addicted; strung out.

Horn. To inhale a drug; *see also* Snort, Sniff.

Hot. Likely to be arrested; known or wanted by the police.

Hot shot. Bag of poison sold as "legitimate dope" used intentionally to kill someone.

Hustle. Any way of making money (or procuring supplies) other than a straight job; e.g., dealing drugs, prostitution, pimping, etc.

Into. Interested in; occupied with.

J. *See* Joint.

Jack-off. Inject drugs a little at a time by releasing pressure on the pacifier part of the way in order to get the drug into your system slowly; a really stupid person; to masturbate.

Jam. Cocaine.

Jive. Dishonest, untrustworthy; "bullshit."

Joint. Marijuana cigarette; penitentiary.

Jones. Heroin habit.

Juice. Alcohol.

Junk. Heroin.

Junkie. Heroin addict.

Key. Kilo, q.v.

Kick. To stop using drugs—usually heroin.

Killer. Really good; *see* Heavy, Far Out.

Kilo. A kilogram (2.2 pounds), usually of marijuana.

King Kong. A big monkey ($200 or more a day heroin habit).

Lame. Stupid, foolish, unhip.

Leapers. Stimulants, especially amphetamines.

Lid. One ounce of marijuana.

Loaded. Very stoned; *see* High; also, sick.

Looking. Wanting to buy heroin; *see* Cop.

Loose. Uninhibited; careless; relaxed; not together; may be amusing, but is not trustworthy.

"M." Morphine.

Man, the. Police; also, someone to buy drugs from.

Make it. To make love; to go somewhere: "Let's make it up to Haight Street."

Mellow. Happy, relaxed.

Meth. Methedrine or methamphetamine; speed.

Mighty Joe Young. See King Kong.

Mike. Microgram, usually refers to LSD dosage.

Miss. When the drug accidentally misses the vein because the needle wasn't in right.

Narc. Narcotics agent, undercover cop.

Natch. Short for natural—without drugs.

Needle Freak. Someone who enjoys injecting almost anything; one who gets a sexual "flash" from the injection.

Negative. General emotional level on a bummer.

Nickle. Five dollars; five dollars' worth of a drug.

Nixon. Low quality or "shitty" street dope.

Nod. Get sleepy from heroin or other depressants.

Nod out. Pass into euphoric state in which the head nods to the chest and is jerked back, only to be repeated.

"O" or Op. Opium.

O.D. An overdose of heroin or barbiturates. Resultant respiratory depression may kill.

Off. Stoned; also, to kill.

On the Street. Not in jail; also, public knowledge.

On Top of It. In control of a situation.

Out of Sight, Outtasight. Usually very good, pleasurable situation: "Outtasight dope, man."

Outfit. A device for shooting heroin consisting of an eyedropper and pacifier or syringe, and a needle; *see* Fit.

Outrageous. Really good or really bad; exceptional; may be very amusing; highly unconventional.

Overamp. Take too much of a stimulant.

Oz. Ounce.

Pad. House or apartment; place where you live.

Paper. Small packet of dope; a prescription; also, a bad check: "He's out passing paper."

Paregoric. Camphorated tincture of opium, used to help "kick" a heroin habit.

Peace Pill. See Angel Dust.

People. One's friends or connections; the common mass, usually without political power.

Per. Prescription.

Piece. Gun; ounce of a drug, usually heroin.

Pig. Policeman.

Pinhead. Skinny joint; tiny amount.

Pinned. Pupils of the eyes contracted from heroin.

Pipe. Large vein.

Plastic. Phony, artificial, insincere.

Popped. Arrested.

Pop a pill. Swallow a pill.

Positive. General emotional state on an emotional "upper."

Psycho-fucking-delic. Amazing, incredible; *see also* Far Out.

Pusher. Drug dealer.

Quarter. Twenty-five dollars.

Ragweed. Bad marijuana.

Rainbows. Tuinal. A barbiturate; mixture of Amytal and Seconal.

Rank. Unfair, dirty.

Rap. Talk.

Red. Panama Red (good marijuana); also a barbiturate (Seconal).

Reds. Seconal (a barbiturate).

Reefer. A partially smoked marijuana cigarette.

Rig. See Outfit.

Righteous. Good, fair, honest; pleasant, enjoyable.

Right on. I agree; something one can agree with.

Rip off. To steal.

Ripped. Extremely stoned; *see* Fucked up; also, one who has had something stolen.

Roach. The butt, or last part, of a joint.

Roach clip. See Crutch.

Rock. Large crystals of cocaine or heroin; also, Alcatraz.

Rush. Strong, pleasurable feeling that follows taking a drug; *see* Flash.

Scag. Heroin.

Scene. Atmosphere; local situation; what is going on.

Score. To obtain anything, usually drugs or sex.

Script. Prescription.

Script Docs. Physicians who will supply ethically questionable prescriptions and who make a living from writing excessive prescriptions.

Set up. Arrange for a person to be arrested by planting dope on him; or, the police trying to buy dope from him.

Shit. Heroin; also used to mean any kind of drug; also, an exclamation, generally negative.

Shooting Gallery. A house or apartment where people go to shoot drugs when they have no other place to go; a communal drug hangout.

Shoot up. To inject drugs.

Shuck. Lie, phony story; "con."

Shut down. When one's sexual partner wants no more of the relationship.

Sick. Needing a shot of heroin.

Sister. Any female, usually black or Chicano; also, Cocaine.

Skin-pop. To inject drugs subcutaneously.

Sleeper. A sleeping pill.

Smack. Heroin.

Smeck, Schmeck. Heroin.

Snitch. Informer; to inform on someone to the police.

Snort, Sniff. Sniff or inhale drugs through the mucous membranes of the nose, usually cocaine, heroin, or speed.

Snow. Cocaine.

Soaper. Quaalude (a sedative-hypnotic with high abuse potential).

Spaced out. Out of touch; not all there: "I'm so spaced out I can't remember what day it is"; usually secondary to strong, prolonged drug use.

Speed. Amphetamine or methamphetamine (powerful central nervous system stimulants).

Speedballs. A combination of stimulants (or "rippers") and depressants (or "downers") taken together, usually cocaine and heroin or speed and barbiturates.

Speedfreak. Someone who takes a lot of speed, usually intravenously.

Spike. Hypodermic needle.

Splash. Speed, amphetamine, or methamphetamine.

Split. To leave, go away.

Spoon. About a gram of drugs.

Stash. One's supply; also, a hiding place; to hide something.

Stoned. See High.

Straight. Someone who doesn't use drugs; anybody who has a middle-class mind, burr haircut and polished black shoes (which may indicate a "narc.").

Strung out. Addicted; dependent on a drug; in bad shape.

Stumblers. Downers (central nervous system depressants, especially barbiturates).

Sunshine. Good orange-colored tablets of LSD.

Tab. Tablet.

Take off. To rob: "Let's take off a bank"; also, to get high.

Taste. A small amount of a drug; one dose.

Tie off. Apply pressure on the vein so it will stand out and the injection of the drug will be easier.

Together. In control of oneself or of a situation; composed; *see* Cool.

Toke. One puff on a joint.

Tracks. Marks or scars on the arms and body from injecting drugs; needle holes.

Trick. Something done to make money; act of prostitution; also, someone who is "used" to make money from.

Trip. An experience on a drug, usually a psychedelic.

Truckin', keep on. Self-confident strut with hips and pelvis held forward; similar to "cake walk" or "sunshine steppin'."

Turn a trick. Act as a prostitute.

Turn on. To take a drug; to give someone else a drug; to make someone aware of something.

Uncool. Conspicuous, blatant, stupid.

Undercover Pigs. Plainclothes police dressed to look like whomever they're trying to arrest; usually dressed like "hippies."

Unreal. Surprising; *see* Far Out.

Up Front. Honest, candid, blunt; explicitly desiring sexual contact.

Uppers. Stimulants, amphetamines.

Uptight. Worried, angry; *see also* Straight.

Using. Currently taking any drug.

Wake up. The first shot of heroin of the day.

Wasted. Extremely stoned; also, hurt, injured or sick; malnourished because of an extended "speed" run.

Water. Speed.

Weed. Marijuana.

Weirded out. Having your mind blown; surprised; confused; *see* Blow your mind.

Wiped out. See Wasted, Stoned.

Works. Equipment for injecting drugs; *see* Fit, Outfit, Rig.

Working. Getting money for dope; also, prostitution.

Yellows. Nembutal (a barbiturate).

Yen. Dope craving after one has been "clean" for a while.

Zap. To put someone or something "down" (from Buck Rogers's comic-book expression).

Zonked out. Really loaded; overdosed.